UNIVERSITY OF NORTH CAROLINA AT CHAPEL HILL

DEPARTMENT OF ROMANCE LANGUAGES

NORTH CAROLINA STUDIES
IN THE ROMANCE LANGUAGES AND LITERATURES

Founder: URBAN TIGNER HOLMES

Distributed by:

UNIVERSITY OF NORTH CAROLINA PRESS
CHAPEL HILL
North Carolina 27514
U.S.A.

NORTH CAROLINA STUDIES IN THE
ROMANCE LANGUAGES AND LITERATURES
Number 205

LE VAIN SIECLE GUERPIR

A Literary Approach to Sainthood through
Old French Hagiography of the Twelfth Century

LE VAIN SIECLE GUERPIR

A Literary Approach to Sainthood through
Old French Hagiography of the
Twelfth Century

BY

PHYLLIS JOHNSON
and
BRIGITTE CAZELLES

CHAPEL HILL

NORTH CAROLINA STUDIES IN THE ROMANCE
LANGUAGES AND LITERATURES
U.N.C. DEPARTMENT OF ROMANCE LANGUAGES

1979

Library of Congress Cataloging in Publication Data

Johnson, Phyllis, 1937-
   Le vain siecle guerpir.

   (North Carolina studies in the Romance languages and literatures; no. 205)
   Bibliography: p.
   1. French poetry—To 1500—History and criticism. 2. Christian hagiography. 3. Christian saints in literature. I. Cazelles, Brigitte, joint author. II. Title. III. Series.

PQ178.J64   841'.1'09352   79-10678
ISBN 0-8078-9205-X

I.S.B.N. 0-8078-9205-X

IMPRESO EN ESPAÑA

PRINTED IN SPAIN

DEPÓSITO LEGAL: V. 1.594 - 1979   I.S.B.N. 84-499-2817-6

ARTES GRÁFICAS SOLER, S. A. - JÁVEA, 28 - VALENCIA (8) - 1979

"O merveille, qu'on puisse ainsi faire présent de ce qu'on ne possède pas soi-même, ô doux miracle de nos mains vides!"

Bernanos, *Journal d'un Curé de Campagne*

PREFACE

This study is the result of a long-term project which was initially two separate enterprises on the part of the authors. Professor Cazelles' intent was to analyze the value of spiritual infancy in medieval hagiography, while Professor Johnson wanted to investigate the role of epithets in the structure of French Saints' Lives. During the 1968 Summer Session at the Institut d'Etudes Médiévales in Poitiers, France, the authors discovered the similarity of their inquiries and decided to combine their efforts. Subsequent discussions brought into relief the importance of early French hagiography, and the two parts of this study are the result of the authors' combined research. In their final versions, the corpus and the Appendices are the responsibilities of Professor Cazelles and Professor Johnson, respectively.

Professor Cazelles is grateful to Professor Jacques Le Goff for having inspired her, many years ago, to study the manifestations of popular piety. Professor Johnson wishes to thank the staff of the Honnold Library for their help, and Pomona College for giving her the funds necessary to conduct her research. Both authors are indebted to Dr. Uitti for his advice, to the members of the Institut de Recherche et d'Histoire des Textes for their invaluable information, and especially to Dr. Sam Borg, without whose comments and editorship this study would not have reached its present form.

Claremont and Stanford
May, 1978

TABLE OF CONTENTS

INTRODUCTION

This study is intended primarily for scholars and graduate students in the field of Old French literature, but it is hoped that specialists in theology and intellectual history may find something of interest in this literary approach to sainthood. Vernacular hagiography, drawing upon the Christian literary and oral traditions, folklore and superstition, mirrors popular belief. Translating, or more precisely, adapting the Latin Lives of the saints, the vernacular hagiographers of the twelfth century respond to the needs of an unsophisticated audience for stories which illustrate Church dogma. It is at once clear that the French Lives, being works of vulgarization, are indicative of the mentality of the listeners as they react to the deeds of a holy hero, admiring religious greatness in its combat against evil.[1] As much as the public feared the supernatural, they believed it: the popular appeal of the saint stems from such an ambivalence between the abnormal and the uncommon.

Our exploration of vernacular hagiography, therefore, aims at defining the essence of holiness in its relation to heroism, at analyzing the reasons for the appeal of an extraordinary character upon the ordinary man. What inspires the French hagiographer are

---

[1] Raoul Manselli (*La Religion populaire au moyen âge. Problèmes de méthode et d'histoire* [Institut d'Etudes Médiévales Albert le Grand: Montréal, 1975]) puts into relief the interest of works of vulgarization for an understanding of popular devotion and mentality. In Peter F. Dembowski's words, vernacular hagiography is "a precious and ... still hardly-tapped source of our knowledge about the popular aspects of the cultural history of the Middle Ages ... a kind of necessary counterbalance to an "aristocratic" view, according to which only the clerical, Latin *maiores* are worthy objects of attention for a serious historian of medieval thought" ("Literary Problems of Hagiography in Old French," *Medievalia et Humanistica*, 7 [1975], 126).

the Latin sources of a Life and an audience which has no knowledge of Latin. [2] To the intellectual historians and theologians, we shall say that the twelfth-century thoughts and doctrines affect vernacular hagiography to the extent of the French poet's knowledge or comprehension. What is common to all vernacular lives is the notion that sainthood is reserved for an elite intermediary between God and man. The impact of the saints upon the audience depends on the didactic nature of the French poems. Always edifying, the twelfth-century Lives are sometimes appealing for reasons more sentimental than moral. The value of the saintly heroes, demonstrating first the value of Christianity, suggests also the recognition, on the part of the poet, that credulity does not arise if there is no verisimilitude in the story. Persuasion demands a coherent argumentation, for without consistency, the hero, holy or lay, cannot exist in the mind of the audience. Uncommonness, not improbability, is obviously the first condition of a good heroic portrayal. So does it go with the saint, and vernacular hagiography, like any other genre, follows the conventional rules of literary success, despite or besides its religious elements.

That this study is mainly directed to scholars in French, and particularly in French literature, is explained by the nature of vernacular hagiography whose vulgarization is a concession to legend. The quality of fiction, like that of dreams, enables man to escape reality. In the case of hagiography, saintly greatness brings earth closer to heaven. The vernacular adaptations of Latin Lives, as suggested by Joseph de Ghellinck's remark, add more fancy than their models:

> Les vulgarisateurs populaires continuent à préférer la légende enchanteresse à la sèche exposition véridique, et il faut reconnaître, en dépit de l'histoire, qu'ils l'agrémentent plus d'une fois avec un talent capable de peindre les âmes au naturel. L'impression faite sur les esprits par ces pièces

---

[2] The texts of the *Vitae* are collected in the volumes of *Acta Sanctorum* published by the Bollandists (Brussels, 1643 ff). They are analyzed by the publications of the Bollandists, *Analecta Bollandiana* in an on-going series, as well as by René Aigrain, *L'Hagiographie* (Paris: Bloud & Gay, 1953), Hippolyte Delehaye, *Les Légendes hagiographiques*, 3rd ed. (Brussels: Société des Bollandistes, 1927), and Jean Leclercq, *L'Amour des lettres et le désir de Dieu* (Paris: Le Cerf, 1957).

populaires, souvent naïves, dont s'inspirent du reste les sculptures ou les vitraux de nos églises, est pour beaucoup dans la mentalité médiévale. Habituellement sans valeur historique, elles demeurent parallèles aux vies latines, qu'elle dépassent dans l'attention populaire. A ce titre, en raison même des questions très diverses qu'elles soulèvent et du jour qu'elles jettent sur l'âme médiévale, ses aspirations, ses craintes, ses conceptions, elles ont droit à être rappelées dans une histoire de la littérature du moyen âge. [3]

Embellishment of veracity, and not submission to historical fact is what makes vernacular hagiography conducive to a literary approach. Our interests are concentrated on the virtuosity which enables the French hagiographer to combine rationality and imagination, so that his story praises uncommonness without disregarding the lack of cultural sophistication of the audience.

At the outset of this study, it was the use and value of epithets related to the hero that attracted our attention. If such words as "the good," "the sinner," "the handsome" were revealing of the definition of saintly heroism, it was necessary to list them as the reading of the texts progressed. The qualification of "saint" is of course predominant in the portrayal of each character, and so are other attributes like "the apostle," "the monk," "the abbot," suggesting that the social status, along with the moral and physical beauty, is of importance in the description of the hero, but too external and imprecise to lead to any conclusion other than that the saint is given a reputable position on earth. Those chosen by God as intercessors are already part of the ecclesiastical elite in rank. However interesting, the tables of epithets fall short in the analysis of vernacular adaptations, since the same qualifications are found in the Latin *Vitae,* and since they do not provide any insight into the embellishment which characterizes the French legends. Expanding the limits of our study, we then paid particular attention to the portrayal of the saint. This examination brought into relief the recurrence throughout the corpus of various narrative themes, setting forth both several types of saints and interesting variations in the treatment of each type. In the portrayal of his hero, the ver-

---

[3] Joseph de Ghellinck, *L'Essor de la littérature latine au XIIème siècle* (Brussels: Desclée de Brouwer, 1955), pp. 421-422.

nacular poet accentuates one or two of the qualities traditionally associated with sainthood. In the subsequent divisions of our study, we attempt to show how the vernacular Lives are inspired by, or differ from the conventional topics of Latin hagiography.

Retreat from the worldly vanity, appraisal of abstinence and isolation, thirst for abnegation or martyrdom, such are the main elements which define virtue in the context of Western hagiography. The history of Occidental sainthood, as it is carried through the Christian literary and oral transmission, the Latin culture, and the doctrine of the Fathers of the Church, [4] is of great importance in the evaluation of twelfth-century French hagiography. The different types of vernacular heroes reflect the evolution from eremitism to Western monasticism, and the importance theology attributes to the study of sin. However indebted to tradition and evolution, the French poems are in no way bringing new insight into the spiritual definition of sanctity. Their interest lies, it appears, in their interdependence with profane literature, and in the way they shed light on the mentality of their audience.

The vernacular portrayal of the saintly hero has much to offer to those interested in legends and folklore. On that subject, the bibliography is relatively sparse. Despite a recent shift of focus, starting with an abundant investigation of the literary value and meaning of the *Vie de Saint Alexis,* twelfth-century French hagiography has inspired mostly historical, philological and stylistic research. [5] Yet French hagiography is more than a mere translation of Latin texts or transmission of devotional legends. Indeed it contains a rich documentation concerning the practical values of

---

[4] The *Dictionnaire de Théologie Catholique* by Vacant, Mangenot and Amann (Paris: Letouzey, 1939) presents what the doctrine of the Fathers elaborate under the article "sainteté" (vol. 14). There are three steps in the definition of sanctity: a negative aspect of absence of sin, by avoidance or purification; a positive aspect of interior renewal under the action of the Spirit; a dynamic aspect manifested in the heroic practice of virtues (p. 843). Three degrees of sanctity can then be discerned through an increasing order of values: sanctity is granted 1) to the members of the Church ("sainteté commune," p. 851) 2) to those who practice the rules of perfection stated by Christ ("sainteté plus parfaite," p. 852) and 3) to those who strive to imitate, as perfectly as possible, Christ's love for God and others ("sainteté héroïque," p. 853). It is this imitation of Christ, or heroic sanctity, which appears to inspire vernacular hagiographers.

[5] We refer the reader to the Appendices for the bibliography of each Saint's Life.

devotion, the twelfth-century view of greatness, the survival and adaptation of feudal heroism, the preeminence of faith or charity, the representation of individual or social salvation. E. Auerbach and E. Curtius have long established the overwhelming importance of the public in the process of medieval literary creation.[6] Examining the Anglo-Norman character of early vernacular hagiography, some specialists have clarified the differences between the clerical audience of the Anglo-Norman writers and the illiterate Continental listeners,[7] an indication of the popular appeal which, in the French legends, contributes to the making of a saint. The only appropriate way to assess the narrative value of those poems requires an exhaustive examination of twelfth-century French hagiography.[8] Only one critic, to our knowledge, has attempted to consider all the extant Lives:[9] in his comparison between the Latin and French versions,

---

[6] E. Auerbach, *Literatursprache und Publikum in der lateinischen spätantike und im Mittelalter* (Bern: F. Verlag, 1958). E. R. Curtius, *Europäische Literatur und lateinisches Mittelalter* (Bern: F. Verlag, ed. 1961). See also Paul Riché, "Recherches sur l'instruction des laïcs du IXème au XIIème siècle," *Cahiers de Civilisation médiévale,* 5 (1962), 175-182, and Etienne Delaruelle, "La Culture religieuse des laïcs en France aux XIème et XIIème siècles," *Miscellanea del Centro di Studi Medioevali,* 5 (1968), 548-581.

[7] A. T. Baker, "Saints' Lives Written in Anglo-French: Their Historical, Social and Literary Importance," *Transactions of the Royal Society of Literature of the United Kingdom,* New Series 4 (1924), 119-156.

O. H. Prior, Preface to *Cambridge Anglo-Norman Texts* (London: Cambridge University Press, 1924).

Johan Vising, *Anglo-Norman Language and Literature* (London: Oxford University Press, 1923).

Mary Dominica Legge, *Anglo-Norman in the Cloisters: The Influence of the Orders upon Anglo-Norman Literature* (Edinburgh: Edinburgh University Press, 1950).

J. D. M. Ford, "The Saints' Life in Vernacular Literature of the Middle Ages," *Catholic Historical Review,* 17 (1931-1932), 268-277.

S. C. Aston, "The Saint in Medieval Literature," *Modern Language Review,* 65 (1970), xxv-xlii.

[8] Thanks to the extensive card-index and files of the Institut de Recherches et d'Histoire des Textes in Paris (IRHT, under the aegis of the Centre National de la Recherche Scientifique), it became possible to cover all the material known, that is the twenty-four Lives dealing with nineteen saints, considering the five duplications. In listing the critical editions of these texts, we have shortened their titles and distinguished between the names by a Roman numeral for reasons of clarity in the presentation and in the quotations used in our analysis.

[9] Josef Merk, *Die literarische Gestaltung der altfranzösischen Heiligenleben bis Ende des 12. Jahrhunderts* (Affoltern am Albis: J. Weiss, 1946).

Josef Merk's approach is helpful in discerning the originality of the vernacular text. For our inquiry, Merk simplifies the question, when it is relevant, of borrowings from Latin sources. Merk, working chronologically, undertakes a linguistic exploration of the Lives, but does not intend to analyze the elements of a convincing portrayal. Our method does not proceed by saint, like Merk's, but by narrative themes and comparisons of their treatments through textual analysis, respecting the chronology of composition as much as data permit.

Although entirely published, the twelfth-century poems seem to have escaped the notice of critics, with the notable exception of a few well-known Lives such as *Alexis* and to a lesser degree *Brendan*, hence our assumption that the reader is unlikely to be familiar with them. The two sections of this study attempt to offer first an aesthetic analysis of French hagiography, and secondly, positivistic data gathered around each Saint's Life. For all 24 poems, listed in the Appendices alphabetically, this documentation includes 1) data on the provenance and historical sources of each poem, 2) relevant facts about the author, if known, 3) its date of composition, 4) a descriptive catalog of the manuscripts, 5) a brief account of the major scholarly works on each Life, 6) a factual description of its poetic form, and 7) a narrative summary. There is no new material contained in these Appendices: they merely summarize the present state of knowledge on the subject. Such information is intended both to clarify the arguments of our aesthetic analyses and to constitute a reference work for further studies on French hagiography. The purpose of our aesthetic analyses is obviously not to present new facts of dates or attribution of the texts, nor is it to propose corrections in the reading of the manuscripts. By quoting extensive passages in the original language and inserting these quotations in glosses that appraise the portrayals of the saints, such

---

The present state of research has allowed us to add many corrections to what Merk presents as twelfth-century vernacular hagiography. He studies fifteen saints, five of whom did not actually inspire the twelfth-century French hagiographers. On the other hand, nine saints are missing in his inventory: Bon, Catherine, Edward, Evroul, Genevieve, Gregory, Hildefonse, Silvester, and Theophile. Moreover, two versions do not appear in his study; following our abbreviations of the critical editions and their titles, they are: Edmund I and Marie II. We hope that our approach, resulting from a close inquiry into the entire corpus, is in a better position to present a true account of twelfth-century vernacular hagiography.

commentary aims at a synthesis of all the elements which contribute to the elaboration of saintly heroism.

Two French poems of the ninth and tenth centuries, those of *Eulalie* et *Léger*, give succinct clarification on the relationship between heroism and sanctity. [10] Both martyrs share a common respect for chastity and prove their internal strength in a negative manner, as they obstinately condemn the world. Both recountings glorify the victory of eternal life and the full meaning of a death that transforms the heroes into intermediaries between earth and heaven. Documents of the early need for vernacular preaching, those two brief homiletic texts are less a biography of the saints than a celebration of heroic times. In the twelfth century, the increasingly expanding distance between such historical saints and spurious, literary heroes, without suppressing the exemplary significance of hagiography, nevertheless transforms its presentation. [11]

The religious ideal of the saint works against the world; his literary existence is presented to the world. For the sake of their audience, the persuasive hagiographers must consider the effect of too morose an instruction. Vulgarizing is acknowledging popular reality, but in hagiography, the challenge is that the reality of the saint is extraordinary and in constant conflict with the ordinary reality of the listeners. The success of the story, therefore, derives from the art of combining the exceptional with the plausible in the portrayal of the saint. An impressive saint has to seem both edifying and real, self-assured yet compassionate, outstanding in stature yet not lacking a minimum of personable qualities. In that respect the predictability emanating from a successful portrayal rests on the talent of the hagiographer for infusing life into a stereotyped hero, adding human dimension to a character in essence inflexible, and inventing

---

[10] Albert Henri, "Séquence de Sainte Eulalie," *Chrestomathie de la littérature en ancien français,* 2nd ed. (Bern: Francke, 1960), pp. 2-3. Jos. Linskill, *Saint Léger: Etude de la langue du manuscrit de Clermont-Ferrand, suivie d'une édition critique du texte avec commentaire et glossaire* (Diss. Strasbourg, 1937). It seems that there are no extant hagiographic poems in eleventh-century French literature, with the exception of the Urtext of the Alexis.

[11] Karl D. Uitti distinguishes between the two aspects of historical and literary saints in "The Old French *Vie de Saint Alexis.* Paradigm, Legend, Meaning," *Romance Philology,* 20 (1966), 263-295.

realistic details and enticing adventures without disrupting the coherence of the story.

Vernacular hagiography shows an increasing interest in fiction, adding to the textual and oral sources of the Lives elements obviously borrowed from profane literature. Throughout the twelfth-century poems, such amplifications respond to a need for adapting the original and feudal ideal of heroic sanctity to a society in full transformation.

The organization of this book arises from the basic notion of sanctity understood as consecration, an apotheosis which dignifies a religious elite above the common. In *Eulalie* and *Léger* one sees emerging already the spatial and temporal distance that characterizes such distinction: both heroes condemn the world and value death over life. What is obviously a rejection of paganism in the historical context of those two Passions, becomes throughout the twelfth-century poems a repeated contempt of worldly vanity. To flee the world, *Le vain siecle guerpir,* is an expression borrowed from one text but which appears in every vernacular Life.[12] In this study, as in its title, the formula summarizes the underlying idea that remoteness is necessary to the preservation of virtue, and that holiness cohabits solitude. Eager to dwell on the evils of society, aware also of the anachronism of eremitic ideals, the French hagiographers of the period choose between, or combine, the two elements inherent in the concept of sanctity. Inclined sometimes to portray virtue as a denial of the world, they praise in the saint his powers of abnegation, poverty and renunciation of all earthly pleasures. In other instances, the main qualities of their heroes stem from a defiance of the world which inspires the saints to confront tormentors and sinners, or more charitably to show compassion for the miseries of humanity. The two parts of our aesthetic analysis are an attempt to explore the portrayal of the saint in accordance with such a combination of isolated and communicated holiness.

---

[12] *La Vie de Sainte Geneviève de Paris,* Lennart Bohm ed. (Upsala, 1959), line 419. Voiced in approximately the same terms, this concept pervades every vernacular Life and invariably qualifies the hero's vocation. Referring to the notion of flight from the world, we use the shorter expression *fuga mundi* while aware that this Latin formula refers, according to many intellectual historians, to a joyous self-sacrifice, and not to the contemptuous attitude implied in most vernacular saints' withdrawal.

The first part investigates elaborations on the concept of sanctity as a flight from the social world. At the outset of their stories, the hagiographers recount all the premonitions that are indicative of an unordinary destiny. That the saint is an outstanding individual is evinced by the exemplary value of his performance on earth. Almost invariably, the hero manifests a precocious disposition for practicing the virtue of asceticism. Chastity, poverty and obedience exert their irresistible appeal upon the young saint-to-be, and despite some temporary obstacles — familial or social objections — he soon chooses to regulate his life on fasting and prayers. Such characteristics are analyzed in the first chapter, an examination of the urge which leads the hero to withdraw from the world. Zealous to become a true follower of Christ, the *ascetic saint* strives to avoid society and to escape its sinful practice, resorting to a more austere mode of life. Taking refuge in the monastery, protected by a set of rules designed as a shield against temptations, the ascetic saint can then devote his existence to God.

Monasticism, a Western adaptation of eremitism, is one medium in which to fulfill a religious vocation. Some of the heroes, however, respond to a call that attracts them towards a greater reclusion, a retreat inspired precisely by the first hermits of the primitive Church. The *hermit-saint* leads a retired life, forsaking all social commitments as did the anchorites of early centuries, or setting a small community of cenobites in an untamed, sometimes hostile, environment. The second chapter considers the import of eremitic traits in the portrayal of the saint. Searching the reason for which the call of the desert could still be of current interest for some twelfth-century hagiographers and their public, one finds an explanation in the disenchantment aroused by the increasing wealth of monasteries. Accordingly, gradual stages of 'desertion' remove the hero from both the secular and regular institutions. In his search for true austerity, the hermit-saint contends with nature in its untamed elements, a wilderness that brings his endurance and miraculous talents to test. Inserting natural forces within their edifying tales, the hagiographers add a cosmic dimension to the moral lesson. Unlike the ordeal of Chrétien de Troyes' heroes, this sojourn in elemental solitude never coincides with debasement because of the ennobling effects of prayer. The narrative theme of desertion presents eremitism as a reconciliation of man and nature.

When he professes his contempt of the world, the saint also affirms his longing for the everlasting bliss of Paradise. As a pilgrim, he moves towards an unknown destination, assured at least that heaven is his goal and will put an end to transitoriness. The voyage away from civilization does not neccessarily end in the desert, and the third chapter analyzes the wanderings of *the traveller-saint*. Progressing along the road of life, or roaming through the dismaying wonders of the Other World, the traveller-saint directs his course to the East. Such 'orientation,' in its concrete meaning, dwells on the utopian and nostalgic belief that time and space have altered the original purity of God's disciples. Eager to find a new Eden, perhaps even some promised land, the hero embarks on a journey which brings about ordeals and adventures in profusion. In a cycle of stops and starts regulated by allegorical numbers and elements, this pilgrimage widens the distance between the hero and reality. Only a few traveller-saints ever return to, or remain, in the West, an 'occidentation' which valorizes the saints' social integration, and consequently modifies the concept of isolated holiness.

The second part of our aesthetic analysis gathers all the narrative themes which relate the saints' holy deeds in the moving or enlightening effect they exert on others. To those who witness the outstanding qualities of such individuals, the discovery that vocation relies on selflessness might prove to be salutory, or fatal, if they perceive the saint's virtue as a threat to their own values. Communicated holiness starts when circumstances bring people face to face with the saints and their concrete examples of virtuous existence. Nevertheless, spatial closeness does not necessarily promote communication. The very uniqueness of sainthood can go against traditions and institutions, and as a result, may provoke dissidence and confrontations. In the pagan atmosphere of the early years of Christianity, the saint fulfills his apostolic mission by defying what he considers impious worship. The fourth chapter analyzes how the saint's obsessive and obnoxious resistance to society attracts upon him the leader's irritated attention. Through this duel, the hagiographer magnifies his hero's internal strength, more that the charitable dispositions usually associated with sanctity. As soon as it becomes visible to the world, righteousness, it seems, unfolds a spectacular manifestation, as evinced either by the dramatic punishments inflicted upon the impious, or through the ostentatious effect of the conversions inspired by the saint's exemplary behavior. Remote from the world, the hermit or the traveller-saint suffers notoriety unwillingly, and his celebrity is usually posthumous. In the Passions, however, the holy man gains recognition before death, and through his heroic disregard for torture. Object of compassion and bewilderment for the faithful, *the martyr* is exemplary in an exclusive fashion, inasmuch as virtue remains aloof both to most witnesses in the context and to the hagiographer's public. Moreover, virtue is here demonstrated in a passive way, and displayed through the unequal combat between the bare-handed victim and his tormentor. Such disproportion, even more theatrical if the saint is a female thrown into a male and menacing world, alters the feudal concept of virtue as virile strength. The exemplary value of sainthood ceases being necessarily the result of external superiority; consequently, virtue may coincide with physical feebleness.

In the fifth chapter, the analysis of communicated holiness is devoted to the question of salvation, as some Lives dwell on the salutory effect of sainthood upon a weakened humanity. The saint strives to convert his fellow sinners, for his apostolic mission consists of self-denial and self-sacrifice in order to bring others closer to God. Altruism begins when the holy hero shows compassion toward mankind, a feeling which might move both the saint's witnesses and the hagiographer's public. Pity and concern, two characteristics almost incompatible with an epic notion of virtue, add humanistic dimensions to the portrayal of the saint. When the story relates how the hero is himself a *repentant sinner,* sanctified through the psychological transformation and perfecting of the individual, virtue is made even closer to the public, accessible to all, and no longer the sole attribute of an elite.

By the end of the twelfth century, social and religious changes entail a new interest in the concepts of conscience and individualism. [13] Vernacular hagiography partly and perhaps inadvertently reflects these changes in the way it increases the psychological identification between the saintly model and the audience. The sixth and last chapter examines the conditions and the values of

---

[13] M. D. Chenu, *L'Eveil de la conscience dans la civilisation médiévale* (Montréal: Institut d'Etudes Médiévales, 1969), and Colin Morris, *The Discovery of the Individual, 1050-1200* (New York: Harper and Row, 1972).

the saint's portrayal as *mediator*. These Chronicle-Lives reduce the distance between the model and the public in that historical facts, and sometimes geographical data, are in such poems the causes of a more concrete interaction of the kingly saint in the affairs of the world. The second version of *Thomas Becket* — a contemporary chronicle — exemplifies however how historicity plays no role in the process of humanization. When the hero becomes more real and more merciful, according to a power of mediation which brings heaven on earth, it is in virtue of emotive reactions of fatigue or joy through which the portrayal, no matter the textual and historical sources, displays that although divinized, the saint retains a human dimension. To be imitated as well as admired, he thus shows to the faithful an accessible road towards God. In this case, heroic deeds become less important than good deeds, according to a maturation and spirit of charity that infuse life into a stereotyped hero.

In the centuries to come — and we mention briefly two thirteenth-century examples — the hagiographic genre develops a growing interest in melodrama. The hero's feebleness is a concession to realism, without contradicting the essential definition of sainthood as extraordinary excellence. Persuasion, a high priority in didacticism, is realized in pathos when the hagiographers exploit the romanesque atmosphere that transforms a helpless individual into a champion of virtue, despite the maleficient forces of the universe.

During the twelfth century, the vernacular poems portray the saint's greatness in relation to the social world. The question to be resolved concerns the aesthetic value of the various forms of flight from the world. Even if the tendency seems at the turn of the century to depict a hero involved in the problems of society, the saint remains an isolated case of valor. The different chapters of this analysis focus on the literary and psychological merit of the portrayals of saints, in order to discover the elements which determine the didactic quality of a Life. The outcome of a hagiographic text is at all times known: it is only its presentation, its thematic structure, and its psychological coherence that are indicative of the hagiographer's talent. This study attempts to elucidate the relations between the poems and the public, and to construe the impact of a hero escaping the world upon a world craving for heroes.

PART ONE

THE INDIVIDUAL PERFORMANCE OF THE HERO-SAINT

Chapter I:

THE ASCETIC SAINT

Medieval hagiographers uniformly describe sainthood as the imitation of Christ, and saintly heroism as an effort toward voluntary poverty. In Roman and Merovingian times, the Christian attained sainthood through martyrdom. Consecrated by a redemptive death, he reached eternal life and brought new strength in a time of sorrow, repeating the first and universally meaningful Passion. Carl Erdmann has carefully examined the warrior-saint in Merovingian times, showing how militancy formed the first step of apostleship. [1] Such a spiritual battle enhanced the Christian concept of faith based on victory, in the concrete sense of conquest and domination. History offers many examples of the *Militia Christi*. Royal conversions brought about thousands of baptisms, proving that the religious conviction of one leader did not allow much individual choice. Almost no room was left for tolerance in the early Christian tradition. In the sixteenth century, the Jesuit movement still retains a military overtone. One of the literary heroes inspired by the Jesuits clearly demonstrates the junction of intolerance and apostleship. In Corneille's play by the same name, written in 1643, Polyeucte destroys the pagan statues and strives to dismiss from the world any remnant of false adoration. Because of his insulting manner he merits death. From the Christian viewpoint, Polyeucte, as his numerous martyred ancestors, deserves the attribute of saint.

---

[1] Carl Erdmann, *Entstehung des Kreuzzugsgedankens* (Stuttgart: Kohlhammer, 1965).

Although they do not overthrow the pagan image, both Sixtus and Laurence in the *Passion de Saint Laurent* [2] cause its destruction. The former addresses it even while referring to its deafness, the latter presents a Christian argumentation in order to demonstrate how false is its brilliancy:

> "Ymage qui n'os ne [ne] veiz,
> Tu qui la fole gent deceiz,
> Destruite soies e confondue!"
> Une grant part est donc chaue
> De l'orible temple Martis.

(*Laurent*, 211-215)

> "Tel deu qui est mu e sort,
> Car d'or sunt, d'argent et d'araim,
> E si sunt sort, mu, e vain.
> Sainte Escripture idles les nunme
> Car faiture sunt de main d'unme;"

(*Laurent*, 434-438)

Idols in *Laurent*, an icon in the narrative of *Alexis*: the role of the image demonstrates the medieval need for icons as opposed to idolatry. [3] Vernacular hagiography uses the imaginary to instruct

---

[2] D. W. Russell, *La Vie de Saint Laurent. An Anglo-Norman Poem of the Twelfth Century* (London: Anglo-Norman Text Society, n.º 34, 1976). A summary of the narrative and additional data are presented in the Appendix.

[3] Einar Ronsjö, *La Vie de Saint Nicolas par Wace: Poème religieux du XIIème siècle publié d'après tous les manuscrits, Etudes romanes de Lund*, n.º 5 (Lund: Gleerup and Munksgaard, 1942). This poem clearly demonstrates the magical power of the saint's portrait and its superiority over the pagan idols. In one episode a man dares to break Nicholas' effigy. Nicholas does not punish him, knowing that this anger has its reason, for the icon has failed to protect the man's material possessions. Consequently, Nicholas pursues the robbers, and the man is thus led to put his trust in the saint again:

> Sempres reçut cristienté
> Pur l'amur et pur la bonté
> Seint Nicholas que son aveir
> Li out fait des larons aveir.

(*Nicolas*, 715-718)

This particular legend reduces sainthood to a simple remedy against chance and the wheel of Fortune. See the narrative summaries of *Alexis* and *Nicolas* in the Appendices.

through images. As a linguistic representation, the legend does not differ from the pictorial interpretation found on the walls of the churches. The image is allegorical in the sense that it implies a movement of interpretation from abstract to concrete.

In his fight against idols, the warrior-saint rebukes a long-established tradition and a definite social hierarchy, and unhesitatingly accepts to pose as the defender of truth through martyrdom. Polyeucte consents to be banished from a Corneilian-feudalistic society, although his position as leader and husband places him high in the social order.

Certitude and fortitude are the obnoxious manifestations of saint-hood. Sainthood belongs only to a select group of people following in Paul's steps in order to establish foundations on earth for spiritual victory, which they attain through ecclesiastical domination. The *Militia Christi* combines material strength and religious intransigence, manly qualities required of a true witness. Leo Spitzer and E. R. Curtius have elaborated a now traditional parallel between the heroism of Polyeucte and Alexis. [4] Both saints incarnate the physical powers representative of such a social and moral stature since etymologically *virtus* means virile integrity. However Alexis' sainthood does not proceed from the striking action of a soldier but rather from his degree of passivity and resistance.

George offers a better example of the true *miles Christi*. The two extant twelfth-century vernacular versions are entitled *Vita Beati Georgii militis* and *Passio Beati Georgii militis et martyris*. [5] The *Vita*, falsely attributed to Wace, closely resembles Simund de Freine's *Passio*: in both cases, George defies the pagan order and diminishes its power of seduction by demonstrating Christian superiority. In the Passions of George and Laurence, the idol's ugliness demonstrates at once that falsity equals evil.

The sainthood of the hero is revealed in three symbolic stages: his social background of nobility, his refusal to compromise with the world, and his total acceptance of the consequences implied in such contempt for terrestrial laws.

---

[4] Leo Spitzer, "Erhellung des Polyeucte durch das Alexiuslied," *Archivum Romanicum*, 16 (1932), 473-500, and E. R. Curtius, "Zur Interpretation des Alexiusliedes," *Zeitschrift für romanische Philologie*, 56 (1936), 113-137.

[5] The narrative summaries of the two versions of George are in the Appendices.

This attitude of defying the world originates in the Pauline concept of conversion as a total and irreversible change from pagan, sophisticated culture to Christian, dedicated involvement. Like Paul, Polyeucte rebuts the pagan surroundings by couching his argumentations in Greco-Roman logic. The warrior-saint does not hesitate to confront a well-organized establishment with a superior, although invisible, reality. In fact, he stands more as an enemy of civic order than as a substantial religious threat, for the principal characteristic of the primitive church was its underground existence. Every Christian was then destined to become a saint, since he was sooner or later compelled to emerge into the open. Paradoxically, the primitive church owed its survival to the martyrdom of its members. Its mystical power changed the blood of death into streams of life, thus laying the foundations of hagiographical edification.

As long as the primitive church needed to defy the world in order to conquer it, the *fuga mundi* appeared as a *contemptus pagani mundi*. The anonymous author of the *Passion de Saint Laurent* develops this idea of confrontation from the seventy-four lines of the prologue to the actual occurrence of martyrdom. In fact, the psychological movement which pervades the poem turns its original melancholy into final joy. Victory over death celebrates the almighty power of God, but points up especially the negative value of terrestrial time:

> Que vaut [desir]? que vaut voleir?
> Que vaut delit c'um puisse aveir?
> Que vaut la joie de cest munt?
> Trestoz deliz a nient revunt;
> Tot vient de nient, a nient revert.
> Ki trop i prent, son tens i pert.
>
> (*Laurent,* 43-48)

> Lorenz dit: "Ne plorer, amis,
> Mais tais tei et si te esjois.
> Car la ou vois, arai vitoire;
> El ciel m'est aprestee gloire,
> Lasus ou li archangre sunt."
>
> (*Laurent,* 772-776)

Reviving the *vanitas vanitatis* sung in Ecclesiastes (see *Laurent,* 29-30), the story of Laurence is presented as a didactic exemplum in which the only events are the diverse tortures inflicted on him, and the sole progression relies on a growing confrontation between the Christian community and its enemies. Decius Caesar has decided to destroy the primitive church, seeking primarily to destroy its chief, Syxtus, in order to disperse the other members. Aware of Decius' intention, Syxtus has time to nominate his successor, Laurence, and also to hide the material possessions of the church from Roman greed:

> L'or de l'iglise et tot l'argent
> En vessele et en vestement,
> ...
> Toz les povres a asemblé,
> L'aveir lor a por Deu doné.
>
> (*Laurent,* 147-148, 151-152)

For the real treasure flourishes not on earth but in heaven, and Syxtus shows through this act of charity that Christian strength does not lie in palpable representations but in an invisible richness. Saintly nudity becomes even more obvious against the Roman display of wealth during the first confrontation of Decius and Laurence:

> Decius mult se esleeça
> Por le[s] tresor[s] qu'il coveita;
> Demande et enquiert ou il sunt,
> E saint Lorenz riens ne respunt,
> Car il voloit le felon tirant
> Conmoveir en ire par tant.
>
> (*Laurent,* 259-264)

Decius' cupidity inspires talkativeness whereas Laurence's silence is a clever and almost non-Christian calculation for unleashing Decius' anger and at the same time bringing his pagan avidity to light. The message in the poem is a denunciation of material possessions and power. Hence the misunderstanding raised by the notion of treasure:

> "Envers nos deus te humelie,
> Fai lor honor et sacrefise
> Ou de ton cors ferai justise.
> N'afier tant en tes tresors

Ke l'en a hunte maint ton cors;
Car ja n'iert ton tresor si grant
K'il contre mort te soit garant."

(Laurent, 581-587)

"Veirs est, en mon tresor m'afi,
Que nule peour n'ai de tei.
En cil m'afi en qui jeo crei.
En mon tresor ai esperance
Que tei ne dot ne ta faisance.
Crei al tresor celestien
Que ne dout torment terrien."

(Laurent, 603-609)

The fourth chapter will dwell further on the interest and social ramifications of the relationship between the saint and the pagan. But already the fight which confronts the warrior-saint and the pagan leader tends to celebrate in the former the virtue of integrity achieved by asceticism against illusory possessions. [6]

From the time ecclesiastical powers tended to coincide with terrestrial domination, history presents a slow and inevitable process of deterioration. [7] Among the members of a now well-rooted community which has incorporated the temporal powers of the world, isolated personalities begin to refuse a peace of mind that seems too much like spiritual defeat. Either through revolutionary tendencies or from a nostalgia for simpler times, those Christians seem to condemn the world by avoiding it. Sainthood obviously cannot be realized by means of martyrdom; it now seeks a new way to

---

[6] Hans Sckommodau in his article, "Das Alexiuslied. Die Datierungsfrage und das Problem der Askese," *Medium Aevum Romanicum Festschrift für Hans Rheinfelder* (Munich, 1963), pp. 208-304, and pp. 325-338, and Edith Simon in her book, *The Saints* (London: Weidenfeld and Nicholson, 1968) both state that it is the influence of Manicheism that brought about a wave of asceticism against evil, matter, lust and woman, four elements progressively illustrated by the story of Alexis.

[7] Concerning the erosion of monastic ideals subsequent to growth of the secular powers of the Church, see R. W. Southern, *Western Society and the Church in the Middle Ages* (London: Harmondsworth, 1970), pp. 230-236. Nostalgia for purer times depreciates progress through the traditional *ubi sunt* motif, a topos implicitly expressed in the ninth-century poem of *Eulalia*: the use of grammatical tenses — past or historical present in the first part, actual present in the second — increases the distance between a vanished heroic time and the temporal reality of the audience.

perfection by silently dismissing the conventional criteria of a good life. Solitude is the first step toward total dedication to God. [8] Since the ecclesiastical authority has been invaded by social laws and pragmatic compromises, the new saint seeks isolation and silence far from civic evils. Denouncing superfluous wealth encouraged by such a hierarchical situation, denouncing too social power as deviation from spiritual strength as well as theological rhetoric as a useless derivative of evangelic articulation, the saint chooses to live a marginal existence in a retreat where he will not be contaminated by these terrestrial deteriorations.

In this respect, asceticism consists of an interior movement towards voluntary poverty. Pre-Christian religions and Greek philosophers had already foreseen its power as a catalytic means for meditation. Although Plato encouraged temperance rather than abstinence, his dualistic concept celebrating the eternity of soul left room for transcendental mysticism. The ancients had a definite conception of the world. Some scorned it but accepted it, others enjoyed it but had a clear knowledge of its limitations.

Christianity has adapted these dualistic tendencies in creating Christian realism, which is a pragmatic transformation of Stoic determinism into Providence, of Platonic virtue of knowledge into knowledge of virtue. Christianity has also liberated humanity from the burden of mortality in introducing the idea of redemption. To lead a Christian life is to follow Christ's steps, away from the evil toils of material possessions. Christianity invests creation with a new value, as long as matter is used and transcended in theosophic terms. The notion of *contemptus mundi* expresses both a mistrust of worldly and egotistic enrichment, and a yearning for the divine rewards of heaven and eternal bliss on which the vernacular hagiographers will insist at length. Asceticism is one means to arrive at the state of selflessness required by the Scriptures. Etymologically, the word ἄσκησις refers to a practice, almost a profession, that turns a negative set of rules into a profitable display of acts. Formed in a monastic atmosphere, Christianity paved the way to heaven

---

[8] Not always: Nicholas is a saint working in the world, but, as will be shown later, his civic awareness remains very limited. He possesses all the attributes of the conventional hero of hagiography, observing a devotional fast during the first years of his existence, giving away his inheritance at his parents' death, and observing the rule of chastity throughout his life.

with well defined steps of corporeal conquest achieved through contempt. One must disregard the body, the product of a fallen human being, in order to perceive the soul, the unique remnant of God's image. The Christian writers were to dwell on that distinction and to enumerate the sins — naming is already knowing. Only then would an ascension be possible toward a perfection which was first described in terms of profitable interdictions. Salvation for a Christian was originally the act of martyrdom which took man out of the world and its imperfections; later, martyrdom was logically replaced by asceticism as a necessary withdrawal from the world and its temptations.

Donald Howard explains why the enumeration of sins inspired further classification: "The origins of this classification are shrouded in the obscurity of a widespread predilection, during the early Christian period, to make conventionalized lists of vices and virtues. The number seven, because of its mystical properties, made the seven-fold list an appealing one; but the number three had mystical properties too, and was often used in a schema for classifying evils." [9] For man, in the medieval mentality, is incapable of permanence: he either progresses or regresses in the scale of beings. [10] Such instability will become even more apparent when the saint is studied in relation to nature. [11] Many are the tales which illustrate the danger of an excessively long sojourn away from social life: Chrétien describes, for example, the fast mental deterioration endured by his hero Yvain in the midst of the forest.

This classification of sins provides material for determining the full implications behind asceticism. The lust of the flesh, of the eyes, of life; gluttony, avarice and vainglory; [12] the desire

---

[9] Donald Roy Howard, "The Contempt of the World: A Study in the Ideology of Latin Christendom with Emphasis on Fourteenth-Century English Literature," Diss. Univ. of Florida 1954, pp. 53-54.

[10] See the analysis on the medieval concept of time by Jacques Le Goff, *La Civilisation de l'occident médiéval* (Paris: Arthaud, 1964), p. 397, and by Richard Glasser, *Time in French Life and Thought* trans. C. G. Pearson (Totowas, New Jersey: Manchester University Press: 1972), pp. 50-69.

[11] See our discussions about the role of elemental reclusion and travel in Chapters Two and Three.

[12] Lester K. Little ("Pride goes before Avarice: Social Change and the Vices in Latin Christendom," *American Historical Review*, 76 [1971], 16-49), explains how the eleventh century witnesses a shift in the notion of the most deadly sin. If pride was the highest sin, it is soon replaced by avarice

to have pleasure, to be rich, to be important: such are the three orders of sin which are counterbalanced by the three monastic rules of chastity, poverty and obedience. From this tripartite set, two directions are possible, which lead man either downward or upward, depending on whether he follows his irrational, instinctive and animal impulses, or submits them to the love of God. The triple temptation becomes, in the twelfth-century expression, "the world, the flesh, and the devil." Howard analyzes the theological writers of the period to show which solutions they brought to counteract these evil tendencies:

> We conquer the devil when we resist his suggestions; we conquer the world when we do not lust after prosperity nor fear adversity; we conquer the flesh when we neither extinguish its desires in necessary things nor indulge in its enticements. [13]

Having defined the basic temptations, the twelfth-century writers suggested how to conquer them. In vernacular hagiography, the world's evil — lust, prosperity, adversity — is depicted in realistic detail. To be good or to do good is to avoid both the material and the social world. The consequences are described in the term asceticism as a deprivation of superfluity, a restraint of natural desire for possessions, and an internal struggle against vain recognition, all elements which put the Christian ethic under a psychological structure of interdictions. This is why the dogmatic level of hagiography appears so static, even nostalgic. The poet of the *Passion de Saint Laurent,* despising worldly vanities, evokes the wheel of Fortune [14] where time incessantly acts against prosperity. Hence the *ubi sunt* motif already noticed in this poem.

---

in a progressively commercialized Christian society. The Councils of the twelfth century attacked simony primarily.

[13] Hugh of Saint Victor, in *Patrologia Latina,* 177, p. 585, quoted by Howard, *op. cit.,* p. 79.

[14] The treatment of time differentiates legend and tale, but its concept can create, within the legend, two levels of duration, either chronological or eschatological. For instance, time in the Passions measures an anterior and therefore better state of sainthood. This medieval pessimism is only applied to profane time, where change tends to be for the worse. On the other hand, contemporary time assumes a positive value to the strict extent that it coincides with the liturgical year, regulated by the repetitive cycle of Christ and saints.

Asceticism is not always to be envisaged as a lack of individualism. When the medieval man accepts the struggle against his evil tendencies, controlling the three categories of sin through the three monastic rules, he implicitly recognizes some degree of individual power. The importance of will, in close dependance on the matter of choice, allows man to fulfill his humanity. [15] In the portrayal of Laurence, there is no choice, in so far as his existence is driven by an irresistible movement of ascension. Unlike the twelfth-century theologians, most vernacular hagiographers at that time interpret individual choice as being a disastrous affirmation of the ego, an option that might feed the natural impulse for selfishness and hinder man's potential function in life. The saint's role is instrumental, and the holy man must, more than anyone, take heed of God's will upon him.

The difference between individual choice and divine selection is clearly exemplified by the story of Gregory. [16] By choosing to live as a knight, in a movement of search for his identity, Gregory encounters only obstacles. Even if he finally discovers the secret of his origin, the way in which he finds his mother is a denunciation of stubbornness. As soon as he allows destiny to direct his vocation, Gregory receives a divine sign to show him the way. Seventeen years of query pass before the saint's ultimate function is revealed. A miraculous event in Rome draws the Christians' attention to a still unknown and mysterious man of God. Destined to become Pope, Gregory does not believe the Roman messengers, for fear of reviving his former ordeals. The episode of the key, a symbol of his dismissal from the world, is also the sign for Gregory's recognition of God's voice:

---

[15] Giles Constable ("Twelfth-Century Spirituality and the Late Middle Ages," *Medieval and Renaissance Studies*, 5 [1971], 27-60) states that the importance of personal will, the emergence of an individual concept of virtue, are the points which made the twelfth-century spirituality appealing to a fifteenth-century man (p. 32). Robert Javelet clarifies the distinction between *posse* and *velle* (*Psychologie des auteurs spirituels du XIIème siècle* [Strasbourg: Much. Le Roux, 1959]) by showing how power was considered by twelfth-century theologians as the natural and unreliable instinct, while will corresponded to the rational desire for virtue (p. 31).

[16] Gerta Telger, *Die altfranzösische Gregoriuslegende nach der londoner Handschrift zum ersten Male herausgeben. Arbeiten zur romanische Philologie* n.º 5 (Paris: Droz, 1933). All the subsequent allusions to the life of *Grégoire* refer to the summary presented in the Appendix.

"Par cel saintisme anuncement
Ça nus unt tramis veirement
Li chardunal ici pur tei,
Pur pastur fere de la lei,
Par nun de sainte obedience."

(*Grégoire,* 1977-1981)

Nothing in these words appears to be for Gregory a sufficient proof that Satan is not hidden, once again, behind this relation. He has not seen any angel and cannot perceive the saintly order of this message. When replying that he will not leave his retreat unless the key to his chains be found, Gregory expresses a determination that defies human power. So the concrete proof of the key, miraculously found inside a fish, is evidence of God's calling. No terrestrial force could have allowed man to discover a key in the bottom of the sea. Selection takes the form of obedience, whereas choice was up to the then unlucky product of Gregory's will.

The narrative theme of martyrdom, a commemoration of heroic times, portrays the saint in martial terms, as a champion of the true God denouncing all signs of corruptability and falsity. In a less dazzling manner, the ascetic saint shows an identical urge for condemning a corrupted, if less threatening, world. Compared to the pagan aggressivity, the mundane evils do not directly menace the saint, although he sees them as an unpropitious medium of meditation and likely to cause spiritual death. Guided by Christ's example, the ascetic saint responds to a call that pulls him out of his social environment. The representation of asceticism, in twelfth-century vernacular hagiography, expresses an undeniable if silent message of disapproval directed against the erosion of Christian ideals. A work of propaganda and apology, vernacular hagiography criticizes the pragmatic motives of society while praising as ominous exceptions all efforts which restore a more austere mode of life. Imprecations concerning marriage, property, power and pleasure, avarice, simony, concupiscence, cupidity, curiosity, envy, pride, ambition and honor are thus stressing the exemplary value of abnegation. In twelfth-century hagiography, sainthood cannot be achieved otherwise than through an initial movement toward abstinence and self-denial. *Alexis,* the first vernacular hagiographic text of the time,[17] clearly exemplifies how the road to perfection starts with a departure from the social world.

Alexis, as well as Polyeucte, strives to imitate Christ's achievement of victory attained through humiliation. In many ways the life of Alexis reproduces the life of Christ, an identification emphasized by the image of his divine affiliation. 'Man of God' is in fact the appellation given to Alexis throughout the *Vita,*[18] as if no other name could define more properly the qualities bestowed on him. Man of God, and son of Euphemien, Alexis belonged, according to the Latin writer, to a noble and wealthy Roman milieu. Born and raised to become an active member of that society, he came of age and married a young girl of equivalent distinction. Up to that point, no mention is made of Alexis' attitude concerning his own life. Evangelic eloquence and sudden flight occur on the same day, radically transforming what was before filial obedience and individual passivity, and consecrating henceforth Alexis' vows of silence and solitude. In the portrayal of the saint the appearance of heroism is juxtaposed to the quiet presence of the woman, and is therefore produced through the contrast of two opposing forces. The wife to be, on one hand, the future saint on the other, respectively represent two contradictory worlds of imperfection and potential greatness. Although the woman remains inactive and unnamed in the *Vita,* she serves as a literary device underlying Alexis' sudden vocation.

This is not to say that the woman will play this role in all of the hagiographic poems.[19] Especially within the Passions, women who witness the martyr's ordeal usually convert to Christianity, sometimes prior to their husbands. When the hero is described in epic terms, the woman is seen as an obstacle between him and God. In the lives of Alexis, Gregory and Giles,[20] the woman is a substantial or alleviating force which marks a turning point within

---

[17] Christopher Storey, *La Vie de Saint Alexis* (Paris: Minard, 1968).

[18] *Acta Sanctorum,* Jul IV, 251-253.

[19] Five times it is a woman who inspires the hagiographer. Compared with the total of twenty-four poems, this proportion indicates that her role as protagonist in the story is not negligible.

[20] Alphonse Bos and Gaston Paris, *La Vie de Saint Gilles par Guillaume de Berneville* (Paris: Société des Anciens Textes Français, 1881). The summaries given in the Appendix clarify the exact role played by female characters.

the poem. In the story of Edward,[21] the hero's marriage does not bring any change in the narrative. He is obliged by his people to choose a wife and, perhaps because the hagiographer is herself a woman, this episode only emphasizes the resolve of both Edward and his wife to remain chaste. Edward explains to her at length why he will not consummate the nuptial bonds. She joyfully answers:

> "Or desirez le mien desir,
> Kar jeo ferai vostre plaisir.
> Cum seignur vus honurerai
> Et chastement vus amerai."
>
> (*Edouard*, 1381-1384)

Evroul[22] does not encounter any resistance either, when he proposes that he and his wife live separately. He married her to obey his parents, but long before, and his precocity is here to attest to it, he was attracted by simplicity over wealth, asceticism over pleasure. After the wedding ceremony, he has accomplished his duties as a husband. His decision does not occur on the first night, as it had for Alexis. On the contrary, he hesitates for days:

> Einsi pensa mout longuement
>
> (*Evroul*, 321)

> Pensout touz jours sanz sejorner
>
> (*Evroul*, 336)

He remembers Paul's words — the evangelist's admonition to re-nounce self-indulgence — and strongly desires to leave society. First, he keeps these thoughts secretly in his mind:

> Ne ne dist son proposement
> N'a parent, n'ami, n'a sa fame.
>
> (*Evroul*, 322-323)

---

[21] Osten Södergard, *La Vie d'Edouard le Confesseur, poème anglo-nor-mand du XIIème siècle* (Upsala, 1948). See our Appendix.

[22] Ferdinand Danne, "Das altfranzösische Ebrulfusleben. Eine Dictung aus dem 12 Jahrhundert nach dem Manuskript 19867 der national Bibliothek zu Paris," *Romanische Forschungen*, 32 (1913), 748-893. See our Appendix.

> Ains le retint bien en son cuer.
>
> *(Evroul, 352)*

> Dedens son cuer mult bien se coevre.
>
> *(Evroul, 367)*

The more he reminds himself of his duties as a son, a husband, and a noble, the more he despises this kind of life. Within his heart, and during his indecision, he feels a progressively stronger need for change:

> Mes touz jours pensoit il de s'ame,
> Comment qu'ëust des biens assez
> ...
> Du bien fet plus s'esjoïsset
> Que du temporel, s'il croisset;
> Et les fes des sainz anciens
> Retint et n'en oublia riens.
>
> *(Evroul, 324-325, 329-332)*

The hagiographer announces here that his hero wants to walk in the footsteps of the saints. We are also informed which kind of sainthood he will achieve. But the movement of *fuga mundi* is not that simple when it concerns a courteous young man:

> Einsi commencha a penser
> Et en son cuer a retenser,
> Ou sa compaigne le dira,
> Ou sans son sëu s'en ira.
>
> *(Evroul, 375-378)*

However, this long conflict is revealed as useless, since the wife agrees wholeheartedly to live a pious existence. She admires her husband for having voiced her own secret desire. She also recognizes his superiority in a declaration which makes Evroul's delicateness all the more courteous:

> Et ne pourquant plus digne est homme
> Que n'est la fame, — c'est la somme.
>
> *(Evroul, 521-522)*

In his introduction Danne indicates that the author is a monk (p. 752): the above quotation, and especially Evroul's subsequent quest, corroborates this fact. Whereas Evroul takes his ideal from other saints' deeds, it is his example that his wife wants to follow and she asks for Evroul's advice. The saint recommends charity, sobriety and chastity (ll. 453-454), after a definitive retreat from the world:

> Miez nous vaudret si aprester
> Et fuir tout sans arrester.
>
> (*Evroul,* 441-442)

For both, the burden of a courtly life becomes too intolerable, and escape consists in going elsewhere to live "une estrange et sainte vie" (l. 475). Up to that point, the portrayal of Evroul undergoes three transformations: a pious adolescent, a sagacious youth praised by his parents and by King Clotaire, and a mature man aspiring toward privacy and obscurity.

The crossing of the threshold of the nuptial room materializes Alexis' entrance into another world. Intimacy and privacy are not in Alexis' case subject to temptations. They simply stand as a still too familiar and familial stage which the saint must avoid, if he is to fulfill the mission he has just become aware of. He instructs his wife, in the Latin text, as if to formulate out loud and for himself the terms of a superior commitment. Freedom is seen as a refusal of filial obedience or marital bonds in order to attain the divine liberty conferred upon God's sons. Out of the definite limits of the nuptial room, Alexis undertakes a long journey at the end of which he will return to Rome and confine himself in an even more restricted area. The meaning of the journey will be studied in the third chapter, but it can already be noted that the evolution of the hero follows a spiral movement, from a static situation as a noble heir, to the contemplative position as a poor mendicant, through the active years of pilgrimage. The saint suffers a symbolic process of humiliation through which he is first presented in the full light of the upright, epic attitude, then on his knees outside the door of the church, and finally lying in the shadow of the most obscure recess of his own home.

An identical pattern is found in the first French version, although a close comparison between the *Vita* and the *Vie* shows in the latter a literary accomplishment achieved through the power of invention and emotion. [23]

The manuscript containing the *Vie* of Alexis, often referred to as the Hildesheim or Saint Alban's Psalter, was intended for Christina, anchoress of Markyate, whose life partially resembles that of the saint. After a close study of the illuminations found here, as opposed to the traditional ones which portray the father failing to recognize his son, the Pope visiting Alexis' death bed, the relatives mourning, or the humble staircase, Otto Pächt concludes: "What has been chosen for illustration are thus the very scenes which were of topical interest in a book destined for Christina, scenes which could be understood as allegories of her own actions." [24] Such a variation in pictorial topics leads him to state that the composition of the Hildesheim version has been completed around the year 1120. [25]

Despite the insistence placed on chastity in this manuscript, the predominant themes of Alexis's life are humility and poverty, in contrast to his aristocratic and wealthy surroundings. The structure of the poem rests upon the dramatic tension between the worldly and the divine. Such a dichotomy never appears however in the character of Alexis: his only emotion is that of joy attained through an ascetic existence, and neither his parents' grief nor his wife's lamentations ever affect this single-mindedness of purpose. [26] For

---

[23] See our Appendices for the data concerning the Latin source and the first two versions of *Alexis* (*Alexis I* and *Alexis II*).

[24] That is to say, the beginnings of his wanderings and the circumstances which surround the marriage night, the refusal of the spouse and the departure. See Francis Wormald, C. R. Dodwell, and Otto Pächt, *The Saint Alban's Psalter* (London: The Warburg Institute, 1960), pp. 139-140.

[25] *Ibid.*, pp. 142-143. C. Storey notes that MS A is scarcely less anterior (p. 28).

[26] Howard S. Robertson ("*La Vie de Saint Alexis*: Meaning and Manuscript A," *Studies in Philology*, 67 [1970], 422) speaks of Alexis' struggle as an effort "to attain sanctity in the face of temptation." It seems too strong an assertion, in our view, inasmuch as there is no explicit dilemma on the part of Alexis. The episodes of the nuptial night, of the inopportune veneration by the people of Edessa, of Alexis' fear to be recognized by his parents, emphasize less Alexis' potential weakness than his actual strength. If the appeal of the flesh and of the world has no effect on the saint — he in fact condemns it as a source of sadness — it might well seem legitimately alluring to the public: for the ordinary man, worldly entanglements are indeed seductive, but not so for a man of God whose joy remains proportional to his liberation from earthly motives.

the *virtus* remains a power of resistance, a faculty of terrestrial renouncement, in the name of God, through the imitation of Christ. Therefore steadfastness does not equal harshness, and the model proposed here offers a unique way of escaping a pragmatic world.

The French poet first describes the noble and social distinctions which belong to Euphemian and his wife. In the *Vita* this point is not neglected, although the generosity of Alexis' father is much more prevalent:

Fuit Romae vir magnus, et no-bilis Euphemianus nomine, dives valde, et primus in palatio Impe-ratoris ... Hic namque erat jus-tus et misericors, eleemosynas multas pauperibus erogans.

(*Vita*, 251)

Si fut un sire de Rome la citét;
Rices hom fud, de grant nobi-
[litét.
Pur hoc vus di, d'un son filz voil
[parler.
[E]ufumïen — si out a num li
[pedre—
Cons fut de Rome des melz ki
[dunc i ere[n]t;
Sur tuz ses pers l'amat li empe-
[rere.

(*Alexis I*, 13-18)

This example notwithstanding, the modifications in the *Vie* indicate a more elaborated emotive world. One crucial scene is that of the marriage night; there is no mention of Alexis' reaction in the *Vita*, while in the *Vie* it is known that he approaches the marriage re-luctantly:

Vespere autem facto dixit Eu-phemianus filio suo: Intra, fili, in cubiculum et visita sponsam tuam. Ut autem intravit, coepit nobilissimus juvenis, et in Chris-to sapientissimus instruere spon-sam suam, et plura ei sacramenta differere.

(*Vita*, 252)

Ço dist li pedres: "Filz, quar t'en
[vas colcer
Avoc ta spuse, al cumand Deu
[del ciel."
Ne volt li emfes sum pedre co-
[rocier;
Vint en la cambra ou er[e]t sa
[muiler.
Cum veit le lit, esguardat la pul-
[cela;
Dunc li remembret de sun seinor
[celeste,
Que plus ad cher que tut aveir
[terrestre.
"E Deus!" dist il, "cum fort
[pécet m'apresset!

S'or ne m'en fui, mult criem que
[ne t'em perde."
Quant an la cambra furent tut
[sul remés,
Danz Alexis la prist ad apeler;
La mortel vithe li prist mult a
[blasmer,
De la celeste li mostret veritét;
Mais lui est tart quet il s'en seit
[turnét.
"Oz mei, pulcele! Celui tien ad
[espus
Ki nus raens[t] de sun sanc pre-
[cĭus.
An ices[t] secle nen at parfit'
[amor;
La vithe est fraisle, n' ad durable
[honur;
Cesta lethece revert a grant tris-
[tur."

(*Alexis I*, 52-70)

Silence and obedience on one side, preaching and self-assertiveness on the other, differentiate Alexis' attitudes as a son and a husband. The *Vie* elaborates extensively on the inner workings of the saint's mind, and the narrative is made more vivid by the use of the historic present in conjunction with the preterite: "As he sees the bed, he looked at his wife." [27] Dramatic tension becomes even more vivid during the setting of Alexis' flight from home: it happens "ensur[e] nuit" (*Alexis I*, 75), adding an air of mystery to what is already mystical. [28] His disappearance provokes a greater amount of lamen-

---

[27] Karl D. Uitti, "The Old-French *Vie de Saint Alexis*: Paradigm, Legend, Meaning," *Romance Philology*, 20 (1966), 289, and "The Clerky Narrator Figure in Old French Hagiography and Romance," *Medioevo Romanzo*, 2 (1975), 394-408.

[28] Robertson notes the similarity in the language that describes this first flight and the second one, "Ensure nuit s'en fuit de la ciptet" (l. 189), when Alexis strives to avoid the veneration of the people of Edessa. The critic, along with Uitti, stresses how "the narrative mode yields to the dramatic as Alexis [becomes] for the first time a physical presence" (p. 423). Even more dramatic is the fact that such physical presence, a manifestation of corporeal embodiment, desintegrates as the young man departs from home and undergoes a complete physical transformation. He no longer exists for his wife, since her understanding is limited by her need for concrete percep-

tation in the French poem, according to Pächt's calculations. [29] His death elicits Euphemian's chagrin at having lost a son in the *Vita,* an heir in the *Vie.*

All the differences mentioned point out the importance of familial structure and the feudal system at the time of the *Vie.* The emotional motifs, sparse as they are, nevertheless show the differentiation between the Latin text and the French poem: in the *Vita,* Alexis is a one-dimensional man, a monolithic figure, a universal Man of God, in the *Vie,* more human, Christ-like rather than God-like, [30] and more individual.

Alexis' example, in the context of the *Vie,* provides material for what the early twelfth century regarded as true asceticism. All the saint's energy is devoted to the struggle against terrestrial temptations. Since the saint himself never shows any hesitation as to the aim of his efforts, the mourning displayed by his relatives opposes his strength to their weakness. [31] Moreover, the vernacular version presents a Christ-oriented construction of the hero through the degree of consciousness which gives rise to his new way of life. Alexis' sainthood is based not only on hieratic contempt directed against his social environment, but also on Christian forgiveness addressed to all manifestations of error:

---

tions, and he becomes so transfigured as to be unrecognized by his own people.

[29] These figures reflect the number of words in each instance:

	father's laments	mother's laments	wife's laments
Vita	58	47	35
Vie	200	230	180

[30] "Aux serviteurs qui se moquent de lui le poète oppose la formule christique toute nue," as Jean Győry remarks in "Hagiographie hétérodoxe," *Acta Ethnographica Academiae Scientiarum Hungaricae,* 11 (1962), 376.

[31] Robertson notes how Alexis "has had no influence on his fellows during his lifetime" (p. 427). The reactions to Alexis indeed show the material and egotistical obsession of his society. For Robertson, such a basic distinction between spiritual and material is lacking in the missing lines of MS L, or not reproduced by MS A. He thus states: "These twelve strophes [111-125] clearly place their emphasis on worldly pomp, emotional involvement with human relationships, and the profit to be drawn from a new advocate with God" (p. 437). The story itself is not altered; what differs is its didactic import, as clarified by Donald Maddox in "Pilgrimage Narrative and Meaning in Manuscripts L and A of the *Vie de Saint Alexis,*" *Romance Philology,* 27 (1973), 143-157.

Ainz priet Deu quet il le lur parduinst
Par sa mercit, quer ne sevent que funt.

(*Alexis I*, 269-270)

Human weakness is described in terms of error and not sin, for the lack of respect shown by the servants, albeit sacrilegious since they maltreat a holy man, is due to a dramatic misunderstanding. Such is the destiny of Alexis. Because of his silence regarding his real identity, he is partially responsible for inspiring the insults. Secondly, Alexis lays himself open to ridicule because of poverty resulting from a reprehensible inactivity. From another point of view, the servants commit a sin as long as they scorn a beggar, an act they would not dare commit against a more powerful man. Respect is therefore a product of hierarchical authority, be it lay or ecclesiastical. Sainthood as asceticism calls for a double rehabilitation of openness and simplicity.

The main transgression that has invaded the world appears to be arrogance. Pride is worthless when attached to terrestrial values and egotistic vanity. [32] In the *Voyage of Brendan*, [33] it is taxed as a deadly sin which sends people directly to Hell:

Enfern prïed vetheir oveoc,
E quels peines avrunt ileoc
Icil felun qui par orguil
Ici prennent par eols escuil
De guerreer Deu e la lei,
Ne entre eols nen unt amur ne fai.

(*Brendan*, 65-70)

Accorded a more clement treatment, the followers of Satan, the fallen angels of the Old Testament, must stay away from God's Paradise and live in the Paradise of Birds in a shameful bestial shape. Nevertheless, their punishment is not too harsh, compared to Judas' torments or other monstrous reincarnations. But the point

---

[32] When Little speaks of the shift from pride to avarice at the end of the eleventh century (see note 12 above), he refers to Latin theology of the time. *Brendan* is one example of the distance between vernacular hagiography and theology, since in the context of the story pride still comes before avarice.

[33] E. G. R. Waters, *The Anglo-Norman Voyage of Saint Brendan by Benedeit* (Oxford: Clarendon Press, 1928). See our Appendix.

here is that arrogance deserves punishment. The beatific state of angels turns into the nightmare of having to receive a carnal body, and the transitory step of human embodiment becomes an eternal damnation of sensorial pain.

Compared with the causes of worldly pride and its consequences, asceticism claims the greatness of poverty. To avoid the physical rewards which accompany pragmatic ascension, it is necessary to flee the world, to renounce its honors, and to distinguish the illusive brilliancy of false light:

> "Ki de cest mund fuit le delit,
> Od Deu de cel tant en avrat
> Que demander plus ne savrat."
> Pur oc guerpit cist reials eirs
> Les fals honurs pur iceals veirs —
> Dras de moine — pur estre vil
> En cest secle cum en eisil.
>
> (*Brendan,* 24-30)

The ascetic flees from the world into another miniaturized world with new rules and new walls. The following lines of *Brendan* describe how he reluctantly allows himself to be elected abbot of the monastery:

> Prist e l'ordre e les habiz,
> Puis fud abes par force esliz.
>
> (*Brendan,* 31-32)

Already there is a hint of the denunciation claimed by hermits or saintly citizens against the deterioration of monastic practices before their reform. Above all, the quotation clarifies a duality in terms of election. Human preference does not prevail over divine choice and the more demanding the renunciation, the more extended its influence:

> Par art de lui mult i vindrent
> Qui al ordre bein se tindrent:
> Tres mil suz lui par divers leus
> Munies aveit Brandan li pius,
> De lui pernanz tuz ensample
> Par sa vertud que ert ample.
>
> (*Brendan,* 33-38)

Such is the significance of the conventional outline for a saint's life. His noble extraction will emphasize his subsequent abnegation. Poverty and obedience will take place during a preliminary step of internal preparation. Devotion and virtue will then lead to the proclamation of his sanctity, sometimes against his will and sense of humility, sometimes by way of preaching or, after death, through the process of beatification and devotion. The *fuga mundi* which is the first step of asceticism is thus narrowly related to the *imitatio Christi*. Like the life of Christ, the life of the saint undergoes three stages: he first strives for perfection through a contemplative and silent period of preparation; he is then propelled or willing to preach to the world how to reach God; [34] his influence continues after death, a death even more admirable when sacrificial.

Edmond presents a clear example of this Christly imitation. In Piramus' version, [35] there are three stages in Edmund's development. The first involves a mandatory time of preparation, when the hero learns how to be a king and a saintly chief. The second part shows his involvement in the concrete and geographical world of England, and the way his preaching is carried beyond words through his exemplary mode of life. Thirdly, his passion and death bring the country closer to redemption. However, the other version of *Edmond* [36] describes in a more obvious way how the saint imitates

---

[34] *Geneviève* (Lennart Bohm, *La Vie de Sainte Geneviève de Paris* [Upsala, 1955]) shows this dual aspect of preparation/preaching throughout the two stages in the poem. Her withdrawal from the world is related as follows:

N'avoit cure del los del mont,
Qu'ele set bien que il confont
Cels qui en lui metent lor cure,
Si com reconte l'Escripture,
Qui dit que nus ne puet servir
Le mont et a Deu parvenir.

(*Geneviève*, 571-576)

Her fame then causes her to return to the world. Unlike many vernacular portrayals, Geneviève exerts a saintly influence through an active, rather than verbal, preaching. Perhaps the date of the poem (c. 1200) explains why her initial contempt for the world later turns into involvement.

[35] Hilding Kjellman, *La Vie Seint Edmund le Rei, poème anglo-normand du XIIème siècle par Denis Piramus* (Goteborg: Wettergren and Kerbor, 1935). See our Appendix.

[36] Albert Nabert, *La Passiun de Seint Edmund. Ein anglonormannisches Gedicht aus dem 12. Jahrhundert* (Greifswald, 1915). See our Appendix.

Christ. Asceticism is perceived as a complete dedication which inspires the saintly king to give up this world in order to save it. It is therefore during the episode of his passion that such an equation is realized:

> N'est pas muable cume li vent,
> Jhesu [Crist] siut hardïement.
> Par passiun e par turment;
> Tut [e feiz] mais en cruiz ne pent.
>
> (*Edmond I*, 773-776)

Although the crucifixion as such does not occur, there is a metaphorical use of the tree to which the felons attach Edmund. Then his trial takes place:

> Devant Inguar lur avüé,
> Si cum Jhesu nostre salvere
> Devant Pilate le jugere
> Fut encusé de grant manere.
>
> (*Edmond I*, 784-787)

The felons proceed to throw off Edmund's clothes, re-enacting in that very action the sacrilege committed against Christ after his judgment. [37] Explicit allusions to the New Testament thus reinforce the holy identification between the saint and Christ. Nicholas, for example, repeats the miracle of the multiplication of bread, and so does Genevieve, as well as twice allaying a tempest. For the hagiographer's public, such references are a clear indication of the commemorative and imitative function of sainthood.

The saint became a Christian example in so far as his spiritual quest for Christ was to be emulated, should the faithful succeed in defeating temptations and attain divine revelation. Witnesses, intercessors and models stood between God and the twelfth-century man: such are the reasons for a progressively increasing number of saints, as if God had by then disappeared to a far-removed heaven. The structural device of refraction by which imitation of the saints mimes the saint's imitation of Christ demonstrates how popular devotion felt the need for a more humanized standard. In this

---

[37] The sainthood of Edmund is also attested through the subsequent comparison with Sebastian's martyrdom (*Edmond I*, 813).

respect, asceticism offers a simple if not easy formula for reaching perfection.

Abstinence is the first condition for fulfilling any spiritual quest. [38] The ascetic saint first of all rejects the feudal order and its useless battles by means of which virility leads to individual pride. The battles waged by sainthood, although individual, strive to celebrate God's superiority. The intercessive nature of the saint places heroism in the perspective of instrumental interference. In *Grégoire,* the abbot tries to convince his pupil that the best way to overcome his fate is to stay in the monastery:

> "K[e] abes seies de cest mustier,
> Ke malfesant ne chavalier."
>
> *(Grégoire,* 891-892)

There is, in these lines, a denunciation of knightly vanity which foreshadows the atmosphere of *Don Quixote.* Gregory is alienated by a shameful origin and his first desire is to seek his parents. To do so, he begs the abbot to make him a knight, to give him the exterior attributes ("De chevalier les garnements," [902]) which complement his physical beauty. Again the abbot admonishes him:

> "Si tu meines chevalerie,
> T'alme sera tute perie."
>
> *(Grégoire,* 1015-1016)

Soon enough, Gregory encounters these predicted ordeals. He comes to assist a beautiful widow, countess of a country prey to invaders and enemies. Stricken by Gregory's beauty and bravery, she welcomes him into her home, only to discover that she sinned with her own son. Remembering the abbot's advice, Gregory gives up his knightly attributes:

> Ses garnemenz trestuz jus mist
> Si se revest[e] de povres dras

---

[38] Genevieve follows her own vocation of silence from the age of 15 to 50, during which time she observes a rigid fast and constant flagellation (*aspre vie,* 806), eating only twice a week on Thursdays and Sundays, drinking only water despite her ill health. The bishops then beg her to lead a normal life in order to be useful to the city. She follows their advice and leads an active existence until her death at the respectable age of 80.

Si se remet de halt en bas,
E si cum povres e chaitifs
S'en [est] fuï hors del païs.

(*Grégoire*, 1610-1614)

Humiliation and abstinence are the first two steps which will allow Gregory to overcome his fate and accomplish his divine destiny:

Ja de peissun ne mangerai
Ne de vin mais [io] ne bev[e]rai.

(*Grégoire*, 1703-1704)

He does not know what kind of vocation is bestowed on him and before his final consecration, Gregory spends seventeen years as a hermit. From this point on, the hagiographer no longer refers to Gregory as *li bon pechiere* but as *saint apostoire*.

With Brendan, abstinence marks the beginning of a long journey:

"E enz el nun al saint Espirit
Juine faimes que la nus guit,
E junum la quarenteine
Sur les treis jurs la semaine."

(*Brendan*, 131-134)

The disregard of material pleasures is accompanied by a characteristic contempt for any familial bonds:

Vait s'en Brandan vers la grant mer
U sout par Deu que dout entrer.
Unc ne turnat vers sun parent:
En plus cher leu aler entent.

(*Brendan*, 157-160)

In order to flee the world, Brendan literally dismisses society and chooses to confront natural dangers. For asceticism assumes here the concrete form of pilgrimage which measures the corporeal endurance synonymous with sainthood:

Grant curs unt fait li pelerin,
Mais uncore ne sevent fin;
E nepurtant ne s'en feignent,
Mais cum plus vunt, plus se peinent,

Ne de peiner ne recrerrunt
De ci que lur desir verrunt.

(*Brendan*, 1101-1106)

Brendan's voyage symbolically represents the journey of life and the travellers not only assume its ordeals, they welcome them joyfully. The saint must suffer hardships in which asceticism illustrates his fortitude, and Paradise rewards his greatness:

Sainz hoem cum ad plusurs travailz.
De faim, de seif, de freiz, de calz,
Ainxe, tristur e granz poürs.
De tant vers Deu creist sis oürs.

(*Brendan*, 1177-1180)

Chi ci estrat, mal n'i avrat,
Ne dunt mals vent ja nel savrat,
Ne chalz, ne freiz, ne dehaite,
Ne faim, ne seit, ne suffraite.

(*Brendan*, 1765-1768)

Similarly the *Vie de Saint Gilles* describes in physical terms what ordeals the saint endures in order to attain perfection. Fifty years after the French versions of *Alexis* and *Brendan* — Gaston Paris dates Guillaume de Berneville's poem around 1170 at the earliest [39] — the conception of asceticism has not changed drastically. It is still based on physical endurance bound up with noble lineage. For Giles belongs to an aristocratic environment which Guillaume adapts for his Anglo-Norman audience. The necessity for a royal peer to beget heirs is part of Giles' dilemma. Between the barons' legitimate request that their prince realize his duties and Giles' own aspiration toward a spiritual life, the unique solution appears once again to be an escape from the world and a search for appropriate retreat. Giles' dilemma is centered around the personage of the woman, who does not appear in this text, but still represents the terrestrial vanity and familial bond which could impede the hero from becoming a saint:

Meis crei conseil, si feras bien,
E cume sages te conten:

---

[39] *Gilles*, xxvii.

Fais ço ke nus te loerum,
Si pren la fille a un barun.
(*Gilles*, 295-298)

The first movement of avoidance on Giles' part is presented as interior withdrawal before his companions' remonstrances. The hero admits to having met a young girl of good fame and appearance, according to the courtly convention:

Jo aim mult une dameisele,
Si est uncor virgene e pucele,
Curteise e bele durement,
E si est mult de haute gent.
(*Gilles*, 351-354)

A few lines further, the poet describes Giles' intense dilemma before the diabolical temptation which incites the hero to visit the young lady. From then on, the woman disappears from the narrative, leaving the reader with two possible interpretations: four times Giles recalls his great sins, although nowhere in the story can any hint be found of that type of weakness. Did he really succumb to what he considers an evil attack of carnal fault? It seems more probable that Giles' declaration was a practical lie by which he reassured his barons while protecting his hidden intentions. The feint was so perfected by the poet that it produced a dramatic turn of events which underscored even better Giles' further determination to leave Greece.

Awareness is the attribute which could describe Giles' personality: he does not want to follow the noble tradition established in a feudal Greece, but neither does he wish to distress his friends. Hence his attitude at the banquet with them:

Gires s'est assis al manger,
Grant semblant feit d'estre heité;
Mut en furent si hume lé,
Ki tant l'orent veu pensif.
(*Gilles*, 586-589)

This scene precedes the night of Giles' departure. The saint flees his entourage, preferring harshness to broadcloth, in a choice of asceticism as obnoxious as Alexis' or Brendan's scorn:

> Gires est en la veie mis,
> Gerpist sa terre e ses amis;
> Il nen ad n'or n'argent od sai,
> Cheval ne mul ne palefrei;
> Il n'en porte ne veir ne gris,
> Meis povres dras de petit pris.
>
> (*Gilles*, 641-646)

The greatness reflected by Giles' decision depends more on his constant effort to preserve anonymity than on occasional expressions of contempt for the world. Unlike Brendan, the saint is perceived as a man for whom poverty is not an end but a means of exercising charity. In this respect the *fuga mundi* movement which recurs at times during the narrative corresponds to the highest level of asceticism, in so far as the flight from the world represents in Giles an authentic desire to be closer to God.

Geneviève pursues an identical effort to remain alone. The young girl is reared in a humble environment — a little house, Nanterre, a rural existence — which she decides to leave:

> Chies son pere fu puis lonc tens,
> Tant qu'i li vint en son porpens
> Que le vain siecle guerpiroit
> Et de ses gens departiroit.
>
> (*Geneviève*, 417-420)

Her departure does not occur by night, nor does she wait for her parents' death. Line 419 of this poem formulates in the title of this study a condensed expression of the elements of the central theme. *Geneviève*, perhaps because of its date, summarizes all the complex values implicit in the flight from the world. *Le siecle guerpir* [40] would be imprecise in so far as in some cases the saint returns to the world. So does Genevieve. *Le vain siecle* is more precise since it incorporates the variations of *vanitas vanitatis* which discards the useless aspects of life, its deteriorated features of hierarchy and statism, its

---

[40] *Le siècle guerpir* may mean the occurrence of death, as one such expression can be found in the same account:

> La morz ne fait pas grant demore.
> A sainte Genevieve vint,
> Le siecle guerpir li covint.
>
> (*Geneviève*, 2610-2612)

negative elements of paganism, heresy and sin. In the story of Geneviève, *le vain siecle guerpir* corresponds to the legitimate boredom that futility arouses in her:

> Ne velt que li siecles l'acoille,
> N'ele ne velt lui acoillir.
> . . .
> Ne velt avoir la grant plenté
> Des maux que li siecles norrist.
>
> *(Geneviève,* 422-423, 426-427)

She lives an ascetic existence, thirty years long, of fast and flagellation. When asked to serve the community, she promptly obeys and carries out her civic duties.

In the same way Giles flees from prominence to obscurity but returns, if necessary, from obscurity to prominence. Before he accepts election as abbot of a monastery, he opposes the people's celebration. The hagiographer has already described his hero's early inclination for generosity. After having given his cloak to a poor child, Giles has to endure the admiration of his playmates.

Gregory displays a similar precocity since, at the age of twelve, he shows an outstanding disposition for purity:

> Ainz fud humbles e pius e duz,
> Amer se fist à tute rien
> E de lettres aprist si bien
> K'à duze ans ne pot trover
> Clere k[e] a li osast desputer.
>
> *(Grégoire,* 770-774)

But the environment does not impede Gregory's spiritual maturity: he lives close to a monastery, under the protection of his godfather. In a movement opposite to the progression of *Gilles,* the events which precede the election of Gregory, forming the very matter of the narrative, cause him to depart from this quiet place into a world that appeals to the young and chevaleresque hero.

If Giles flees from Greece, it is because fame disconcerts him: each time the saint feels the danger of being institutionalized — even for such good causes as healing, comforting and inspiring conversions — he rejects the intrusion of society with all his strength. [41] The world is not described here in the same dark colors as those seen throughout some episodes of *Alexis* or *Brendan:* Giles' environment is rather friendly and lively. However, the life force in Giles springs from a deeper joy. In contrast, popular admiration is felt as a mummification which literally keeps the saint from moving. When sadness occurs, heaviness accompanies it, according to a meaningful association of the words *pensif* and *pesance* (lines 157, 487).

The saintly ideal, in Giles' story, evokes therefore a divinely originated enthusiasm, taken in its etymological meaning of "being lifted by God's breath." Alexis close to the stone of the staircase tends to be petrified, crystallized in his virtue. On the other hand, his family suffers, and Alexis' virtue is achieved to the detriment of others. With Brendan, the saint's image borrows its features from the Celtic material of the poem. The element of the sea participates in the portrayal of a character less monolithic, if less spiritual. Guillaume's hero appears even more mellowed. The world that Giles tries to avoid is constantly threatening his vocation. But he never completely rejects society. In the name of Christ, Giles endures the burden of living for the joy of giving:

> Lui la donai ki la me quist
> Pur amur Deu ki nus tuz fist:
> Ja se leissat il pur nus vendre
> Et des Judeus en la croiz pendre,
> E nus, las! ke faimes pur lui?
>
> *(Gilles,* 183-187)

If there are common characteristics which describe sainthood as the imitation of Christ — the first step being always to flee the world and to live an ascetic existence — divergences appear in its poetic treatment. As shown here, the warrior-saint in the Passions

---

[41] See in the Appendix the episode which describes the encounter of Giles and Charlemagne. The saint unwillingly responds to the emperor's summons, and proceeds to convince Charlemagne that he should confess his sin. On the matter of Charlemagne's sin, see Baudouin de Gaiffier, "La Légende de Charlemagne, le péché de l'empereur et son pardon," *Recueil de Travaux offerts à M. Clovis Brunel* (Paris: Société de l'Ecole des Chartes, 1955), I, p. 490ff, and Rita Lejeune, "Le Péché de Charlemagne et la *Chanson de Roland,*" *Studia philologica, Homenaje ofrecido a Dámaso Alonso* (Madrid, 1961), II, pp. 339-371.

presents an association of power and nobility which places the hero in a feudal society. From this point of departure, and when the story no longer takes place at a time of persecution, the hero's greatness emerges as a denial of the world. Whoever avoids sins is declared a saint. On this level, Alexis and Brendan achieve an individual accomplishment mostly in negative terms. According to the doctrine of the Fathers, this step of sainthood corresponds to avoidance or purification. But Edmund and Genevieve, Gregory and particularly Giles, represent sainthood in its dynamic aspect, what the Fathers describe as "heroic practice of virtues." For this reason their portrayals are more successful, since the hagiographers deal with a dynamic heroism. With respect to asceticism, *Alexis* and *Brendan* celebrate the values of humility, poverty and abstinence. The other four poems mentioned above add to these values the greatness of humiliation and contemplation. *Gilles* is the best example of hagiography understood as a motivation for inspiring other vocations. This particular saint associates spirituality and maturity, an achievement which most of the twelfth-century poems fail to present.

The narrative theme of asceticism elaborates on the concept of *fuga mundi,* a flight from the world which starts as a wariness for all things mundane. In imitation of Christ, the saint-to-be avoids the vain world, sees it as a perilous distraction from the divine, and seeks refuge behind the three monastic rules of poverty, chastity and obedience. Obviously the hagiographers want to stress the beneficial value of selflessness; they do so in a dramatic way, elevating thereby the saint to a heroic stature, whether he martially endures death or chooses to lead a stoic mode of life. The intent of such dramatization is clearly to accentuate the admirable virtue of the character, holy by way of divine selection, and extraordinary in all respects. The greatness embodied in these portrayals derives from their inexhaustible need for God, from a compulsive and fanatic urge to declaim the pagan heresy at the price of martyrdom, which becomes, in the ascetic, an obsessive quest for the private joys of meditation. Accordingly, sainthood is a state of splendid isolation, and as such, beyond the reach of ordinary people to whom it displays its dazzling merits.

CHAPTER II

THE HERMIT-SAINT

The validity of eremitism is often called into question. On the one hand, laymen believing in the good neighbor policy condemn the apparent selfishness of eremitic isolation. On the other, churchmen debate the role of isolation and solitude in regard to the more urgent needs of Christendom. To lead a good Christian life, from both points of view, implies a certain degree of giving, and how can a hermit secluded in a desert or forest fit into this scheme? The solution depends on the definition of the individual's role in a community. Between the duties of the ecclesiastics and the spiritual powers of the monks, two degrees of efficacy are attained for the benefit of the communion of saints. [1] Christian orthodoxy resolves what could be a potential dilemma between secular and regular by sanctioning both as a legitimate imitation of the life of Christ. [2] The ecclesiastic dignitaries exercise an essential function of propagation and apostleship, as long as their action serves the cause of Christianity. Monasticism calls those who prefer to work for the Church in a less visible way. Both the monk and the cleric accept hierarchical obedience and live within a well defined framework.

---

[1] All members of the Church constitute what the doctrine of the Fathers calls "sainteté commune." The living and the dead are united by this communion of saints in which the heroic actions of the elite atone for the sin of the rest.

[2] The distinction between spiritual and temporal is not formulated as contemplation versus action before the late twelfth century. And they never conflict since the two stages are complementary as M. E. Mason emphasizes (*Active Life and Contemplative Life. A Study of the Concepts from Plato to the Present* [Milwaukee: Marquette University Press, 1961], p. 75).

Eremitism does not essentially differ from this religious cohesion, yet neither can it be assimilated to it. The main distinction between eremitism and asceticism derives from a mode of life which, in the hermit's case, is more marginal. The hermit-saint did not originally live in a community. He imitated an ideal established by the Desert Fathers.

During the first three centuries which witnessed the early struggles of Christianity, the three main nuclei of patristic writings centered on specific elaborations. The Greek aptitude for mysticism, the Latin disposition for preaching, and the Syriac culture which adapted Greek mysticism and Semitic traditions are the geographic points whence the Christian doctrine began its development. The Syriac culture produced the tradition of the Desert Fathers, who practiced asceticism achieved through reclusion in the manner of John the Baptist. Eremitism encouraged solitude and meditation apart from the social world. The first hermits did not relate to a communal life, even though they served the Christian community since the first Desert Father was fleeing persecution in order to save the religion. Then, from Egypt, the ideal spread over the Gallic ground up to Ireland, becoming progressively institutionalized as well as socialized within a monastic frame. Peter F. Anson, who studied the question thoroughly, summarizes this process:

> It was from Gaul that the solitary life found its way into the Celtic churches of Brittany, Ireland, Wales and Scotland. During the fifth, sixth, and seventh centuries, monasticism based on the observances of the Egyptian and Palestinian eremitical or semieremitical type took root in the North-Western countries of Europe, and was adapted to the temperament and character of a different people. The hermit or anchorite remained the normal species of ascetic, but a curious type of monastic feudalism was evolved, based on property and carrying spiritual authority, whereby abbots and even abbesses wielded considerable jurisdiction over bishops. [3]

Historically eremitism precedes monasticism and gives birth to Christian asceticism. During the eleventh and twelfth centuries,

---

[3] Peter F. Anson, *The Call of the Desert. The Solitary Life in the Christian Church* (London, 1964), p. 54.

however, there is a recrudescence of eremitism, a revival which attests to a growing discomfort aroused by the deterioration of monastic ideals. [4] Eremitism, a quest for isolated mortification, is paradoxically unachievable, as its cyclic development explains it. Seeking total reclusion, the hermit unwittingly draws others — monks or laymen — to witness and admire such endeavors. The cycle thus goes through the following stages: first, the retreat of an individual; then, the arrival of other individuals and the subsequent creation of a small community; thirdly, the desire to flee, this time from that community, when it becomes too large to fulfill the individual's need for privacy. In the early years of Christianity, these solitary characters were called anchorites (one who retires) or hermits (one who dwells in the desert), and were particularly numerous in Egypt. Isolated or grouped in small clusters, they wanted to attain a physical, moral and spiritual self-controlled balance, regarding which there was yet no institutionalized rules:

> One of the hermits was chosen as a sort of spiritual director. Although generally referred to as *abbas* in the Latin translations of the travellers' tales, it would convey a wrong idea to give him the title of abbot. The Hebrew *rabbi* or the French *maître* give a better conception of his status, because he wielded no jurisdiction over the solitaries. [5]

Later, "the *eremites* became *coenobites,* men living in common, under a common rule, with a common head; and then the development of the monastic institution fairly began." [6] To extend this quotation from J. B. Brown, it is adequate to say that the monasteries created a community inside the community; that monks were considered as active and recognized members of the Christian society; that monastic rules coincided with civil laws, and sanctity, with the strict observance of those laws. [7]

---

[4] Hermits and recluses, according to J. M. Bienvenu ("Pauvreté, misères et charité en Anjou aux XIème et XIIème siècles," *Moyen Age,* 72 [1966], 389-424, and 73 [1967], 5-34), were fleeing a certain way of life more than society. Around 1100, they were seeking voluntary poverty.

[5] Anson, *op. cit.,* p. 17.

[6] James Baldwin Brown, *Stoics and Saints* (New York: Macmillan, 1893), p. 106.

[7] The solitary saint is called a hermit, as opposed to the monk living in a community. But *monachus* etymologically means "one." As Jean Leclercq

Certain saints' lives of the twelfth century, revealing an increasing malaise as regards the very purposes of monasteries, celebrate sainthood through the realization of eremitism. It corresponds to a stronger attack derived from the eleventh-century theologians. "Monastic life with all its observances is but a preparation for that higher goal, the solitude of hermitage" : [8] institutionalized monasticism, as seen by Peter Damian, lessens charismatic exaltation in so far as it goes too often hand in hand with progressive wealth and declining discipline. According to Louis J. Lekai this movement incarnates a healthy "reaction to prevailing standards of monastic life, a spontaneous protest against the comfort and quiet daily routine which no longer presented sufficient challenge to souls yearning for the heroic life of the Desert Fathers." [9] The first step of monastic renewal consists in returning to a more simple and remote life of poverty and silence.

Eremitism comprises not a revolution but an evolution of sainthood which will closely imitate the Desert Fathers' achievement in incorporating its worthwhile elements within the contemporary world. [10] In the Lives which praise the movement of desertion, the 'desert' is represented by nature, poverty begins with privacy, and

---

shows (*Etudes sur le vocabulaire monastique du moyen âge, Studia Anselmiana* n.° 48 [Rome: Pontificum Institutum S. Anselmi, 1961]), monasticism was to combine solitude and unity (p. 26).

[8] Louis J. Lekai, "Motives and Ideals of the Eleventh-Century Monastic Renewal," *Cistercian Studies,* 4 (1969), 3-20.

[9] *Ibid.,* 11.

[10] Charles P. Weaver, *The Hermit in English Literature from the Beginnings to 1660* (Nashville, Tenn.: George Peabody College for Teachers, 1924), compares the Oriental and the Western hermit, describing the latter as one who gives counsel to all and is the object of pious veneration (p. 52). The hermit-counsellor constitutes a bond between heaven and earth; in vernacular hagiography he also brings together the forest and the city, nature and man. So the legendary hermit is more an object of wonder than a pretext for hierarchical feudality. Etienne Delaruelle explains how the twelfth-century hermit identifies himself with the involuntary poor, whereas the good Christian was satisfied with the virtue of generosity ("Les Ermites et la spiritualité populaire," *Miscellanea del Centro di Studi medioevali,* 4 (1967), 212-241, here 228-229). On this level the popular audience could be more pleased by the hermit-saint than by the ascetic. They could also recognize in the portrayal of those hermits some of the many recluses numbered among the famous characters of profane Celtic literature. Such identification, reducing the distance between hagiography and fiction, also results in rooting the saint in the legendary components of the Other World.

silence signifies 'romantic' ecstasy. [11] Such a dismissal of social convention allows the hagiographer to christianize the pagan features of rural solitude and furnishes subsequent narrative themes such as the flight towards elemental solitude and the redeeming quality of a sojourn in the wilderness.

Between the bounded habitat of the monks and the natural dwellings of hermits, the difference is one of environment. Along with the limits imposed by the Rule, the concrete boundary of the monastery encloses one in a miniaturized society, thereby defining holiness in terms of immurement. Even Alexis, although his long-term effort tended to autonomous retirement, chose to end his life in the confinement of a staircase. The rhythm of his existence was determined by that of the familial household. The hermit, on the other hand, has only the natural cycle of day and night to regulate his existence.

Compared to the conception of asceticism, eremitism appears as a movement of *fuga mundi* from the walls of the monastery. No longer satisfied with the security provided by the monastery, or dubious of its spiritual qualities, the hero embarks on a journey towards a greater reclusion. In *Brendan,* two personages correspond to this original 'desertion,' those of Barintus and of the abbot of the Albian island: [12]

> Barinz out nun cil ermite,
> Murs out bons e sainte vitte;
> Li fedeilz Deu en bois estout,
> Tres cenz moines od lui i out.
>
>   (*Brendan,* 75-78)

---

[11] Studying the role of the hermit in German literature, and particularly in romanticism, John Fitzell (*The Hermit in German Literature* [Chapel Hill: University of North Carolina Press, 1961]), examines the poetic, psychological and metaphysical significance of such a personage. Hermithood represents "the apotheosis of the isolated individual, suffering out of love for humanity under standards of life with which he will not compromise — yet embodying undying hope for redemption in the future." (p. 119). The three steps — rejection of society, individual struggle with nature, ecumenical expectation — are the very components of vernacular sainthood. In this chapter, however, the hermit-saint inspires above all the didactic level of contempt for the civilized world and the poetic appraisal of the natural world.

[12] See our Appendix.

The extent of Barintus' solitude is moderated by the numerical precision of his followers: but this remark must be related to the meaning of line 76, which demonstrates the saintly value of Barintus and the degree of his exemplary excellence. What is particularly interesting in the following line (77), is the detail of the forest which introduces a new element into the elaboration of sainthood.

The hermit flees the wall of the monastery to take refuge in the dense forest. The forest could serve as an analogy for the liquid aspect of the sea that symbolizes most of Brendan's environment. In the context of the story, the *terra firma,* less perilous a medium, is thus an obstacle to heroism. The forest could also be related to the wall of the monastery in that it assures an immediate protection against any social temptation. Yet this natural environment is far from being a secure one, for it leads Chrétien's Yvain to insanity, and induces Tristan and Isolde into forgetting the rules of civilization. In *Brendan,* the travellers are well aware of the debasing effects of wilderness. In one episode, the group is forced ashore in an unknown country. A stream and a tree are the two elements noted by the hagiographer, and both can be related to the traditional romanesque landscape:

> Al chef del duit out une arbre
> Itant blanche cume marbre,
> E les fuiles mult sunt ledes,
> De ruge e blanc taceledes.
>
> (*Brendan,* 491-494)

During the Middle Ages, the progress of civilization was accompanied by the taming of the wilderness: in order to conquer nature and to establish cities it was necessary to carry out large-scale, periodic cuttings in the forest. [13] The extensive remains of the forests offered a natural shelter for the best and the worst. The phenomenon

---

[13] Describing the spatial and temporal structures of the Middle Ages, Jacques Le Goff (*La Civilisation de l'occident médiéval* [Paris: Arthaud, 1964]) sees the forest as the physical Western reality: "La religion née en Orient à l'abri des palmes se fait jour en Occident au détriment des arbres, refuge des génies païens, que moines, saints, missionnaires abattent impitoyablement. Tout progrès dans l'Occident médiéval est défrichement, lutte et victoire sur les broussailles, les arbustes..., les futaies, la forêt vierge, la "gaste forêt" de Perceval." (p. 169).

of brigandage continued in France and in England as long as these unsafe localities were used by various refugees. But along with such a manifestation of evil, another threat was felt to be more menacing for the common man. The forests were inhabited by the fairies and witches of folklore who, being neither human nor angelic, were made responsible for all kinds of irrational and inexplicable occurrences. The danger of the forest was that its attraction tempted the innocent. Once lost in its darkness, the wanderer could very rarely come back to a normal life. The tree which dominates the Paradise of Birds in the tale of Brendan possesses this dual quality of external magnificence and implicit threat in its white and red coloration:

> De haltece par vedue
> Muntout l'arbre sur la nue;
> Des le sumét desque en terre
> La brancheie mult la serre
> E ledement s'estent par l'air.
>
> (*Brendan*, 495-499)

The tree also presents a bridge between earth and heaven, since its roots plunge deep and its branches reach high into the sky. Through a symptomatic personification, the poet insists on the fact that the tree seems to grow by its own will. White and tall, the trunk could possibly allow one to ascend and to perceive the mysteries of the sky. At the same time, its branches so thickly intermingled forbid such a venture and project opacity and darkness. While providing shelter for the beautiful birds, this tree in fact protects the fallen angels:

> Umbraiet luin e tolt l'esclair,
> Tute asise de blancs oiseus —
> Unches nuls hom ne vit tant beus.
>
> (*Brendan*, 500-502)

The forest is either a refuge or a purgatory. [14] If the hermit flees the social world to avoid its temptations, he nonetheless encounters

---

[14] Jacques Le Goff (*Ibid.*, pp. 169-170) enumerates the types of people who live in the forest to avoid civilization deliberately: "Le désert, d'ailleurs, c'est alors la forêt. Là se réfugient les adeptes volontaires ou involontaires de la *fuga mundi*: ermites, amoureux, chevaliers errants, brigands, hors-la-loi." Because of its composite population, the forest becomes a universe of wonderful or terrifying legends in the medieval imagination.

other threats inasmuch as during his prolonged contact with nature, he risks the deterioration of his humanity into bestiality. [15] Such is the theme of the Wild Man and the significance of Merlin, so enclosed in his solitude that he finally turns insane.

With this in mind, it is not surprising to see the reaction of Brendan's peers in front of a tall and silent old man:

> Hastivement, e nun a tart,
> Ast vus currant un grant veilard.
> Poür oussent, ne fust l'abit —
> Quar moines ert — mais rien ne dit.
>
> (*Brendan*, 655-658)

Two unusual elements provoke their fear: first, this personage is described as running, which is not logically consistent with his age; secondly, he maintains a frightening silence, and once again this device creates a misunderstanding comparable to the dissension that causes the servants to mistreat Alexis.

This silence is soon explained by the mode of life which regulates the Albian monastery. It has attracted a group of hermits who voluntarily isolate themselves on an island in order to imitate their patron saint by leading an exemplary existence devoted to prayer and contemplation. Brendan has to wait for the propitious moment before inquiring about their identity; until that time communication is by way of gesture:

> As altres dist par sun signe
> Vengent vedeir leu mult digne.
> Cum alouent, l'abes ad quis
> Quels leus ço seit u se sunt mis;
> Mais cil se taist, respunt ne fait.
>
> (*Brendan*, 665-669)

> Meinent en lur abeïe
> Brandan e sa cumpainie;

---

[15] Richard Bernheimer (*Wild Men in the Middle Ages* [Cambridge: Harvard University Press, 1952]) notes how the existence of the Wild Man raises a theological problem within the medieval system (p. 5). When such a personage appears in the legend, he is presented as a holy man. In vernacular hagiography, the solution is always to sacralize the inexplicable.

Servise funt bel e leger
. . .
Puis vunt manger en refraitur,
U tuit taisent fors li litur.

(Brendan, 695-697, 699-700)

The charitable welcoming, along with its pious manifestations, give
to the hermits' silence a Christian dimension which precludes any
allegations in incivility. If the Albian monks achieve a true asceticism made possible partially by an eremitic life, they still live a
communal existence comparable to that of Barintus' followers. Two
other characters in *Brendan* illustrate an even more remote seclusion: Mernoc and Paul.

The former was originally a member of Barintus' community,
but he decided to leave this peaceful retreat for a locality yet unde-
termined and which would later be described as Paradise:

Ço fud Mernoc, qui ert frerre
Del liu u cist abes ere,
Mais de ço fud mult voluntif,
Que fust ailurs e plus sultif.

(Brendan, 85-88)

Solitude is the first step of the eremitic concept and Paul incarnates
what is not developed in the tale concerning Mernoc. Paul, contrary
to the Albian monks, is not reluctant to break the silence and to
explain how he too left the retreat in the woods. A boat had mysteriously guided him to the rock where he settled ninety years
before. His exterior appearance becomes an object of wonder among
Brendan's companions, although it could have frightened them by
its anti-social element:

N'ad vestement fors de sun peil,
Dum est cuvert si cum de veil;
Reguard aveit angelïel,
E tut le cors celestïel;
N'est si blance neifs ne clere
Cume li peilz d'icest frere.

(Brendan, 1535-1540)

The wilderness is in fact immediately tamed through a divine sign
which consecrates eremitism as a superior state of being. At the

same time, the process of returning to the original nudity known by man before his fall marks an opening toward the Renaissance context of humanism. No longer shameful, nudity proclaims the beauty of the body as long as it is nourished by celestial food. In the scale of animal symbolism, the nutrient-bearing otter serves as an intermediary betwen the Upper World and the Other World. Similarly, good sea-serpents fight bad ones — the griffin versus the dragon — in order to save the travellers lost in the midst of elements which remain too formidable to be understood. Sometimes an evil mark of dispersion, elsewhere a blessed proof of multiplication, the abundance of animals in the poem celebrates the marvels of the world. The *Summa theologica,* and later Ignatius' *Spiritual Exercises,* tend to subordinate accident to necessity, and turn the pagan features of nature into Christian celebrations of Creation. It is difficult to decide whether Brendan's hagiographer intended to christianize the Other World or simply enjoyed narrating its folkloric details for their own sake. In any case, the poetic level of the story is heavily indebted to the *imram* genre from which the Latin version of the *Navigatio* takes its context. [16] Benedeit converts this pagan and romantic background even more in order to produce an edifying legend. The pagan elements manifested through joyful interactions between man and nature foreshadow the more directly classical oriented sources of Renaissance humanism:

> Brandan lur dist: "Freres, savez
> Pur quei poür oüt avez?
> N'est pas terre, ainz est beste
> U feïmes nostre feste,
> Pessuns de mer sur les greinurs.
> Ne merveillés de ço, seigneurs.
> Pur ço vus volt Deus ci mener
> Que il vus voleit plus asener.
> Ses merveilles cum plus verrez,
> En lui mult mielz puis encrerrez;
> Mielz le crerrez e plus crendrez,
> A sun comant plus vus prendrez."
> *(Brendan,* 467-478)

---

[16] E. G. R. Waters, *The Anglo-Norman Voyage of St. Brendan by Benedeit* (Oxford: Clarendon Press, 1928), lxxxi.

The experiences of the unknown are here not joyful, but frightening. In Brendan's logic, everything is matter for Christian instruction. A faith based on fear deepens when confronted by nature, and such is the message carried by the eremitic level of Brendan's life.

In the life of Gregory, eremitism assumes a quite different meaning. The *fuga mundi* movement is really a flight, more so than a quest, inasmuch as the world constantly threatens the saint. [17] In his struggle to discover his identity Gregory is condemned by fate to learn the details of his birth under dramatic circumstances. He then decides to flee his familial and social environment to avoid sin and Hell:

> "De si grant pechié sui chargié
> Que [là] ne voil mais demurer,
> U hoem me puisse unkes trover;
> Ains vois querant un hermitage."
>
> (*Grégoire*, 1732-1735)

The fisherman who dislikes everything that concerns the hero does not take Gregory's words seriously, but decides jokingly to have his wish realized to the letter. The following morning, they sail to a remote rock in the middle of the sea. There the fisherman locks Gregory to iron chains and throws the key into the water. This stylite-like period will last seventeen years:

> Dis e set anz sur cele piere,
> K'[unques] n'en out altre maisun
> Fors le nu ciel e le perun,
> Unkes nuls hoem nel regarda,
> Neis li culvert qui l'ensera.
>
> (*Grégoire*, 1808-1812)

The hagiographer's skill consists in presenting one of the best plots of the vernacular narratives. That Gregory survives seventeen years of fast is of course part of the miraculous aspect of potential sainthood. But it is not accomplished without pain:

> E de feim fud mult anguissus
> E de mangier bien desirus,

---

[17] See our Appendix.

Dunc reclamat parfitement
Le veir seignur omnipotent.

(Grégoire, 1815-1818)

He survives thanks to the rain water which collects in a cleft of
the rock. Not a direct intervention of heaven but the natural
elements are thus the reason for his survival. The poet takes great
care, however, to note that:

...grant peine suffri li sire
Enz en la mer sur le perun
Ainz qu'il ëust remissiun.

(Grégoire, 1836-1838)

From line 1839 to 1908 the hagiographer explains what has happened in the outside world which relates his story to this particular
episode. The Pope has died, and the clerics are seeking an explanation for the message brought to Rome by an angel. They
happen to encounter the fisherman responsible for Gregory's exile.
Offering them dinner, he opens a fish and finds the key to Gregory's
chains. Symbolized through such concrete objects, the link between
events is not fortuitous. The clerics are now able to interpret the
angelic message, while the fisherman realizes the extent of his
sin and remembers Gregory's fate. In his mind there is no doubt
that the hero has died of hunger. But Gregory is still alive as the
process of the legend demands. His physical condition is so deplor-
able that several days of rest are required before the saint's next
and last trip. Thus all the elements are presented in a logical
succession. The hermit has little by little lost his clothes:

Tuit li peri sa vest[ë]ure
Unkes n'[en] out de coverture,
Ne par iver, ne par esté
Fors sul le ciel e la clarté.

(Grégoire, 1831-1834)

According to the ascetic tradition evoked earlier in the case of
Paul and the abbot of the Albian Island *(Brendan)*, Gregory ap-
pears to the messengers as a hirsute and almost disincarnate hero.
His appearance is that of a wild man:

> Il n'ad char gueres sur les os
> Ne de drapel fil en son dos,
> Tut est veluz cum une beste
> Des piez amunt iusc'à la teste.
>
> (*Grégoire*, 1943-1946)

There is no fear, however, but a veneration on the part of the messengers which inspires them to kneel before the saint. He alone is aware of the hidden significance of their act. The angelic message brings the certitude of God's affirmation that Gregory is forgiven and has no longer to fear the disastrous effect of calamity. Seventeen years of eremitism here emphasize that perfection is the product of divine obedience accomplished through the silence and solitude of carnal purification. [18] Moreover, eremitism indicates in this narrative that a movement of self-sacrifice is the only springboard to self-identification: Gregory was striving to know who he was on earth. God shows him what he will be in heaven.

In the desert or on a rock, the hermit is surrounded by natural elements. His greatness comes from his resistance to whatever temptation might occur. Sooner or later he becomes notorious enough to attract followers and imitators. There is an isolated case, mentioned in the Life of Edward, which refers to a hermit dwelling in a hole and to his role as intercessor between Edward and Saint Peter. The hagiographer explains the reasons which inspired the hermit to choose such a refuge:

> Suz tere vuleit eschiwer
> Que plus vit sur tere regner:
> Orguil, folur e cuveitise,
> Haür e tres male cuintise;
> Pur ço que tut guerpir vuleit
> Ço que plus sur tere veeit,
> Pur ço suz tere se tapi.
>
> (*Edouard*, 2119-2125)

Although traditional, the role of this particular hermit is ambigous, since Edward's kingship shows no evil. Such a discrepancy between a flight from worldly vices and a world allegedly dedicated to virtue

---

[18] Allegorical numbers play an important part in the making of a saint, as will be shown in the third chapter.

progresses as the hermit transmits Saint Peter's message. The apostle wants to deliver Edward from his vow. Instead of the pilgrimage intended by the king, he asks him to build a monastery:

> Si enrichisse ma maisun
> De moines de religïun,
> Riches edifices m'i face,
> E jo metrai el liu ma grace.
>
> *(Edouard,* 2175-2178)

Edward is considered a man of integrity. The hermit stands for complete poverty. Yet, the divine intervention of the apostle brings a notion of temporal wealth where, up to then, all elements celebrated renunciation. Edward carries out his new vow and the monastery successfully develops its lands:

> Fist le mustier, fist maisuns faire,
> Riches rentes al liu atraire.
>
> *(Edouard,* 2695-2696)

If the character of the hermit appears in twelfth-century vernacular hagiography, he does not assume an outstanding role. With the exception of Gregory, he remains in the background of the story, and his mission is to emphasize and sometimes to define the protagonist's sanctity. Gregory endures seventeen ascetic years, confined on a barren rock: in this case eremitism has nothing in common with romantic ecstasy. It is a period of necessary contrition, almost a methodical attainment of spiritual rebirth.

A third aspect of eremitism is evident in the legends of Evroul and Giles. With these saints it is a period which occurs at a certain time during their lives, and shows their personal preference for solitude. These two characteristics describe a more authentic disposition for a retreat within the self.

Evroul manifests an early need for simplicity. He has decided, in agreement with his wife, to leave the French court and to enter a monastery. There, he first enjoys peace. But his reputation soon interrupts it:

> Si que a peine estet il gueres,
> Qu'il n'eust bien grant compagnie
> De grant gent de chevalerie,

Qui touz a lui se conseilloient
Et son conseil lui demandoient
Et troubloient sa conscience.

(*Evroul*, 780-785)

Such a phenomenon is not unusual within hagiography; it goes along with the nature of sainthood and occurs even though the saint is a champion of solitude. That the hero strives for privacy is notable enough to attract multitudes. Some of the saints — Giles for example — place their civic duties above their own aspiration for reclusion. [19] The story of Evroul follows an identical pattern. The Benedictine monastery of Deux Jumeaux loses its attraction when it no longer promotes silence. The saint declares to the community that he has decided to seek a deeper solitude elsewhere:

Aler m'en veil en .i. desert;
Quer qui a dieu de coer desert.
Deit foir le bonban du monde.
...
Cil qui loing en desert habite,
Il poet vivre plus saintement.
...
Quer je m'en veil de ci aler
Priveement et avaler
En bois ou en une forest.

(*Evroul*, 799-801, 804-805,
809-811)

Especially when arising out of sanctity, admiration does not allow for privacy. Evroul's words have provoked great enthusiasm among the Benedictines who want in turn to follow his example and settle in a desert:

"Alez devant! nous vous suivron
Et ovec vous nous en fuiron."

(*Evroul*, 821-822)

This anecdote illustrates one remark made at the beginning of this chapter: eremitism does not always signify solitude. The *abbas*

---

[19] See, in the last chapter, the analysis of the saint's social integration.

is a spiritual director for reform and is sometimes *abbas* despite
his own volition.

Setting out for Montfort, they flee society ("de cest monde
la malice," 918) and enter the forest to build a little community:

> Si ont lez arbres donc plessiez
> Et brisiez et fet la meson,
> Ou eulz furent cele seson;
> De branches firent leur maneir.
> ...
> Closture i fist et forte et fiere
> Et cloistre de cele maniere.
>
> (*Evroul*, 936-939, 943-944)

The cutting of the forest symbolizes several elements: first, it is
the consequence of an escape from the richer monastery; secondly,
it marks a taming of the wilderness, as much as it signifies the
renunciation of nature *(closture);* thirdly, here is the outset of a
new organization materialized by the fence.

Eremitism does not occur in any other way through this narrative. It is interesting to note how the hagiographer is conscious
of all the problems raised by such a setting. Soon after the monastery is built a man comes to claim the land and to force the monks
out of this territory. He accuses them of simulating their vocation
so as to steal more easily the possessions of others. Evroul answers
with a long and elaborate sermon which begins with these words:

> Et dit, que pas ne sunt tourné
> En ce bois par forcenerie,
> Mes pour miez amender leur vie,
> Non pas pour usurper leur terre,
> Mes pour dieu devotement querre.
>
> (*Evroul*, 992-996)

It is not immediately convincing for the man that the monks have
only a pious intention in mind. But it is not too convincing for
a modern reader either. Perhaps it was feared that the monks'
skill as land managers, where they usually succeeded very well,
might attenuate the original movement of *fuga mundi* which was
intended to avoid prosperity. But this conclusion may be out of
context. The rest of the story, from line 1211 to the end, praises

Evroul's miracles and the good influence his community continued
to have on the country:

Il est donquez et temps et eure
De ses miracles raconter.

(*Evroul*, 1206-1207)

If these miracles are mandatory in the process of vernacular
sanctification, one can only regret that the hagiographer needs
over three thousand lines, compared to the one thousand which
covered the actual story of Evroul, to enumerate what seems to
be a dry account of chronicles. Such an enumeration precludes
poetic relevance and displays a lack of invention.

Through a more elaborate conception of eremitism *Gilles* succeeds in presenting a satisfying account of both its dogmatic repercussions and its narrative interest. The hermit-saint imitates Christ's
time of preparation covered by His first thirty years and His forty-
day retreat. Giles' desire for reclusion is a consequence of genuine
interiority. His penchant for contemplation does not hinder his
charitable disposition towards others. Remote, self-sufficient and
immersed in the pursuit of God, the character of the hermit tends
to become a monolithic figure in most of the vernacular Lives. In
choosing a hermit-saint as his protagonist, the hagiographer runs
the risk of depriving his hero of the dynamic elements essential in
a successful legend. In *Gilles*, however, the urge for reclusion is
never detrimental to the progression of the story nor ill-suited to
the psychology of its hero.

The Christly significance of Giles' existence is suggested through
the seven steps which mark his development toward perfection.
Of these seven degrees two belong to the eremitic concept of
fuga mundi seen as a necessary time spent in the desert, far from
civilization. The background of the narrative places Giles in Greece,
although neither history nor fiction clearly explains this geographical location. The first movement of desertion from society sends
Giles from Greece to the south of France, where the saint satisfies
his need for solitude. After this flight and before his consecration,
Giles leads a solitary existence, modelled on that of the Desert
Fathers. The Latin text as well as the French version reflect this
trend toward seclusion which began to appeal in the ninth and
tenth centuries. Gaston Paris presents evidence to prove the his-

toricity of a Giles around the end of the seventh century. [20] Although he agrees that Giles had undoubtedly never been in Greece, E. C. Jones calls even the existence of the saint into question:

> Somme toute, la *Vita Sancti Aegidii* nous apparaît comme un document forgé au Xème siècle et dans un but tendancieux. Les éléments qui la composent ont été suggérés, pour la plupart, par les faits et les circonstances de ce temps. Elle recèle peut-être une tradition reliant l'église de Saint-Gilles et son fondateur au Vème siècle et à Saint Césaire d'Arles; elle aurait d'authentique peut-être le nom de ce fondateur; elle ne nous apprend cependant rien d'historique sur ce personnage." [21]

Poetic fiction and hagiographic demand weave the texture of the Latin *Vita*. The author borrows a name, chooses a place, and invents around them enough holy evidence to strike popular imagination. The French version similarly voices the hero's discontent for secular pleasures:

> Le los del siecle est trespassant:
> Trop s'i delitent li alquant;
> Jo ne m'i quer ren deliter,
> Meis guerpir le e esluigner.
>
> (*Gilles*, 535-538)

Giles' asceticism, as seen in the first chapter, brings about a divine joy frequently endangered by the demands of the world. The hero's cycle of enthusiasm and sadness is determined by his eagerness for reclusion and the repeated intrusion by others. Friendly but harrassing, Giles' barons accuse their leader of being unfit. They disdainfully suggest he become a monk, if he feels indeed too weak a man to administer his land:

---

[20] Alphonse Bos and Gaston Paris, *La Vie de Saint Gilles par Guillaume de Berneville, poème du XIIème siècle publié d'après le manuscrit unique de Florence* (Paris: Société des Anciens Textes Français, 1881), lxxii.

[21] E. C. Jones, *Saint Gilles. Essai d'histoire littéraire* (Paris: Champion, 1914), p. 61. Giles is important in this study of vernacular hagiography mainly because of his didactic and narrative interests. The written process of the legend is proven to come entirely from oral invention. It shows how popular imagination, here the sole point of departure, does not necessarily rely on reality. It is not devotion for the saint that inspires the legend, but the love for legend that creates a likeable saint.

"Garde, sire, ke hom ne die:
A mult feble heir est revertie.
Tu fais semblant d'ume sultif,
La terre gastes a estrif.
Mar fud tis cors e ta beuté
Quant il nen ad en tei bunté.
Si tu n'oses terre tenir,
Va tei en un buissun tapir
E deven moigne en un muster,
Kar tu nen as de el mestier.

(*Gilles,* 321-330)

Within this feudal code of ethics goodness and beauty are depicted in terms of exteriority. Social actions constitute the measure of epic strength, and the bad and the weak are associated with a reprehensible tendency for solitude and inactivity. Giles' guilt comes from his lack of interest in his lands and men, and the barons are unable to realize the saintly value of such a disposition. On the other hand, Giles despises terrestrial possessions which, in his mind, lead to temporal temptations. The flight from the world appears to be a contempt directed against feudality. But Giles' kindness makes him depart silently from Greece so as to avoid any display of scandal. Away from his social function, he seeks to fulfill the Christian duties which are his only joy.

In sailing for another and yet unknown land, Giles strives to avoid the rules of ostentation and seeks a place to develop his inward disposition for prayer and solitude. But Giles cannot help being a miracle-worker.[22] During the tempest which assaults the boat, he saves the sailors by means of a prayer which results in a clement wind and brings the travellers to the shore of an unknown island. This episode bears resemblance to those of Brendan, with the folkloric if not Celtic traits of wilderness:

Vit terre, ce lui fud avis,
Meis il ne sout en quel pais.
Un yle und devant eus veut.
...
De sus trovent une funtaine.

(*Gilles,* 921-923, 938)

---

[22] See our Appendix.

It is not the holy land of *Alexis,* nor the epic land inherited by Giles, but an allegorical island which coincides with the first stage of the hero's journey. On this island, imprecisely located in the Mediterranean Sea, the fountain is midway between civilization and wilderness. It provides food for the little old man soon discovered by the sailors:

> Le trovérent en oreisun:
> Lunke barbe ad, le chef ferant,
> Petiz hum fud ne guéres grant,
> Mult fut meigres e senz colur,
> Taint del soleil e del labur.
>
> *(Gilles,* 946-950)

The discoloration of his complexion, followed by the contradictory notation of line 950, illustrates the type of life led by the hermit. If compared with the earlier description of Giles, it suggests how asceticism transforms and transcends physical appearance into a more disincarnate embodiment. According to the romanesque tradition, young Giles' complexion is exceedingly fair:

> Jam jamque foris scintillabat indiciis intus succensa lampas charitatis.
>
> *(Vita)*[23]

> Li emfes Gires fud mult bels,
> La flur des autres damoisels
> De cele terre u il fud né:
> Bloi out le chef, recercelé,
> La charn out blanche cume leit,
> Les olz rianz, le nés ben feit,
> Cléres les denz, la buche bele;
> N'out pouint de barbe en sa mazele.
>
> *(Gilles,* 55-62)

The portrait is one of the characteristic additions by the French poet. In the Latin text, Giles radiates a luminous charity. But Guillaume de Berneville feels free to insert religion in a literary framework, creating thereby a saint who is heroically appealing. In comparison with this pictorial device, the hermit is for Giles

---

[23] *Acta Sanctorum,* Sept. I, p. 229, col. 1.

a living example of the physical deterioration consequent to divine dedication. One reason which explains the sailors' attitude and differentiates it from the reaction of Brendan's followers before the similarly wild appearance of the Albian island's abbot, is that this hermit is first seen praying. His leanness and ugliness proceed from his eremitic mode of existence:

> Unkes fors vus home ne vi,
> E faz ici ma penitence
> En jeunes e en abstinence.
> Jo ne manjuz mie de pain,
> Nepurquant sui haité e sain;
> A la fiée truis peissun
> Entre le roche et le sablun.
>
> (*Gilles*, 988-994)

It is not without reason that Giles is sent to this island to disturb a peaceful life of twelve ascetic years. The hermit, nourished according to the irregular occasion of chance, illustrates a reconciliation of man and nature. Far from the unbalanced society oppressed by useless needs and worries, the hermit achieves a poise of mind and body. Eremitism seems here to bring health through temperance and diet. The *fuga mundi,* accompanied by an escape into the wilderness, allows the hermit to know moderation and enthusiasm. He therefore proposes his exemplary life to Giles. The hero seems at all times pursued by a conscientious fear of sin. The hermit shows him a way of avoiding faults through dismissal of the world and its temptations:

> "Jo ne puis de cest ysle aler:
> De tutes parz l'enclot la mer;
> Chastement vif, u voille u nun,
> N'ai de pecher nule achaisun.
> Penser puis jo assez folie,
> Meis, merci Deu, ne la faz mie."
>
> (*Gilles*, 1001-1006)

Although this personage lives alone as he twice recalls (*loinz de gent,* 971, 997), humanity in him has not deteriorated, since his sanctity equals sanity. But his asceticism is limited because of both the natural and miraculous protection which keeps him on the island. The surrounding sea confines him in a place where his nourishment is provided, two circumstances susceptible of decreasing the will power and margin of choice which favor greatness. On his road towards perfection, Giles soon encounters another hermit whose example is a truer illustration of austerity.

Veredemius lives in the middle of a forest, on top of a bare and inaccessible rock:

> A un hermite est assenez
> Ki manait haut en un rocher,
> A peine i pot hume aprocer;
> Haut fud li munz e ben grevus
> E a munter ben anguissus.
>
> (*Gilles*, 1256-1260)

Above the world and the common man, the holy man cares enough for his fellow men to cure those who are good-hearted. The structural situation of this stylite emphasizes the spatial distance which separates holiness and the norm. Miracles take place at the foot of the rock where the faithful and the sick stand, while the saint himself remains on the top.

Prompted by the irresistible desire to meet Veredemius in person, Giles strives to climb and finally finds a staircase dug into the stone. This physical effort marks the way by which Giles begins his ascent toward sainthood. Unlike Alexis', this staircase appears at first to be miraculously reserved for the hero. Secondly, it projects him onto the spiritual summit of asceticism mixed with apostleship. The renown of the two saints becomes widespread enough to attract a multitude and, eventually, to bring a new episode to the tale. After one particular miracle, which Giles performs in Veredemius' absence, the hero decides to leave in order to avoid the hermit's admiration:

> Mais kant orrat ceste nuvele,
> Il me voldrat plus honurer
> E sa bunté sur mei turner.
>
> (*Gilles*, 1432-1434)

As long as Giles was leading a life subordinated to a person whom he considered superior to him, he found divine satisfaction in this subordination. Although he hesitated at length before healing the knight, Giles was compelled to accomplish the miracle as a reward for the knight's display of belief. In the flight from prominence to obscurity such a decision provokes a spiritual and narrative development. To flee a long-hated celebrity which follows each of his miracles, Giles departs again in pursuit of another quiet abode.

The second stage of Giles' eremitism also takes place in a forest, near a fountain and under a tree. Giles shows a determination of mind which leaves no doubt as to his present holiness. He scorns the natural resources that surround him, preferring to live on prayers rather than food:

> Nen ad hume oi ne veud,
> Ne ne mangad mie de pain,
> Ne nule ren ki fust de grein,
> Ne il ne vit char ne peissun;
> De racines e de kerssun
> Enz el desert vesqui meint jur.
>
> (*Gilles,* 1490-1495)

The vegetarian aspect of his limited nourishment contrasts with the first hermit's way of life, in which fish is permitted. If the hagiographers insist so much on fasting, basic for any saintly accomplishment, it is because of the striking effect it could have on their audience. It can be noted also that such a marvel is described in negative terms, as if the enumeration of goods discarded by the saint could make his greatness all the more admirable. Unlike Veredemius, Giles has not chosen a high location for his abode but a trench that he covers with twigs and branches. The only messenger capable of reaching Giles' reclusion among the vegetation is a deer. On a mystical level, the animal is used as an intermediary between Giles and God. Recognizing at once the significance of the deer, Giles allows himself to drink its milk:

> Tant cum iloc el desert fud,
> Del leit de la bisse ad· vescud.
>
> (*Gilles,* 1521-1522)

Like the miraculous manna of the Old Testament, the deer is a divine guarantee of the righteousness of man.

On a narrative level, however, the deer marks the entrance, or return, of the social world inside the hagiographic frame. If the forest represents a location of peace far from the city and its social disturbances, it also provides a rich resource for the hunters. A royal entourage has decided to pursue the deer. To denounce the cruelty of man chasing the weak and to protect innocence from feudal depravation, Giles manages to receive the arrow intended for the deer. In return, the mysterious animal, more human than the hunters, refuses to eat as long as the saint is hurt. The communion of man and God thus occurs in the forest through the intervention of a motherly deer.

Guillaume de Berneville dwells on the hunters' amazement when discovering Giles' abode. The natural beauty of the trees and of their blossoms and fragance is celebrated in a humanistic fashion, creating thereby the most poetic passage of the narrative:

> Virent le liu durement bel:
> Tut l'unt purpris li arbreisel
> Ki planté furent en virun
> E portent fruit en lur saisun:
> Cooinz, permeins, pesches e fies
> E alemandes e alies
> E autres fruiz assez plusurs,
> Ki jettent les bones flairurs.
>
> (*Gilles*, 1921-1928)

In this paradisiac atmosphere of the scene nature is praised for its own sake. Moreover, the presence of the deer and the prostrate position of a hero, weakened by pain, add to the moving innocence of an Eden discovered and already fading away. During this ephemeral but beneficial vision, the soul, not the intellect, instinctively knows the happiness of reverie, as if a hidden part of the now silent hunters were longing for an ideal retreat they have just destroyed. Here the desire for imitation is not inspired by a precise fear of Hell: it comes from a certain type of meditation where prayer, according to Bremond's study, becomes poetry. [24]

In a comparison similar to Bremond's distinction between *animus* and *anima*, Bachelard notices how the latter is: "Le principe commun de l'idéalisation de l'humain, le principe de la rêverie d'être, d'un être qui voudrait la tranquillité et par conséquent,

---

[24] Henri Brémond, *Prière et poésie* (Paris: Grasset, 1926), p. 218.

la continuité d'être." [25] Before this miniaturized world, where the key word is silence, intimacy is felt as a power of permanence. The recognition of immortality goes hand in hand with the discovery of the concrete limits of this symbolic cave. The vegetative life led there by Giles finally marks the union of God and nature since, "Demeurer dans la grotte, c'est commencer une méditation terrestre, c'est participer à la vie de la terre, dans le sein même de la Terre maternelle." [26] The greening of the desert breaks with the folkloric tradition of the menacing wilderness by humanizing and even sanctifying it:

> Entre le Rodne e Munpellers
> Ert le pais large e pleners
> De granz deserz e de boscages;
> Assez i out bestes sauvages,
> Urs e liuns e cers e deims
> Senglers, lehes e forz farrins,
> Olifans e bestes cornues,
> Vivres e tygres e tortues,
> Sagittaires e locervéres
> E serpenz de mutes manéres.
> Gires n'en prent nule pour,
> Einz se fie en sun bon seignur.
>
> (Gilles, 1229-1240)

Earlier in the narrative Giles' has to confront an unwelcoming forest which is seen as an epitome of flora and fauna. But the bestiary exists to celebrate all the more the saint's audacity and God's favor. The mythological elements of the quotation create the atmosphere of a desert not frequented by man but by animals, tamed not by civilization but by sacralization. Just like Francis of Assisi's well known love for Creation, Giles' communion with nature tends to bring man back to the desert. Eremitic 'desertion' is thus an effort to sanctify society. The narrative image of the forest as a desert adapts the Oriental tradition to Western reality. Humanism penetrates, by way of sacralization, the heretofore rejected features of paganism:

---

[25] Gaston Bachelard, *La Poétique de la rêverie* (Paris: Presses universitaires de France, 1960), p. 74.

[26] Gaston Bachelard, *La Terre et les rêveries du repos* (Paris: José Corti, 1948), p. 209.

Jo ai oi sovent cunter
K'en bois soleient converser
Li seint hume religius.

(*Gilles*, 1809-1811)

And it is in *Gilles* that the union of folklore and eremitism successfully presents the apostolic dimension of sainthood. The *fuga mundi* theme is not related to a mere contempt of the world. It permits the hagiographer to describe in dynamic terms the internal journey of his hero. In studying the saint as traveller, we intend to show how events can alter the portrayal of sainthood, creating a saintly legend where apostleship precedes apology. Already the hermit-saint is eroding the monolithic figure of the ascetic hero.

CHAPTER III

THE TRAVELLER-SAINT

Whenever the saint decides to move away from a locality which he deems unpropitious to his quest, he embarks on a journey both spiritual and spatial in character. The narrative theme of desertion elaborates on the beneficial elements of solitude and silence. As praised in vernacular hagiography, the hermit-saints emulate the early models who, in the Eastern tradition, sought a state of contemplation by leading an existence which disregarded the needs of the body. For the Eastern mind, holiness was less a denial of humanity than a heroic glorification of humanity: Saint Anthony's greatness stems from the fact that he rises above his humanity through voluntary sacrifices and corporeal discipline. [1] What was, in the East, a systematic search for incorruptibility, gradually became a struggle against sin and evil: the Western adaptation of eremitic holiness thus assumed a negative turn inasmuch as the flight away from civilization was perceived as the only means of escaping corruption. Whereas the Desert Fathers thought that divinity was to be discovered within the self, the Western saints believed that divinity was outside, and that perfection could be reached only when there was a certain distance between the world and the self.

Eremitism, in this respect, represents a way to cut oneself from the known world. Not necessarily a complete isolation — indeed, most examples of hermits stay in communication with a monastery, a spiritual leader, or other individuals — eremitism is a re-creation

---

[1] See the Life of Saint Anthony in *Vie des Pères du désert, Lettres chrétiennes*, n.º 4 (Paris: Grasset, 1961) and the analysis of André-Jean Festugière in *Les Moines d'Orient* (Paris: 1961).

of the internal solitude achieved by the Desert Fathers. The more detached from worldly reality, the more inclined they are to devote their life to contemplation and prayer. As it is described in the *Vie de Saint Gilles,* eremitic experiences are an attempt to return to a pleasurable state of harmony with nature. It is, in fact, an effort to reproduce the conditions of Paradise on earth which was made impossible by the original sin. Some of the saints celebrated in twelfth-century French hagiography aspire precisely to rediscover, or re-establish, this Paradise, and their voyage away from civilization does not end in the desert, but aims at some promised land, a new Eden which the heroes tend to place in the direction of the East. Such 'orientation,' in its concrete meaning, dwells on the utopian and nostalgic belief that time and space have altered the original purity of God's disciples. In accordance with the primitivistic tendencies of their time, the twelfth-century hagiographers choose among the many models of holy men those whose life is devoted to a *peregrinatio* which brings about ordeals and adventures in profusion. Describing the dismaying wonders of the Other World, the hagiographers can thus instruct and enrapture their audience at the same time.[2] The richest source for such tales appears to be the Irish tradition, and the *Voyage of Saint Brendan* abounds with happenings and strange encounters through which the hero reaches maturity.[3] The narrative theme of pilgrimage describes greatness in terms of self-control in the face of the unknown.

The traveller-saints, however, differ in degrees of spirituality according to the various motivations which inspire them to take on a journey. Obviously, Alexis has little in common with Brendan, and shows no interest in a voyage for its own sake. The story of Alexis converges on the hero's native home: at the start of his odyssey, he leaves the familial location where he spent uneventful years of filial obedience. At the end, Alexis is back in Rome, and

---

[2] M. M. Davy compares the twelfth- and thirteenth-century mentality and states that in the twelfth century there was no opposition between Nature and the Upper World (*Essai sur la symbolique romane* [Paris: Flammarion, 1955]). This does not seem to comply with the meaning of travel as represented in *Brendan*. If there is a definite hatred for the illogical, it is because Nature in its wild aspects threatens man. The traveller-saint is victorious over evil, but evil continues to exist.

[3] E. G. R. Waters, *The Anglo-Norman Voyage of St. Brendan by Benedeit* (Oxford: Clarendon Press, 1928). See our Appendix.

finishes his life in the very location which had seemed to him incompatible with his vocation. The distance which he has covered meanwhile represents, more than a mere geographical displacement, an internal voyage of the soul which went through four distinctive stages. These stages can be juxtaposed to the four ages of Alexis' physical and mental life. Infancy and youth, the first stage in Rome, are only briefly evoked for, in *Alexis* as in most Saints' Lives, the early period does not interest the poets, as if it were unnecessary for the public to know anything more than the social surrounding, the miraculous premonitions, and the signs of precocity which announce the future manifestation of holiness. The second stage marks the real beginning of the story. Alexis chooses his own road toward perfection, a decision which consists of a dual movement against his familial surroundings and in favor of another location. In order to avoid too pragmatic a world, Alexis places between Rome and himself a distance judged sufficient for the realization of poverty as a supreme virtue. This time of preparation begins in the Holy Land and ends with Alexis' return on a divinely conducted ship. Under the staircase of his own house, Alexis fulfills the third step of his mission, an exercise in poverty and humiliation, and the fourth stage corresponds to the time of his celebration after death when the saint is finally accorded universal recognition. Alexis himself writes his story, according to a paradoxical process of self-praising which inspires the hero to reveal his own heroism. [4] But this last stage does not constitute the most important part of the poem, although it demonstrates how the twelfth-century notion of sainthood allows a revealing combination of humility and certitude, humiliation and celebration. No value can in fact be realized in secret. The hagiographer works against his own message. Legends are created from hidden achievements and praise mostly unnamed

---

[4] This is particularly true of MS L (Hildesheim). As Donald Maddox demonstrates ("Pilgrimage Narrative and Meaning in Manuscripts L and A of the *Vie de Saint Alexis,*" *Romance Philology,* 27 [1973], 143-157), MS A (Ashburnam) omits the last fifteen stanzas, as well as two major points in the autobiography written by Alexis (reliquary importance of the saint's body, his return to, and beneficial influence on, the city of Rome). The resulting version, lessening the self-praising process of MS L, presents a more austere hero. MS A creates a legendary sainthood whereas MS L, more interesting in regard to Alexis' concrete intercession, produces a saintly legend.

personalities. Thus the two stages of Alexis' existence and the two ages of his mental life that are to be studied here consist of preparation and maturity. Through this diptych of seventeen years of Christly significance Alexis reaches the aim of a quest oriented toward complete asceticism. [5]

Brendan undertakes his travel for reasons which appear less spiritual if not less gratuitous. In the same way as the symbolism elucidated by the Christly significance of the number thirty-four, the mathematical connotations that constantly reappear through the narrative of Brendan first attest to a biblical background borrowed from the original *Navigatio*. [6] The saint and his peers embark on a journey undertaken centuries before by the Israelites of the Old Testament:

> Tendent lur curs vers orïent;
> Del esguarer n'i funt nïent:
> . . .
> Quarante dis en mer halte
> Eisi curent que ne lur pert
> Fors mer e cel qui sur eals ert.
>
> (*Brendan*, 1641-1642, 1646-1648)

In this new quest for the Promised Land, forty days are required before the actual discovery of Paradise, just as it took forty years of wandering in the desert to reach the limits of Zion. The boundless opening of sky and sea represents another desert, empty except for the eager voyagers and the monstrous obstacles they encounter on their way. Wandering is described not only through symbolic numbers and timing but also by virtue of a spatial interpretation suggested by the dichotomy Orient-Occident. As long as the travellers are conducted by an East wind, nothing but perils and

---

[5] Alexis spends seventeen years as a pilgrim in Edessa, seventeen years as an unknown beggar at home, for a total of thirty-four years which Eleanor W. Bulatkin associates with the medieval tendency to calculate inclusively ("The Arithmetic Structure of the Old French *Vie de Saint Alexis*," *PMLA*, 74 [1959], 498).

[6] E. G. R. Waters, "Navigatio Sancti Brendani," in *Brendan, op. cit.* n.º 3. See also J. Hillier Caulkins, "Les Notations numériques et temporelles dans la *Navigation de Saint Brendan* de Benedeit," *Moyen Age*, 80 (1974), 245-260.

ordeals threaten their journey to the point of leading them into the midst of Hell:

> Trestout curent al portant vent
> Chis fait errer vers occident.
>
> *(Brendan,* 897-898)

Even more precisely opposed are the two directions, and this contrast begins with the first day of embarkation. The ship is immediately blown away by an apparently *bon vent* (215) which is in reality evil, as it becomes evident later:

> L'orrez lur veint del orient
> Quis en meinet vers occident.
>
> *(Brendan,* 211-212)

The process of 'orientation' taken in its strictly concrete meaning will start after forty days of erratic wanderings and will mark the true beginning of spiritual travel. But during the more than fourteen hundred lines of the preparation before entry into the waters of Paradise, all the incidents take place as they move further and further West. The spatial dichotomy juxtaposes the marvels of the Other World and the wonders of the Divine World, the Celtic and the mystic dimensions. The human world is confined to the prologue and the epilogue. Studying the Celtic material in Chrétien de Troyes, Jean Frappier remarks:

> L'Autre Monde des celtes — îles élyséennes situées dans la mer occidentale, paradis sous-marins, tertres hantés, palais souterrains — était à la fois le pays des morts, plus exactement de ceux qu'on croit morts, mais qui sont peut-être encore vivants, et celui des dieux, des déesses et des fées ; régions bienheureuses où l'on ne vieillit pas, où le temps s'abolit, où un jour vaut un siècle. Or, et c'est là le trait le plus caractéristique, si une frontière humide, océan, rivière, mur de brouillard, les sépare du monde terrestre, cet obstacle n'était pas toujours infranchissable. Les deux mondes pouvaient communiquer grâce à des navigations lointaines, ou par des passages périlleux, quelquefois de simples gués, ou par une zone intermédiaire que traversait une bête pourchassée, cerf ou sanglier de couleur blanche. Une sorte de solidarité les unissait aussi l'un à l'autre, surtout à l'époque des grandes fêtes saisonnières d'automne

et de printemps. Cependant, si les humains pouvaient entrer dans l'Autre Monde et en revenir moyennant certaines précautions, il ne s'ouvrait pas à n'importe qui, et il était aussi prompt à s'évanouir aux regards qu'il surgissait soudain : l'aventure de l'Autre Monde était réservée au héros prêt à surmonter des épreuves redoutables et énigmatiques, ou au privilégié de l'amour qu'une fée emmenait dans son royaume. [7]

Three worlds are present in *Brendan* but a simple calculation shows that the scale of interest is obviously centered on the description of the Other World. One hundred sixty-eight lines are devoted to the Divine World, two hundred forty-one to the human world, fourteen hundred thirty to the Other World. Considering that Brendan's voyage is intended to be a hagiographic work, one can wonder why the author shows so little interest when his hero wanders in the marvels of Paradise. It is, after all, the aim of seven troublesome years. It is also the climax of the tale, properly situated at the end of the story. Almost four hundred lines, however, are devoted to the endless enumeration of infernal elements. One explanation could be that evil has to be extensively emphasized in order to strike fear into the listeners. Another interpretation is suggested through Brendan's reaction of pity in front of Judas' torments. [8] It underscores the saint's humanity and raises in Judas a repentance that attenuates his evil image. The emphasis placed on Hell and on satanic elements creates a very powerful effect, for, as Milton suggests in *Paradise Lost,* no figure can be more epic nor more heroic than Satan : Ganelon's powerful impact, Dante's *Inferno* are two other examples proving that it is easier to portray evil than to describe a Paradise which is largely ineffable.

The real literary prospect offered by *Brendan* remains the voyage itself, and the elements of an adventure which projects the hero into the enigmatic unknown. Almost all of the Celtic elements enumerated by Jean Frappier appear at some point in the narrative.

---

[7] Jean Frappier, *Chrétien de Troyes* (Paris: Hatier, 1957), p. 59.

[8] Douglas David Owen disagrees with Waters who maintains that the poet attempted to create sympathy for Judas. Owen believes that he wished to emphasize the horror of Judas' crime and to show how he justly deserved his punishment (*The Vision of Hell: Infernal Journeys in Medieval French Literature* [Edinburgh: Scottish Academic Press, 1970], p. 59).

Islands and castles offer their marvels to the travellers, real and unreal at the same time, a reflection of the natural world but nonetheless unnatural. Intermediaries between the magic and the prosaic levels take the form of white animals which have a bestial characteristic as well as a supernatural dimension. It seems that medieval imagination cannot conceive the unknown in other ways than by a distorted imagery of the well known. Threats hinge upon the four elements of nature, but become exaggerated and overpowering. The sweet smell turns into an atrocious ordeal, the magic spring in another embodiment of evil. Correspondences between Celtic and ordinary worlds are indeed established by similar cycles of seasons repeated throughout the seven-year trip. The medieval mind, if deeply attracted by the illogical, had a no less deep horror of the inexplicable, and tended repeatedly to tame the wilderness by giving a logical pattern to apparent irrationality. The saint affirms human supremacy over animalism or spiritism. [9]

One trait of folklorism can be seen in the symbolism of the number forty. It represents not only the biblical period which predisposes the spiritual condition of the seeker, it also insists on the material aspect necessary for such a voyage:

> Ne plus que a quarante dis
> De viande n'i out enz mis.
>
> (*Brendan,* 183-184)

This preparation assumed by the travellers can be compared to the forty years of Egyptian exile and the forty-day fast of Christ in the desert. But in the context of Brendan's embarkation this detail underscores a pragmatic concern for food which will reappear many times. [10]

---

[9] The hero and the saint dominate Nature and read its secrets. Confident in their supernatural powers, the medieval man considered signs, prodigies, miracles as a possible and familiar reality. See Paul Rousset, "Le Sens du merveilleux à l'époque féodale," *Moyen Age,* 62 (1956), 25-37. Jean Larmat shows that Brendan's companions are subject to the emotions and fatigues of the common man. These are realistic portrayals with which the public can easily identify. Their story is a proof that salvation is promised to everyone ("Le Réel et l'imaginaire dans la *Navigation de Saint Brendan,*" *Senefiance,* 2 [1976], 169-182).

[10] Caulkins (see note 6) prefers to interpret the number forty as a period of suffering necessary to the spiritual renewal of the monks before their departure.

At the outset of the voyage, no mention of fasting is yet in order because the travellers are merely portrayed as explorers. The first explanation for this *navigatio* remains, on a very prosaic level, the overwhelming desire to discover the whereabouts of Hell and Paradise. With the convenient pretext of being called by God, Brendan organizes his expedition to satisfy this slightly selfish curiosity. Attracted by an identical longing for reaching before due time the *terra repromissionis sanctorum*, Brendan's followers first enjoy fifteen days of favorable wind. Only after that do they encounter troubles on their route to heaven, as if they had to evaluate, through forty symbolic days of fast, the degree of their eagerness and zeal.

Benedeit tries to rationalize the voyage by mingling gratuitous enthusiasm with pious description:

> Sed quoddam precipuum cotidianis orationibus a Domino impetrabat, ut scilicet paradisum sibi ostenderet.
>
> *(Navigatio,* WATERS, pp. 5-6)

> Deu en prïet tenablement
> Cel lui mustret veablement;
> Ainz qu'il murget voldreit saveir.
>
> *(Brendan,* 59-61)

The exterior motivation of curiosity becomes in the vernacular version an interior movement provoked by the feeling of oncoming death. In order to place his life on the appropriate path towards eternity, Brendan wishes to see the realities of evil and to learn its direct consequences. Unlike the visions of Saint Paul or the prophetic manifestations described in *Revelations,* knowledge of the divine is attained by physical effort rather than through spiritual strength. The meaning of travel points up a noticeable shift in the portrayal of the saint from the moral virtues ascertained by asceticism to the material ordeals endured throughout this geographical quest. The benefit of knowledge turns out to spring from the knowledge of benefits:

> Ainz qu'il murget voldreit saveir
> Quel sed li bon devrunt aveir,
> Quel lu li mal aveir devrunt,
> Quel merite il recevrunt.
>
> *(Brendan,* 61-64)

In this exchange of merchandise, man strives to reconquer the lost paradise and insures during his lifetime the permanent asserts of everlasting property. One characteristic point omitted by the translator of the *Navigatio* allows such a prosaic and nasty remark. In the Latin version, Barintus has succeeded in finding Mernoc's wonderful island but has failed to follow his uncle's ascension into heaven. No explanation is given to clarify this failure and nothing proves that Brendan possesses more qualifications than Barintus. The latter has all the distinctions of a true hermit whereas Brendan leads a life less difficult, if not less devoted. But Brendan alone stands as the hero and the vernacular legend constructs every detail around the discovery of Paradise. Brendan's visit to Barintus furnishes premonitions of what will constitute the literary climax of the poem.

Through the traditional device of ordeals envisaged as stages of preparation, both for the travellers and for the listeners, the Anglo-Norman text tends, more than its Latin source, to emphasize the moral value of hardship:

> Ventus qui eis prosper fuerat, non, ut de more solet, desidiam in eis generavit; sed omnes pro amore Jesu corpora sua laborare cupientes, manus remis apponunt, ut velo ventum retardarent.
>
> (*Navigatio*, 14)

> Pur le bon vent ne se feignent,
> Mais de nager mult se peinent,
> E desirent pener lur cors
> A ço vetheir pur quei vunt fors.
>
> (*Brendan*, 215-218)

One can, however, wonder whether the physical effort displayed by the travellers emphasizes their spiritual eagerness. It seems to be another proof of impatience and appetite, closely integrated to the folkloric aspect of the legend. Greed for visible rewards *(vetheir)* lasts as long as the wind remains favorable, in contrast to the Latin characters who devote their free time to praising any heavenly assistance.

Compared to the journey of Alexis, Brendan's travel presents a different treatment of omens. The wind has led Alexis back to his native land in spite of his own desire for solitude. Obedient to the divine sign, the saint is therefore led to know a solitude superior in meaning and value through a vow of silence and acceptance. Neither obedience nor asceticism constitutes the bases of sainthood for Brendan. Man has here to seek more concrete difficulties such as the numerous delays necessitated by external obstacles. It seem that these obstacles are mainly evoked through the use of suggestive numbers. [11]

Brendan's voyage presents a meaningful recurrence of the number three, connected with both the magical and the mystical. The number may refer to the three days, from death to resurrection, of Christ's Passion, or to the wider symbolism evoked by the Trinity:

> Dist lur l'abes: "Seignurs, d'ici
> Ne nus muverum devant terz di.
> Jusdi est oi de la ceine,
> Cum li filz Deu suffrit peine."
>
> (*Brendan*, 391-394)

In a cyclical movement, *imitatio Christi* consists of faithfully observing the Christian year which is another way of bringing civilization to the untamed. The discovery of the Great Pillar concretizes this notion of taming described here by the architectural aspect of solidification as opposed to liquefaction. On the pillar, which might be an allusion to the pillar of Simon the Stylite, the travellers remain three days:

> Ici estunt desque al terz jurn.
> Messes chantent tuit al lur turn.
> Brandans en prent purpens en sei,
> Ne deit querre le Deu secrei.
>
> (*Brendan*, 1091-1094)

---

[11] We have tried to collect all references in *Brendan* that make use of the number forty, and also to examine the negative and positive significance of the numbers three and two. Because the structure of the poem closely depends on these figures, it seems important to study their relationship with the phenomenon of orientation. But with V. Foster Hopper (*Medieval Number Symbolism: Its Sources, Meaning and Influence on Thought and Expression* [New York: Columbia University Press, 1938]), one should note that in medieval literature, where the predilection for repeating the commonplace persists, the number is more naive than symbolic or philosophical (p. 127).

The hero does not seek reclusion as did the hermit-saints. Brendan decides that this is not the place where God wants him to stay. The group sails on to further discoveries:

> Treis jurz curent tut a plein curs
> Par le chemin qui lur est surs:
> El quart issent de cel calin;
> Forment sunt led li pelerin.
>
> (*Brendan*, 1669-1672)

Once again frightened by a sensory experience, the sailors must undergo three days of fear before knowing joy. This symbolic time of preparation now reflects the religious nature of the trip along with the material ordeal inherent in it. To eliminate any trace of pagan enjoyment, the travellers must experience incertitude and anguish. During the three months required to return home — three months, and no longer seven years — the monks meditate on the true meaning of Paradise. They will bring back a religious message rather than euphoric news.

In comparison with this peaceful tone, the opening lines recount an impatient hunger for immediate compensation:

> Amunt, aval, port i quistrent,
> E al querre treis jurs mistrent.
> Un port truvent, la se sunt mis,
> Qui fud trenched al liois bis,
> Mais n'i out leu fors de une nef;
> Cil fud faitiz el rocheit blef.
>
> (*Brendan*, 259-264)

The poetic rhythm of the first line (259) emphasizes successfully this impatience manifested through a vivid accumulation of erratic actions. Those three days of search could suggest how preparation comes before any sign of divine approval. They seem in fact to create a folkloric atmosphere made even more evident by the precise description of the harbor: color as well as material (*blef*, pale; *liois bis*, grey limestone) and natural elements (*rocheit*, rock) prove how the poem is closely related to a Celtic background.

It is on this rock that a significant robbery will take place. Despite Brendan's warning not to touch any of the rich objects and not to trespass the appropriate limit of nourishment, one of his monks becomes the subject of a brief trial. It is only after three days that Brendan makes public his knowledge of the thief's nocturnal actions, an announcement which provokes an immediate repentance. Here, the number three (line 327) is used to describe the duration of evil (desire for possession) instead of measuring an internal quality of resistance. In this context, the number three is indeed a sign of evil, since the culprit is one of the three bad monks who joined Brendan's expedition at the last minute. Their motivations are not pure, hence the poet's warnings that they will be duly punished:

> Ast vos ja tres curanz adés,
> A haltes voiz Brandan criant
> ...
> "Les dous de vus avrat Satan
> Od Abiron e od Dathan.
> Li tierz de vus mult ert temptez,
> Mais par Deu ert bien sustentez."
>
> (*Brendan,* 188-189, 199-202)

The fate of the two other monks is promptly resolved during the trip through Hell (lines 1200, 1500) and the group enters Paradise with the same number of members originally chosen by Brendan.

In *Brendan,* the number two very often assumes a negative meaning. At one point of the story, the travellers cast anchor and live a sedentary life for several years. During this time, they spend half the year on the Albian Island, and the other half on the big fish. On the Albian island, they find two fountains which provide them with water for drinking and washing. As long as they choose to enjoy such a secure existence, the pilgrims risk forgetting the real purpose of their journey. The vicious circle of duality is here perceived as a temptation of routine, a threat to Brendan's true quest. Should they want to find the proper direction, the travellers had to avoid the East wind. They must now renounce security and confront hardships, away from the pleasant life provided by the two islands and their comforts.

The interest of numerical precisions, in *Brendan,* lies in the fact that they express rather clearly when the voyage undergoes auspicious phenomena. Ordeals and supernatural events are thus quantitatively measured so as to become unequivocal to the understanding of both the audience and the travellers themselves. Their quest aims towards visible manifestations, since they strive to experience a foretaste of heaven. The characters are very human indeed, in their overall quest as in their reactions to various ordeals. Their main anxiety, it seems, is to have to endure hunger. Very often, food is miraculously supplied; the new danger is no longer starvation but intemperance. The motif of food brings to the tale a folkloric dimension, sometimes advantageous, sometimes detrimental to the completion of the voyage.

The heroes of *Brendan* have little resemblance with the true ascetic saints. In this particular story, fasting is not viewed as an indispensable element for the success of the quest. In fact, the pilgrims are more than once allowed to enjoy a real feast. At the outset of their journey, they weather a storm which wipes away their supplies:

> Force perdent e viande;
> Pur oc ourent poür grande.
>
> (*Brendan*, 239-240)

Lucky enough to find anchorage, they begin at once to search for a supply of food (*mesters*, 285). Instead of organizing prayers of thanksgiving for such a landing, they immediately satisfy their hunger:

> Cil aportent asez cunrei,
> E n'en prestrent a nul desrei;
> Tant mangerent cume lur plout.
>
> (*Brendan*, 301-303)

As long as they avoid excess, the travellers do not have to fear for their subsistence. Nourishment is assured, provided that they keep with their religious duties as monks. When they land on the island of fish and on the island of birds, they celebrate Mass, and food and drink are immediately provided them. On the Albian island, however, Brendan realizes that there is a danger in leading a life too dependent on material ease.

When they arrive on the Albian island, the travellers are welcomed by a group of monks who serve them food while the story of Saint Alban, their patron, is read aloud. Of noble extraction, Saint Alban had decided to answer God's calling and to live an ascetic existence as a poor pilgrim. Settled on this island, he was soon surrounded by many followers. Saint Alban was a pure man and it is only after his death that the mysterious food started to be distributed to the members of the Albian community:

> Ici vivum a sanz cure;
> Nule vie n'avum dure.
>
> (*Brendan*, 763-764)

When Brendan discovers how security might impede the progress of their quest and make them forget their mission, the hero starts questioning the value of such a suspicious comfort:

> Dist lur abes: "Fuium d'ici,
> Que ne chaiez meis en ubli.
> Mielz vient suffrir honeste faim
> Que ublïer Deu e sun reclaim."
>
> (*Brendan*, 819-922)

The travellers' fortitude remains intact as long as the good messenger does not forget to bring the *cumrei* (lines 862, 890, 892). Indeed fear and fatigue reappear with hunger. The pilgrims are eager to work and row when physically satisfied. If overnourished, they lie down in a very unheroic fashion. But if undernourished, they simply refuse to move, and it is this inactivity which each time slows down the ship or causes it to stray off course. The longer their starvation — for Brendan's admonition has finally strengthened the monks' will power (981) — the more vivid in the vernacular version is the process of eating:

> Et idriis suis et doliis aqua dulci repletis,
> vento prospero veniente abierunt.
>
> (*Navigatio*, 53)

> D'eigue dulce des funtaines
> Funt lur tunes tutes pleines,
> E de busche se guarnissent.
>
> (*Brendan*, 1001-1003)

The legend of Brendan therefore propounds a paradoxical message. On the one hand, it occasionally denounces the erosion of sainthood when integrated into an overly materialistic environment, and along with the Albian monks, the episode of Paul the hermit (1563-1568) is another example of a comfortable quietude which never really puts Paul's endurance to a test. On the other hand, the poet lingers with complacency over the physical weaknesses and needs of the travellers. As a consequence, the portrayal of the pilgrims is perceived in realistic terms, thus making allowance for the limitations of the common man.

The narrative theme of pilgrimage adapts the movement of *fuga mundi* into a journey which, in *Brendan,* is above all a geographical quest for a new Eden. In this course towards the East, the saint's orientation may also be inspired by a decision to reform and to establish an internal paradise. Examples of repentance, in vernacular hagiography, show how the heroes undertake a trip in order to widen the distance between a past life and a new, regenerated self.

The first version of *Marie l'Egyptienne* describes in lively terms the initial stage during which the heroine acts as a sinner and goes to Jerusalem without any religious intention. [12] After the episode which relates the circumstances of her repentance, approximately one thousand lines are devoted to the second period of Mary's life. These lines offer an interesting account of the process of orientation as it seems to comply with the purification of the sinner. The image of the Virgin has spoken to Mary:

> "Va t'ent au moustier Saint Jehan,
> Puis passeras le flun Jordan;
> El moustier prendras medecine,
> Puis t'en iras en le gastine."
>
> *(Marie I, 555-558)*

The geographical framework of the narrative immediately associates the story with the tradition of the Desert Fathers. Mary is led beyond the Jordan, through John the Baptist's country, in an initial movement of automatic purification brought by the evangelic significance of the river. In the desert *(gastine)* Mary is going to live an existence diametrically opposed to that she has known. She

---

[12] Peter F. Dembowski, *La Vie de Sainte Marie l'Egyptienne, versions en ancien et en moyen français* (Geneva: Droz, 1976). The version we refer to as *Marie I* is called version T by Dembowski. See our Appendix.

used to fear solitude, she now seeks it in order to fulfill not only the Virgin's orders but also her own aspiration. She sleeps on the bare ground and prays in the nearby chapel.

The second movement shows her entrance into the forest. Guided by an interior voice, she continues her peregrination, experiencing nevertheless a growing fear as the forest becomes more savage:

> Vers oriant tint sen chemin.
> Tant ala par jor et par nuit
> A faim, a soif et a dur lit
> Que tant parfont fu el bocaige.
> Toute devint illuec salvaige.
>
> (*Marie I,* 612-616)

As a concrete consequence her clothes are soon torn, her physical appearance loses all the attractive attributes which were once part of her beauty. Her now dark skin reflects the interior purity of a heroine determined to subdue her will and strength of mind, the better to serve God. The ugliness of her body indicates not a transformation but a transcendence of disposition:

> Por chou estoit ele molt lie
> Quant ele souffroit le hasquie.
> N'est merveille se iert noirchie,
> Car molt demenoit aspre vie.
> Plus de quarante ans ala nue,
> N'iert merveille se iert moussue.
>
> (*Marie I,* 659-664)

And through the complacent attitude of the hagiographer in his descriptions of her physical appearance it is possible to discern the passage of time. Forty years of fast consecrate a saintly achievement which places Mary in a new perspective of *imitatio Christi.* Maturity is here the heroic practice of virtues made all the more wonderful by the appearance of Satan. He unsuccessfully tries to have her recapture the memory of her past beauty and life of ease. Mary simply rejects these images in repentance for a period of madness. And so, she continues to live in the midst of the wilderness with no other company than the animals of the desert.

Not far from there, on the outskirts of the forest, lives a group of hermits whose rules are poverty, silence and prayer. Their eremitic ideals are still preserved as they lead a truly ascetic life and withdraw regularly in the midst of the forest to renew an individual contact with God:

> Puis lor ouvroit l'uis dee mostier,
> En le forest les envoioit,
> ...
> El desert vivoient de fruit,
> En Dieu avoient grant amor,
> D'erbe vivoient li plusor.
>
> (*Marie I*, 742-743, 754-756)

The vegetarian and ascetic mode of life which allows these hermits to remain close to their tradition is framed in a context of wilderness, the best environment for meditation. When they go outside the walls of the monastery, it is to avoid routine and ease. Moreover, they flee any contact between each other to be all the more open to God:

> Quant l'un veoit l'autre el desert,
> Fuioit s'en de la ou il iert,
> ...
> Il ne savoit ou il aloit,
> A Damediu se conmandoit.
>
> (*Marie I*, 757-758, 765-766)

The return to the monastery after forty days of retreat is each time welcomed by the superior as a victory over individual temptations associated with eremitic solitude. Having described the reasons for this annual custom, the hagiographer now presents the character of Zozima, a saintly man who begins his wandering by walking alone for twenty days toward the deepest center of the forest. He first rejoices in his successful solitude, then feels a growing apprehension which soon receives the embodiment of temptation. For Zozima has seen a human shape moving not far away in the shadows. He is to encounter danger:

> Quant il ot s'orison fenie
> Turna soi vers destre partie,
> Si resgarda vers orient,
> Un ombre vit son essient
> Qui estoit ou d'ome ou de feme.
>
> (*Marie I*, 821-825)

Several elements in this quotation are worthy of comment. First, Zozima has just finished a prayer for mercy. Secondly, he looks towards the East, namely, in a direction which so often bears a positive religious connotation. Thirdly, he immediately doubts the identity of the shape. The possibility that it might be a woman allows the audience to feel the dramatic situation of a hermit, lost in a forest, subject to demoniac imagination, and yet it is clear to the audience that he is looking in the right direction, since it is precisely here that Mary lives.

The ensuing event undoubtedly conveys humor. Mary is covered only by her long white hair and the hagiographer pauses to note that in this deserted forest it is slightly windy, a threat to her modesty:

El n'avoit altre vestement,
Quant ce li soslevoit le vent,
Dessous paroit le char bruslee
Del soleil et de le gelee.
(*Marie I,* 845-848)

It is not made explicit whether Zozima recognizes saintly asceticism or is merely glad to discover a woman. Nevertheless, Mary is afraid and runs away while Zozima, although aged, runs after her:

Ne garda pas a se viellece,
Molt li est peu quant il se blece,
Par le forest va achoupant,
Molt sovent le va apelant.
(*Marie I,* 853-856)

His eagerness is judiciously described through precipitated movements which contrast with his former attitude. Mary miraculously calls Zozima by name, and, from that moment on, the message and the progression of the story are clear: the only rivalry between the two protagonists consists in proving that the other is the more humble, according to the Eastern tradition of competitive asceticism. Both demand to be blessed by the other; both admire God's greatness in the other's achievement, and both insist on rising last, in deference to the other's greatness.

The process of orientation is associated here with the role of the hermit. Mary desires to be informed about the state of a world she left forty years earlier. In Zozima's words, peace has finally overcome:

> "Mais sainte Eglise a grant besong
> Que por li faichiés orison
> Que Dex li envoit pais durable
> Et le deffende del diale."
>
> *(Marie I, 967-970)*

Mary is moved by Zozima's remark and while she prays for the Christians, another sign occurs in the form of her levitation which once again celebrates the benefits of the flight from the world:

> Ele garda vers orient,
> Drece ses mains, al ciel les tent
> Et Dé proie, le Creatour
> Molt pieument et par amour.
>
> *(Marie I, 973-976)*

Zozima is at first terrified by the phenomenon of levitation which could very well be a demoniacal manifestation. But Mary reaffirms her position as a Christian and even asks to be granted absolution through confession. Her edifying story as a repentant sinner sets the tone for the new relationship between the saintly man and the heroine. She asks him to come back the following year and to bring her communion. She then dies in an odor of sanctity.

The hagiographic content of this particular poem relates the theme of *fuga mundi* to the events arising from a pilgrimage aimed at the imitation of Christ and achieved through heroic combat against sin. There is a series of images which present Mary's ordeal as an example to be followed almost to the letter. These images suggest that sainthood begins with the intervention of the Virgin, is perfected in the spirit of Christ, and for God's love. Sainthood occurs only when man abandons himself to the harshest environment and eliminates existential needs, becoming almost disincarnate. Being so remote, Mary needs Zozima to awaken the consciousness of others and to animate the spirit of the monastery. She consequently inspires the Christian community, the regular and secular orders as well as the layman.

Orientation, as seen in Brendan's voyage and Mary's pilgrimage, allows the hagiographer to describe allegorically the phenomenon of purification that accompanies the flight from the world. The traveller-saints possess the same qualities as the ascetics. They are hermits since they tend, with some differences, to scorn material ease. Mary's trial surpasses Brendan's ordeals inasmuch as she does not seek any terrestrial paradise. Her story also underscores the concept of compassion toward sinners which humanizes the concept of holiness, for sainthood is no longer reserved for those who have never failed. But these saints still evolve in an abstract world. Mary's desertion takes place in Israel, Brendan's 'orientation' occurs in the North Sea. Despite these concrete geographical locations, allegory plays an essential role: it is not so much the aim of travel as the meaning of travelling that prevails here. The concrete details tend to enhance the marvels of Brendan's victories and the wonders of Mary's strength.

Another poem, however, invites the audience to see travel as a necessary mode of purification on the road to perfection. Travel is still presented as an individual performance, while its details are not over-abstracted. This is not to say that the geographical details in *Grégoire* reflect an effort toward identification. On the contrary, the vagueness of the 'seashore', the 'land', and the 'island' ceases only when Rome is cited as the final destination and the place of this sinner's rehabilitation. But travel symbolizes for Gregory an interesting spiritual cure through the process of self-identification.

The structure of *Grégoire* follows three stages of travel which describe the story of a repentant sinner. Gregory's birth is the result of incest. His father's pilgrimage to Jerusalem is not enough to purify the child, perhaps because at the same time the mother is guilty of attempted homicide. A servant finally convinces the mother to spare the innocent infant. Gregory-Moses is abandoned in a fragile boat and confided to the sea. Harbored by the prior of an unspecified abbey, he spends his first twelve years learning from the abbot and living at a fisherman's house near the sea.

The second trip is Gregory's return to his country home. Here begins his responsibility, since he decides to search for his parents and to become a knight, despite his godfather's admonitions. Responsibility accompanies sin in this narrative. The trip from the sea inland, from the abbey to the castle, from a peaceful retreat to a warring city, is a premonition of the nature of his next voyage.

As seen in Chapter II, eremitism in *Grégoire* coincides with a movement of contrition and submission.[13] The hero puts his fate in God's hands and is led to retrace a voyage from land to sea. The retreat he will endure for seventeen years is in a remote and again unnamed place. Gregory settles in the middle of the sea (perhaps the Mediterranean) because of an event which appears gratuitous but bears several connotations. He first arrives at the seashore where he looks for shelter. A fisherman reluctantly accepts him for one night. He might well be the same fisherman who raised the youngster during his first twelve years.[14] The destination of this third trip is a deserted rock from which Gregory will make his last voyage to Rome. Time and space in *Grégoire* delineate the degrees of interior pilgrimage necessary to overcome the fatality of sin and to become a saint. The road to sainthood is scattered with dangers, here more spiritual than concrete.

Concretization will therefore be applied to those poems where the travels both situate the saint in a definite geographic location

---

[13] Therefore the *fuga mundi* is a recognition that terrestrial vanity is here individual misbehavior. Like Chrétien de Troyes' Perceval, Gregory has sinned because of his vain attraction to the flashy world of chivalry. When he repents, he relinquishes these superficial manifestations of identity in order to discover his true self. In comparison with the concrete attributes of the knight, the external aspect of Gregory the pilgrim presents a spiritual disposition:

> E si cum povres e chaitifs
> S'en [est] fuï hors del païs.
> (*Grégoire*, 1613-1614)

[14] A fisherman had announced to Gregory, in a movement of anger, that he was not his father. This discovery had sent Gregory to unhappy adventures and further discoveries led him to flee the social world. Gregory has donned poor clothes. But one day is not enough to leave the imprint of poverty. Hence this fisherman's reaction:

> "Ohi, dist-il, cum il est gras,
> E blancs e tendres suz les dras,
> ...
> Bien me semble tel march[e]ant
> K[i] altri bien vait espiant."
> (*Grégoire*, 1645-1646, 1649-1650)

This is another example of the realistic observations which are typical of this particular poem (See Chapter II).

and illustrate his progressive maturation. Thomas Becket remains, of course, the best example of a saint acting within a specific world. [15] Compared to the remoteness of Alexis' refuge, there is no doubt that his life presents a different form of holiness. Not only space but time participate in the concretization of the poem. Thomas Becket is a figure still familiar, if not close, to the late twelfth-century audience. When he flees England and travels through France, it is out of motivations that are widely known by the people. In the struggle between Becket and Henry, the modern reader sees sainthood as the heroic integrity of an individual. For the French medieval audience, however, it was a struggle between ecclesiastical and royal power. After his martyrdom, Becket becomes the champion of the Church.

Although not at all contemporary, *Geneviève* and *Gilles'* could have been two better examples of sainthood appealing to a popular audience: the former for reasons of sentimental imagery, the latter because he is the product of sheer invention. The sentimental imagery refers to the moving power in the story of a young shepherdess from Nanterre who decides on her own to go to the bishop of Chartres and finally saves the people of Paris. The hagiographer does not dwell on these travels: they seem, however, to suggest three stages of maturity in civic action (see chapter VI).

The final example of concretization regarding the theme of travel is best illustrated in the story of Giles. The temporal and spatial distance is presented as a subjective experience. If the ascetic and the hermit idealize time and space to transcend these earthly factors and to lessen the distance between the Creator and His creatures, the traveller-saint is more directly confronted by specific situations. The treatment of time and space, however, is mostly suggested by numerical intervals: forty, three, and two. In *Gilles'* travel is a progression toward maturity: it really refers to the journey endured by an individual. [16]

---

[15] *Becket II, Edmond,* and *Edouard* are three examples of a chronicle-like hagiography. As such, they portray a hero involved in a specific time and space. In the last chapter their degree of concretization will be studied in relation to the concept of caritative activities.

[16] Analyzing the role of time and space in the later Middle Ages, Richard Glasser notes that: "If, in the early Middle Ages, a moment or

The orientally-directed motion which structures Alexis' first degree of preparation and Brendan's last stage of sanctification turns here into a definite 'occidentation'. Through the seven steps of his Christly existence Giles leaves Greece and settles in the south of France, reproducing the trends of apocryphal apostleship in vogue during ninth- and tenth-century Latin hagiography. In Provence, to which he refers as his country, Giles experiences two periods of eremitism followed by the creation of a monastery. From Provence, he travels to the North in order to meet Charlemagne. By then he is abbot of the monastery because of Floovent's instigation. Under these royal pressures and the threats which endanger the rule of asceticism, Giles' last voyage consists of a quest for privileges. He comes back from Rome, not only with the papal benediction, but preceded by two golden doors which miraculously appear at the monastery. In the geographic structure of the poem two levels of spatiality can be discerned: besides the small twist of orientation to Rome, Giles evolves in the social environment represented by Theocrita, Floovent and Charlemagne. Yet his original aspiration for solitude projects him into the natural world depicted by the forest. Brendan's fluid surroundings are metamorphosed into the solid element of the French land, the trees of Provence, the monastic stones, and finally the miraculous doors. But the monolithic quality of Alexis is absent in this tale. The process of solidification simply anchors Giles' sanctity on this earth.

If the source of vernacular hagiography comes from England, as the dates and origins of the poems seem to prove, the theme

---

a day was selected with particular care, this was a consequence of a symbolic and formalistic mode of thought. Now [in the fourteenth and fifteenth centuries] it was the specific situation, the development of circumstances up to a certain degree of maturity, and external factors in general, that were decisive factors in the choice of a time for action" (*Time in French Life and Thought,* trans. C. G. Pearson [Totowas, New Jersey: Manchester University Press, 1972], p. 110). It is precisely the junction of contemplation and action that is successfully respected in *Gilles,* and this, in the early Middle Ages. The saint's travels allow Giles to discover progressively his mission on earth. Guillaume de Berneville exploits his journey as a symbolic representation of the hero's journey toward perfection. To do so, he does not resort to the traditional numbers. Imagination here corresponds to original invention, apart from artificial formula.

of travel is also one Anglo-Norman feature, developed in *Alexis* and *Brendan* according to opposing treatments of spiritual and physical ordeal. *Marie l'Egyptienne* perceives time and space as the components of a pilgrimage toward sainthood. *Grégoire* emphasizes the necessity of distance in the process of repentance. But 'orientation' remains a movement of escape from transitoriness. On the other hand, 'occidentation' brings the saint back to earthly time and space. Becket is the best example of this involvement in a geographical reality, and the continental writers, Norman (*Grégoire*) as well as French (*Geneviève*) have meanwhile conceived how spatial observations can judiciously emphasize the inner progression of each hero. The concrete details of a chronicle, in such poems as *Edmond, Edouard* and *Becket,* do not, however, at once prove the literary success of a legend. Here again *Gilles',* an Anglo-Norman poem, achieves a harmonious combination of imaginary and credible factors.

Three degrees of interpretation clarify how the element of travel presents the saint in a progressively less abstract universe. There is in fact a predominance of allegory as long as sainthood is the result of merely physical ordeals. The symbolic use of numbers which places the saint in reference to the standard of Christ should itself be subject to caution. [17] But travel brings a new dimension to the portrayal of vernacular sainthood when it describes the circumstances of internal maturity. A flight from the world, or, sometimes, a return to the world, travel is a turning point as soon as it suggests that altruistic care prolongs an individual maturation.

---

[17] Guy Beaujouan ("Le Symbolisme des nombres à l'époque romane," *Cahiers de Civilisation Médivale,* 4 [1961], 159-160) expresses some reservations in respect to the importance of numerical symbolism: Davy (see note 2), Bulatkin (see note 5) and Hopper (see note 11) base their research on apocryphal texts (Beaujouan, p. 161). Obviously, the use of numerical symbolism has little in common with true theology. In vernacular hagiography, the numbers two, three and forty make a clear and superficial reference to well-known episodes of the Bible. Indeed, the term symbolism does not comply with such an artificial device. It is on the contrary an allegorical way of sanctifying the hero's journey. The poems in which the temporal and spatial distance are merely arithmetical generally fail to elaborate on the progression of the story and to portray the hero's maturation.

In this respect, it is interesting to note that no mention of travel can be applied to the Passions. It could perhaps signify that the role of the martyr remains static, inspiring either an immediate condemnation or a conversion of the pagan. When the portrayal of the saint implies a dynamic impact upon others, the hero receives a new dimension. The few traveller-saints who remain, or return to the West exemplify the way holiness may affect society. The element of 'occidentation' consequently modifies the concept of isolated holiness.

PART TWO

THE ALTRUISTIC DIMENSION OF THE
SAVIOR-SAINT

CHAPTER IV

THE SAINT AND THE PAGAN

From our study of the hero-saint as ascetic, hermit and traveller, in the first three chapters, it is evident that greatness is, for the hero, the result of an individual performance. The imperfection of the world impels the saint to seek a place for meditation. In his retreat he strives to develop his capacity for meditation and to spiritualize his existence. His example preaches the valor of humility and abstinence. To be vainglorious or a glutton, in comparison, is to be dominated by the mortal elements of incarnation. Thus the poems stress the negative value of mankind in order to illuminate all the more the transcendental effects of saintly heroism.

Individual performance is by no means equivalent to individualization: Alexis, Brendan and Gregory progressively fade as individuals and emerge as an abstract image of sainthood. Their powers of resistance, their reclusion or eremitism, are part of the geographical and psychological movement of *fuga mundi*. In *Gilles'*, however, the evolution of the genre may be seen in the way the hagiographer expands the conventional outline and makes the legendary pattern more flexible. It is the contact between Giles and society which entails the humanization of saintly heroism.

In the theme of the return to the world, the poets portray various forms of communicated holiness. The hero's reaction to others may be one of compassion, when holiness inspires repentance and admiration, or one of confrontation, if the saint's impact is perceived by others as a threat to traditional law and order. For at times the savior-saint has no opportunity, or shows no inclination, to compromise with those whose behavior he disapproves.

In the context of the Passions, the saint's greatness stems precisely from his power of integrity on the road to martyrdom, a resilience which places him above, rather than amongst, the mortals. In the vernacular Passions, martyrdom introduces elements of tension and dramatization absent in the portrayals of isolated holiness, and heroism is no longer a flight from, but a fight against the world.

During the early years of Christianity martyrdom was the only road to sainthood. In the pagan atmosphere of the Passions, tortures and miracles constitute the bipartite structure of the poems. The events that precede tortures briefly suggest the saint's attitude of defiance. Following the martyr's death the miraculous elements emphasize in a quantitative way the numerous conversions that such a witnessing inspires. On a literary level the secularization of the hero is a matter of communication. The tension arising from the two forces present can either become intensified or disappear.

In *Laurent* the battles which confront the pagan and the saint are represented through the opposing images of darkness and light. [1] The first episode of conversion involves a miracle which restores sight. The pagan Lucillus has been imprisoned because of his leniency toward Christians. Despair and tears cause Lucillus' blindness. But Laurence assures him that conversion to Christianity will bring physical recovery. Lucillus is subsequently granted a dual illumination:

> Lucillus dit: "Loés en soit
> Jesu Crist, cum estre deit,
> Qu'il me deigna revisiter,
> Par saint Lorenz enluminer."
>
> (*Laurent*, 297-300)

The nineteen subsequent conversions are also instigated by a hope for material reward. The celestial light refracted by the saint is thus clouded with earthly solicitude.

Laurence's lack of apostleship is best made explicit through his battles with Decius. Enraged by the saint's obstinacy, the pagan emperor tries in vain to prevent further conversions. But

---

[1] D. W. Russell, *La Vie de Saint Laurent. An Anglo-Norman Poem of the Twelfth Century* (London: Anglo-Norman Text Society, n.º 34, 1976). See our Appendix.

the tortures do not affect Laurence since the fire is miraculously extinguished. Illumination continues to shine forth:

> E dit: "Male nuit est venue,
> En tei iert tote despendue,
> En peine, en peris, en tormenz."
> Idunc lui respunt saint Lorenz:
> "En ma noit n'a point d'oscurté,
> Mes tote reluist en clarté."
>
> (*Laurent*, 820-825)

The author strives to be persuasive and to illustrate falsity and illusion. He admits neither the Roman reality nor the sophistication of paganism. The tension of light and darkness, allegorically depicted, does not create a dynamic portrayal of the hero.

In *Silvestre* the antithetical structure proceeds from the opposition of blood and water. [2] Weakened by illness, the emperor Constantine is advised to bathe in children's blood. But the mothers' grief causes him to seek another solution. He is then told of a certain man whose power derives from water:

> "Oiez, font s'il, la medicine:
> Ou Capitoire est la pecine
> Qui de chaut sanc iert tote pleine;
> E ceste chose est mout certeine:
> Tantost com i sereiz bagniez
> E des dous braz un poi sagniez,
> Qu'autresi sereiz seins e saus
> Com au jor que vos prist li maus."
>
> (*Silvestre*, 111-118)

> "Emperere, fet li seins hom,
> Totes les eves, ce creon,
> Ont cel poer que vos oez,
> E Deus li bons et li loez
> Les sentefia de sa boche,
> E tantost com a l'eve toche
> Li apials de la Trinité,

---

[2] Adrien Planchenault, "*La Vie de Saint Silvestre et l'invention de la Sainte Croix:* poème français du XIIème siècle," *Cartulaire du Chapitre de Saint-Laud d'Angers, Actes du XIème et du XIIème siècles* (Angers, 1903). See our Appendix.

De pechié sont tuit aquité
Cil qui dedenz baptizié sont."

(Silvestre, 363-371)

A comparison between Latin and French clearly shows that the vernacular version lessens the conflict between pagan and Christian by portraying Constantine as a non-violent man.[3] First, he questions the curative value of human blood, whereas, in the Latin version, he follows his counsellors' suggestion. Secondly there is no mention of persecution since the *cortil* (courtyard, 271) replaces the cave in which Silvestre hides from Constantine's misdeed in the *Vita*:

> Sylvester episcopus civitatis Romae ad montem Sirapti persecutiones tuas fugiens, in cavernis petrarum cum suis clericis latebram fovet.
>
> *(Vita, p. 158)*

> "Fei un suen home a tei venir
> Que l'en par non cleime Selvestre,
> E cil t'enseignera tot l'estre
> Com tu vendras a garison.
> Près est d'ici, ce te dison;
> Joste Rome est en un cortil,
> Tapiz chiés un prodome."
>
> *(Silvestre, 266-272)*

Laurent and *Silvestre* present a quite different treatment of the pagan antagonist. If Decius is described through the simplistic equation of pagan/primitive, Constantine is granted enough intelligence to be enlightened on his own. Not satisfied by the prospect of recovering his health through the sacrifice of innocents, the emperor displays a convincing disposition for rationality. Although health is still a reward, conversion has less materialistic bases than in *Laurent*. On the other hand, no dilemma can be found in *Silvestre* since Constantine is immediately convinced of his error: the apostles Peter and Paul inspire him to convert because their advice does not involve egotistic means of cure. Saint Silvester himself is of minimal importance in the story and apostleship is

---

[3] *Ibid.*, pp. 156-158.

left to an emperor who has already shown compassion toward innocents.

If *Silvestre* is concerned with altruistic accomplishment, it is because of the good disposition of the converted pagan. The saint remains inactive and his intercessive power is in itself questionable. There is therefore no conflict between the pagan and the saint. *Laurent* offers a better illustration of such a confrontation. Decius' blindness is caused by imagination. Fascinated by his own dreams — a compulsive desire to dominate, a dogged need to assert his power — Decius remains impressed with no other vision than his own. The images of darkness and light thus refer to the opposite elements of illusion and illumination respectively embodied by the two main characters.

Decius' threats are not only verbal: they are concretely represented by the instruments of torture which, in the pagan's opinion, should be ominous enough to overshadow the saint's radiance. If this plan fails in the story, it nevertheless satisfies the audience's need for dramatization;

> Ceo est mult orible torment,
> Si cumme dient romaine gent;
> Ceo sunt platines de fer granz.
>
> (*Laurent*, 632-634)

In bringing the *laminas* (blades, 631) before Laurence's eyes, Decius hopes to break the saint's resistance. But the reflection of those blades only emphasizes that the pagan blindness derives from false light. Analyzing the expression "a wheel with sharp blades," André Jolles shows how formulae often replace invention:

> Ein Rad mit scharfen Klingen — so ist nicht ganz einzusehen, wie man einen Menschen damit martern soll, aber es ist unmöglich, den Begriff sämtlicher seelischen und körperlichen Foltern besser zu fassen als durch ein Rad mit scharfen Klingen. [4]

---

[4] André Jolles, *Einfache Formen: Legende/Sage/Mythe/Rätsel/Spruch/ Kasus/Memorabile/Märchen/Witz,* 2nd ed. (Tubiengen: Niemeyer, 1958), p. 44.

The hagiographer is not concerned with naturalism. He tries to suggest the saint's integrity and the evils of paganism. He portrays a confrontation between wrong-doing and right-doing. In contrast to Laurence's passivity Decius' illusion causes him to react and to act. If there is not a sustained conflict it is because the two characters are immersed in two dreams so opposed they never really meet. Unaffected by Decius' intimidations, the saint retains his assurance. If we trust the poet:

> Petit covient a sarmoner.
>
> (*Laurent,* 335)

But Laurence's attitude is not consistent with this remark and one hundred thirty of the nine hundred fifty lines of the narrative are devoted to lengthy monologues. This type of verbal battle precludes any chance of recognition, since, in Jackson's words, "verbalizing is non-communication." [5] Thus on the literary level, the wrong-doing entails more dramatization than the right-doing, and marks of humanity are accorded to the pagan, not to the saint.

Georges exploits the same elements of misunderstanding between the antagonists of the story. [6] Persecution is also evoked through numerous tortures that pseudo-Wace's version describes with complacency:

> As os perceier fist glaives faire
> Et tenailles por les dens traire,
> Et rasors por le cuir des chiefs
> Escorchier, fist tormenz et griefs.
>
> (*Georges II,* 33-36)

George is of noble extraction in both versions, hence his disdain for the weakness of the Christian crowd:

---

[5] W. T. H. Jackson, "Problems of Communication in the Romances of Chrétien de Troyes," *Medieval Literature and Folklore Studies: Essays in Honor of Francis Lee Utley* (New Jersey: Rutgers University Press, 1970), p. 50.

[6] John E. Matzke, *Les Oeuvres de Simund de Freine* (Paris: Société des Anciens Textes Français, 1909) called here *George I* or *Passion,* and Victor Luzarche, *La Vie de la Vierge Marie, par Wace, suivie de la Vie de Saint Georges* (Tours: Bouserez, 1859), referred to as *George II* or *Vie.* See our Appendices.

De lui se guaitat chescun ben,
Cum levre fait quant veit le chen.
George fut de noble quer
Ne vout flechir a nul fuer.

(Georges I, 65-68)

The stylistic rupture in line 36 of the above quotation from *Georges II* dramatizes all the more what will be the fate of the insubordinate. In *Georges I*, the hero belongs to the tradition of the *miles Christi* which makes knightly bravery and saintly inflexibility coincide. The bravery tends to become braggadocio, so teasing is George's attitude toward Dacien. It begins with a long monologue in which George recapitulates his desire for poverty *(Georges I,* 104), his disdain for the world (139), and his decision to return to the world in order to denounce paganism:

"Aler voil demaintenant
A l'emperur mescreant
Qui les cristïens esforce
De Deu reneer par sa force.
Jo l'ai nomé emperur,
Meuz pus dire empeirur."

(Georges I, 141-146)

Through the play on words *emperur* and *empeirur,* emperor equals worst. These rhymes forebode the lack of communication between the two antagonists. Tortures succeed insults and George is certain that his ordeal will strengthen the frightened Christians. It does not seem, however, to do so. They secretly carry away George's corpse in the hope of subsequent miracles:

Tut celéement de nut
Pristrent le cors u il jut;
A l'église le portérent
E de bausme l'embausmérent.
Tut de nut fu enfuïz
U maint home est pus gariz.

(Georges I, 1674-1679)

By embalming George, the faithful show that they understand the curative power of the body, if not the value of saintly fortitude. Acting silently in the darkness, the faithful are only shadows. The

obscurity of night reinforces on a literary level their spiritual blindness and stumbling. George's intercessive power is again put in
question.

The saint's caritative influence becomes all the more questionable
as George never persuades Dacien either. Their reasons for living
are mutually exclusive since for George it is to propagate, and for
Dacien to extinguish, the Christian faith:

> Cist mist tut tens peine e cure
> Faire as cristïens leidure.
>
> (*Georges I,* 29-30)

> "Sanz poür e sanz dotance
> Voil enseigner ma creance."
>
> (*Georges I,* 153-154)

George's struggle is directed more against the false idols than
toward the defense of truth, hence the destructive manifestation
through which his virtue is displayed. He ridicules Dacien's belief:

> "Un trunc mu e ciu e surt,
> Qui ne veit, ne qui nen ot,
> Ne qui oïr ne poet mot."
>
> (*Georges I,* 172-174)

Dacien, on the other hand, shows a clemency astonishing for an
emperor to whom George is nothing but an offense. He offers the
saint castles and honors which George at once rejects. The dialogue
deteriorates into reciprocal insults. In Dacien's logic God has no
value since every Christian is poor:

> "Cristïen sunt pain querant
> Pur ceo qu'il sunt mescreant.
> Povres sunt e ben lur faut,
> Car le lur Deu ren ne vaut."
>
> (*Georges I,* 259-262)

When compared with Decius' attitude in *Laurent,* Dacien shows
more rationality. His subsequent arguments suggest the unsound-
ness of such concepts as the Trinity, the Resurrection and the virginity of Christ's mother. Logic for George implies that everything
is meaningful since God is meaningful. The weakness of his an-

swers is particularly noticeable when he proceeds to explain the mystery of the Holy Mother's virginity by comparing it to the stainless light of the sun:

> "Solail, quant il lust sur veire,
> Parmi passe tut eneire,
> Si remaint le veire enters.
> E tut lusant et tut clers.
> Ausi out enfant Marie
> Senz aver la char blesmie."
>
> (*Georges I*, 387-392)

With such arguments, George is obviously unable to convince Dacien, and here again, verbalizing is non-communication. Between the poet and his audience, however, George's polemics are based on irrefutable grounds, and the following incidents substantiate the validity of the Christian faith. After this extensive dialogue, or rather, confrontation of two monologues, Dacien remains so unmoved either by George's arrogance or by his sermon that he simply retorts:

> — George," dist li emperéres,
> "Lapider vus frai de péres."
>
> (*Georges I*, 423-424)

After the first round of tortures the hagiographer is pleased to note that George has not felt anything:

> Ore oëz merveille grant:
> Mal ne senti tant ne quant.
>
> (*Georges I*, 445-446)

> Car, ben sachez sanz mentir,
> Mal ne pout son cors sentir.
>
> (*Georges I*, 465-466)

Logic would require corporal pain to make George a true martyr. But the didactic purpose needs to show first how the wrong-doing is really a non-doing, in order to insist on the superiority of the miracle-worker. As a last resort Dacien decides to put George in a jail. Isolation *intra muros* at first alters the saint's inflexibility. That involuntary solitude paralyzes the hero and reduces the saint to human proportions. For acting is reacting — which is a psychological defense, not an upsurge of spirituality — and stops at verbalizing. This appearance of vulnerability mollifies the rigid character of the saint:

> Mult fu plein de grant puür
> E fu tut tens sanz luür.
>
> (*Georges I*, 475-476)

These two lines suggest man's limitation. But the hero is divinely provided with lucidity, represented by the light which suddenly illuminates the jail. The relation between the martyr and his executioner emphasizes that human communication is alienating. Religious obedience, on the contrary, is the only means of liberation. It is described as a liberation from all carnal vicissitudes. God announces to George that he will be tortured three times before being granted salvation in Paradise. Following this reassurance, George is no longer affected either by the walls of his jail or by the limitations of his body:

> Tant out joie grant al quer,
> Ne pout manger a nul fuer;
> Ne pout dormir en son lit
> Pur la joie de cel dit.
>
> (*Georges I*, 495-498)

After this episode, God's power is made visible. Dacien is irritated by the fact that George suffers no physical harm from the tortures. After having held in contempt the saint's state of vulnerability, he now rages against George's sudden talent for remaining indestructible. Dacien declares that miracles are the work of the devil. In another time, George could very well be accused of witchcraft:

> "George," fait il, "dunt avent
> Que vostre cors nul fer ne crent?
> Qui fait cel enchantement
> Que vostre cors nul mal ne sent?"
>
> (*Georges I*, 561-564)

For the medieval audience, however, the succession of miracles was expected in a Passion, for without miracles, the saint would not become a true witness (μάρτυς). One onlooker, Magnacius, for example, converts because he is easily satisfied with the promise of reward. Along with him, more than one hundred people reject Apollo. Dacien shows no disposition for such credulity. He continues to see miracles as a result of black magic and plans a competition with his own sorcerers:

> Dacïen fu fel e fers,
> Venger se vout volenters.
> Dunt enveat par la tere
> E fist bons enchanturs quere.
>
> (*Georges I*, 595-598)[7]

The confrontation develops into a folkloric duel of spells, a hint of the direction in which Saint George's legend will develop. Simund de Freine adds folklore to the hagiographic element in order to move his public. God becomes more than the King of Heaven, He is also the Ruler of the Earth, able to dominate any Merlin. George overcomes the sorcerer Anastasius in staving off the poisonous effect of the potion: Anastasius then turns from black to white magic.

After having lost two of his best soldiers and magicians in the persons of Magnacius and Anastasius, Dacien has no other recourse than to invent new tortures. He drives sixty nails into George's head and saws his body in two, then boils the parts in hot resin. Even though these actions result in five hundred subsequent conversions, Dacien's imagination is not exhausted. The emperor orders George to go and live in a woman's house:

> Dunt comandat qu'il fut pris
> E chés une veille mis,
> En un bordel mut estreit,
> U nul ben suz ciel n'esteit;
> En un liu u ja n'eust eise,
> Mès la morust de meseise.
>
> (*Georges I*, 726-731)

The author introduces this episode in a way which could conceivably arouse the expectation of a medieval audience for a scene

---

[7] In line 597 the expression *par la tere* defines Dacien's error. The poet suggests that the pagan should seek in heaven what he will not be able to find on earth.

of carnal temptation. But the torture comprises hunger, darkness, and lack of space, three concrete elements present during the prior confinement in jail. Although at first glance repetitive, the episode brings a new type of confrontation between the pagan and the saint. Endowed with common sense, the impoverished widow is a perfect subject for testing George's ability for persuasion:

> "Vedve," fait il, "pain vus faut,
> Car Apolin ren ne vaut.
> Ceo est chose veire e certe
> Par lui avez la poverte."
>
> *(Georges I, 760-763)*

These were the very words Dacien used to scorn the Christians' poverty. The word *Apolin* replaces *Deu* and in both quotations poverty appears to be shameful. [8] The widow unwillingly suffers poverty whereas the saint chooses it in the name of God. Sainthood is still the result of voluntary renunciation. In the Passions, however, heroism stems from confrontation. George decides to enter the world so as to put an end to the fear of the faithful and to ridicule the pagans, risking his own life for the sake of bringing life to others.

In George's opinion, amazing the pagan is converting him. The more wonderful a miracle, the more powerful it appears, especially if it causes material ease. He concocts three miracles which, in a comic way, leave the widow indifferent. The saint brings bread to the table, widens the hut, makes a beam blossom, all in vain since the widow goes on with her routine. Challenged by her silence, he speaks, resuming his previous imprecations against Apollo. The widow finally speaks:

> "Un enfant ai, surt e ciu,
> Nu e clop, ne veit del liu.
> Si vus volez prendre en mein
> De lui faire trestut sein,
> Lui e mei frai baptizer;
> Voil Apolin reneër."
>
> *(Georges I, 803-808)*

---

[8] Compare:

> Dacien: "Car le lur Deu ren ne vaut." *(Georges I, 262)*
> George: "Car Apolin ren ne vaut." *(Georges I, 761)*

Whether trust results from her maternal worries or from a true renunciation of falsity is difficult to say. Conversion is still based on a doubting-Thomas attitude and a need for concrete proof. The irony comes from the event following the child's cure. The now healthy son unwittingly kills the family ox. At this point the positive aspect of the miracle is questionable. The goodhearted saint cannot resist the widow's tears, or justifiable anger, and he grants her wealth as well as health, thus assuring a definitive conversion. She is all the more shocked by George's apparent submission to the emperor's request:

> "En qui se poet Deu mès fier
> Si vus le volez desfier?
> Malement en poi de tens
> Changé vus est vostre sens."
>
> (*Georges I*, 966-969)

The converted Christian acquires an intransigence similar to the martyr's. But despite George's courage, Dacien too remains intransigent. George then tries a new strategy:

> "Mandez," fist il, "un provost
> Qui face venir ci la gent,
> E ceo mult hastivement.
> A tant est la chose mise,
> Veant eus frai sacrefise."
>
> (*Georges I*, 941-945)

To reassure his audience Simund de Freine stresses his own approval of the saint's ruse. Laurence convinces Lucillus by blackmail: here George temporarily abandons his tone of imprecation with immediate success, since Dacien displays great joy over this change of mood. The emperor is disposed to appreciate George, showing a need for friendship rather than for violence. But George is only, like Polyeucte, feigning respect for idols in order to destroy them before a large crowd. More than twenty-five hundred men are gathered for George's sacrifice. For witnessing must be conspicuous, and martyrdom is by nature public. This episode signals a turning point from verbal to active battle. In this scene silence is observed both by the spectators and by Dacien. The confrontation between the saint and the statue of Apollo thus assumes a theatrical nature.

All eyes are now concentrated on the statue, as the hagiographer describes its horrible appearance at great length. George knows how to play with illusion, letting the bestial aspect of Apollo engrave itself in the mind of the spectators. Apollo's ugliness becomes real and sensible to all, although it is described in details too extraneous to correspond to reality. The poet accumulates all suggestive traits that prove its demoniac function:

> Cheveus neirs, pendant aval
> Com le cue d'un chival.
> Front out velu cum un urs,
> Purtreit trestut a reburs.
>
> (*Georges I*, 1024-1027)

Apollo is described as the quintessence of evil. His face is half-horse, half-bear, his mouth is like a dragon's. The poet has transformed a wooden statue into a menacing stereotyped animal that reappears throughout the romances and carries with it the odor of Hell:

> Pendant aval cum bec d'ostur,
> Del nés getat tel fumée
> Com fait meson alumée.
> Buche out large cum seüs
> Dunt issit flambe e fus.
>
> (*Georges I*, 1041-1045)

Menacing only in its appearance, however, the dragon shows fear. George interprets its ugliness as a sure sign of falsity and Apollo immediately admits his wrongs. He knows the fatal outcome of this confrontation: for the saint projects a new light on the physical aspect of the statue, as if it were suddenly made visible to everyone that the idol is a hidden incarnation of Satan. Apostleship is here realized through enlightenment and with the use of words. The verbal confrontation between George and Apollo yields to a true communication with the spectators which is achieved in the silence of revelation.

Except for Dacien: the emperor still remains rational and is deeply displeased to learn that George has used him. In traditional epic vocabulary he accuses the saint of lies and treason. By pretending a new desire to venerate the idol, the saint makes use of

trickery as did Satan when he assumed the likeness of a pagan
god. Here a verbal ruse, there a physical disguise. But George's
deceptive means are justified by the end. For those who are converted — by the thousands, it must be admitted — George's struggle
is valid. For Dacien, who has proven in two instances his merciful
tendency, George's imposture merits nothing less than death. It
pushes Dacien to the limit of anger and almost to insanity, attested
by the refinement of tortures he himself finally executes:

> Quant la bote fu si ardant,
> Mener fist seint George avant;
> Veant totes celes genz
> Mettre fist son pé dedenz.
>
> (*Georges I*, 1172-1175)

He also believes in the power of examples. That is why he forces
the saint's foot into a blazing boot only when all his men are
present to witness it. Since George feels no pain, Dacien resorts
to other expedients such as throwing the saint in the lions' den.

Dacien's ferocity turns his wife against him. Moved either by
the dramatic spectacle of lions running to devour the saint, or
by the pathetic vision of them peacefully licking his feet, she
proclaims her new faith. Dacien is torn between his love and his
tenacity. Despite his grief he tortures the queen to death. In dismay
and confusion he begs George for another miracle which the saint
performs by resuscitating seventeen persons, who narrate how they
suffered two hundred years in Hell for having worshiped Apollo.
Dacien still refuses to believe in God and the hagiographer proposes his own interpretation of such obstinacy:

> Tant fu fel e de mal eire
> Que ses oilz ne voleit creire;
> Treis tant out le quer plus dur
> Que pére qui seit mis en mur.
> Deu ne vout pur ren amer,
> Tant out fel quer e amer.
>
> (*Georges I*, 1531-1536)

Dacien's blindness, caused by his harshness of heart, is contrasted
with the elements that destroy him. In condemnation of his blindness, he is struck by a flash of lightning; and his harshness is

reduced to ashes. Nature kills the pagan by means of an allegorical punishment which exposes his blindness and re-establishes light and order.

The last line of the above quotation mentions the bitterness of the pagan hero. This detail, unintentionally made by a poet at all times determined to denounce blindness, enhances the pagan's character by making him alone credible. Bitterness is here synonymous with sorrow; Dacien becomes conscious of his irreducible solitude. Of course the didactic purpose is to divert man from becoming obsessed with possession. Dacien's worldly treasure, first a material power, corresponds progressively to the few intimate members of his entourage. George succeeds in taking away from Dacien his soldier, his magician, and his wife, successively. The pagan is left alone and looses the battle not only because he is on the wrong side, but because he stubbornly clings to temporal values doomed to destruction. In the struggle which opposes George to Dacien, it is the pagan, not the saint, who projects humanistic traits. Although evil in the context of the poem, the character of Dacien is more elaborate, more psychologically sound than that of the saint. If the overall purpose of the poem gives the prerogatives to George, the portrayals of the two characters are nevertheless disproportionate in interest. The real impact of a Passion proceeds from a presentation of similarly attractive characters. In the poems studied above, neither the martyr, nor the tormentor, succeeds in generating credibility. Drama requires more verisimilitude in both protagonists: the portrayal of the saint needs to be humanized, and it is necessary to present the pagan resistance as an imperative rather than compulsive reaction.

The second twelfth-century version of George, falsely attributed to Wace, couches the confrontation in epic terms. Equally noble, the two antagonists fight over leadership. As in the Passion (*Georges I*), Dacien's obsession motivates the progressive events of the *Vie* (*Georges II*). In striving to establish his military supremacy, the pagan ses in George's inflexibility a threat to civic order. His ensuing anger is thus justified by a legitimate concern for harmony. The portrayal of the pagan divulges a psychological dimension which appears during the first encounter with George. George delivers a sermon denouncing the pagan blindness. Dacien does not listen to the words, so greatly does he admire this handsome young man's audacity:

> "Jorge, ta biauté m'esmuet
> Duel aurai, se morir t'estuet."
>
> *(Georges II,* 87-88)

Quite ready for dialogue, the emperor does not attach importance to George's verbal attack. The first hundred lines depict Dacien as having an enjoyable character, open to compassion and friendship. George on the other hand is not inclined to concession:

> Li sains dist: "N'aies duel de moi,
> Aince de ta vie et de toi.
> Daciens, ton aage deplore,
> Perdus es, nés fu de pute ore."
>
> *(Georges II,* 89-92)

This last insult puts an end to the dialogue. As if seeking martyrdom for its own sake, George ensures his own martyrdom through the epic tone of the offenses which he voices, casting aspersions on Dacien's extraction (*né de pute ore*), and predicting his destiny (*perdu es*), rather than taking his present reality into account. The saint's sarcasm as well as the pagan's increasing anger depict in both an equal capacity for obstinacy, and enlighten their comparable strengths. Their struggle has the same aim:

> "Essample auront mes gens par tei
> De mort, si tendront miaus ma lei.
> Verrai se ti deus te delivre
> De mes mains et te fera vivre."
>
> *(Georges II,* 97-100)

> "Tos siaus qui vendront en m'église
> A moi faire enor et servise,
> Defens les de mort subiteine
> Et de peril et de grant peine."
>
> *(Georges II,* 445-448)

They both strive to become intercessors between their god and the people. Dacien acts in the name of *Agaba, Rache et Apoloine* (*Georges II,* 96) just as George invokes *Jesu Crist, Deu* and *la virge*

(*Georges II*, 437, 69, 73). This version is thereafter a close replica of the *Passion*, with the identical tortures and miracles, verbal and active defiance, and with the final result of George's ascension into Heaven. Dacien's fate, left unknown in the *Vie*, seems to be a progression from anger to madness:

> Le fels d'ire par poi ne crieve,
> Se que il veit forment li grieve.
>
> (*Georges II*, 133-134; 229-230;
> 399-400)

The humanization of the pagan is based on the psychological observation that anger invades man when he feels rejected. The hagiographer refers to *Daciens li fels, le plains d'ire* (*Georges II*, 21). This early characterization at the outset of the poem condemns in the pagan an unbalanced mind, prey to instinctive and uncontrolled impulses. Despite his own effort to pose the equation pagan/ sinner, the author creates a credible hero in so far as anger does not constitute Dacien's first reaction to George. Only when the saint disregards decency does Dacien resort to violence.

Another difference between the two versions is seen in the result of the tortures. In the *Passion* they have no effect on George. Here he suffers greatly, to Dacien's joy:

> Daciens comença à rire,
> Quant il vit du saint le martire.
>
> (*Georges II*, 113-114)

Admiration yields to ire as illustrated by the following exchange of questions:

> "Jorge, bien es por fol tenus;
> O est ti deus? qu'est devenus?"
>
> (*Georges II*, 117-118)

> "Daciens, ou sont ti torment?
> Tes grieves peines et tes manasses?"
>
> (*Georges II*, 130-131)

George then receives divine assistance which keeps him alive and gives him strength to perform miracles. The healing of the widow's child is another means of ridiculing Apollo's helplessness:

"Sors est et mus et ne veit gote.

...

Ti Deus est sors et ne se muet
Ne veir ne parler ne puet."

(*Georges II*, 153; 171-172)

These repetitions of formulae have the effect of a superlative which
reaches Dacien:

"Jorge, se dist lors Daciens,
Vaut donc ti Deus miaus que li miens."

(*Georges II*, 167-168)

In addition to his impulsiveness (in admiration and in anger) Dacien
appears human because obsession is not in his case allegorical.
When he realizes that George's God may not mean disorder, he
voluntarily acknowledges Apollo's inferiority in comparison to the
saint's accomplishment. This interpretation, going beyond the hagiographer's words, stems from George's subsequent attitude. Instead
of seizing the opportunity for dialogue and conversion, he pursues
the struggle and plots an encounter with the idol. Gradually the
confrontation works against communication, creating a thoughtless
and narrow-minded saint.

His breaking of the idol entails, as in Simund de Freine's version, the queen's conversion. If Dacien orders his wife's death, it is
not without grief. Humanity and compassion once again occur
despite the hagiographer's intention and through the contradictory
statements of Dacien's motives:

Daciens pleins de felonie,
En son siege s'ala séoir
Et vost le saint à ce oir.

(*Georges II*, 318-320)

Epic heroes are generally depicted in an upright position: that
Dacien sits down is a mark of discouragement provoked by sorrow
more than by misdemeanor (*felonie*, 318). In the *Vie*, the pagan's
behavior tends, even more than in the *Passion*, to give him a
humanistic dimension as weakness is evidenced through his emotions. He does not execute the tortures himself. As an emperor
he would not consent to deal any longer with a disgraceful and

disloyal enemy. He recalls his wife's beauty but does not hesitate to fulfill his civic duties in having both her and George put to death. As a warrior, he inflicts upon George a punishment that very much resembles an epic humiliation and outcasting:

> "De ma cité, de ma muraille
> Hors il sera trainé sans faille.
> Là vueil-ge qu'il perde la vie
> Où fu ocise Alexandrie."
>
> (*Georges II*, 417-420)

George is understandably pleased by this type of conspicuous humiliation, a sign that he will soon enter Paradise. On the literary level, it is also a proof that the portrayal of a martyr favors neither conversion nor conversation.

From *Georges I* to *Georges II*, the literary divergences play an essential role in the description of Dacien; in *Georges I* inflexible, stubborn and blind, very close to the single-minded Decius of *Laurent*, in *Georges II* emotive, sincere, accessible. If this extrapolation is possible despite the hagiographer's purpose, as we believe it is, the question is now whether some writers are able consciously to depict the pagan in a more credible way.

In the two other narratives which also deal with paganism and persecution, the dramatic elements are intensified by the presence of a female saint. The male martyr is adamant. He shows no care for the world and its imperfection. His only human contact consists in blessing those who imitate him, or in cursing the others. No place is left for compassion since the representation of *virtus* inspires only an apology of virile stature and divine superiority. The softening of the saint is accompanied by an increasing interference of marvel and wonder, when the poet, juxtaposing the heroine and her persecutor, describes a struggle between the handsome and the ugly, the angel and the beast.

Catherine and *Marguerite* each narrate the story and passion of a female martyr. The presence of the woman draws the focus to the disproportionate struggle between the female saint and the evil man. Such a confrontation consequently prompts the audience to a greater participation. The male martyr is portrayed as a man of action; the description of the female martyr can bring a more emotive tone to the narrative, if the heroine is portrayed as a persecuted woman. The pathetic elements are closely associated with feebleness, rousing the spectators' sympathies and their potential predisposition for sadism and masochism.

Catherine expounds its antithetical structure through a trial during which her theological ability undergoes the test of the best dialecticians. [9] The story takes place in Alexandria, under Maxence's tyranny, and Catherine is first presented as a noble and well-educated *pulcele* and *meschine* (*Catherine*, 135, 137) whose knowledge includes terrestrial as well as divine matters. She opts for virginity because terrestrial love is mortal whereas divine love is eternal. Her choice is described in terms of logic, unlike Margaret's decision. The didactic level of *Catherine* dwells on the verbal mastery by which she proves God's superiority. According to William Mac-Bain, this shows "the new vogue for Platonic disputations apparent in the twelfth century." [10] *Catherine* was to gain popularity among a monastic and clerical audience, and the author, Clemence of Barking, certainly did belong to such surroundings. There are no pathetic devices in the narrative, for the heroine's philosophical versatility eliminates from the portrayal any elements of feebleness.

If no pathos can be discerned, it is entirely because of Catherine's unordinary tenacity. Having heard of the persecution of the Christians, she decides suddenly to come before Maxence:

> De sun palais est dunc issue,
> Od soens est al temple venue.
>
> (*Catherine*, 177-178)

Her superiority is based on a self-control which makes the ensuing debate possible:

> Mult out grant duel en son curage,
> Mais bel se cuntint cume sage.
>
> (*Catherine*, 187-188)

In contrast to George or Margaret, the saint retains at all times an attitude of politeness. She respects the present hierarchy (201-

---

[9] William MacBain, *The Life of St. Catherine by Clemence of Barking* (Oxford: Anglo-Norman Text Society, n.° 18, 1964). See our Appendix.
[10] *Ibid.*, xi.

202) and in so doing inspires respect in return. When the pagan rhetoricians are sufficiently convinced to be converted, their conversion leaves Catherine and Maxence face to face. The portrayal of the pagan is here both a failure and a success. His obsession consists in desiring to possess the heroine. As in the case of Decius, Maxence's blindness keeps him from recognizing the true value of the saint. But Maxence has plausible reactions. When his wife is put to death, he displays a sincere sorrow. Here again, humanization emerges in spite of the poet's effort and only in the portrayal of the pagan. Because of Catherine, Maxence is left tragically alone:

> "Chaitifs ore sui, tut deceu,
> Mort et trai et confundeu.
> Or n'arai mais nul reconfort;
> Or ne desir el que la mort."
>
> (*Catherine,* 2195-2198)

> [Il se dejote et crie en haut:
> "Las, fait il, ma vie ke vaut?]
> A mal ure me portad ma mere;
> Jo suis serf et nient emperere."
>
> (*Catherine,* 2387-2390)

Clemence of Barking writes in a convent and for nuns: for this reason, the whole poem celebrates militant asceticism without acknowledging at any time that a pagan could be anything other than stupid, unless converted. [11] Finally, Catherine appears as in-

---

[11] In the evolution of twelfth-century judicial procedures, the theoreticians condemn a type of judgment which effects an alienation of the conscience by transferring to God the proofs of innocence or culpability. This remark seems to apply to the passion of Catherine in which the heroine's attitude is an irrevocable condemnation of Maxence. M. D. Chenu makes the judicial, theological and sociological transformation responsible for the new interest focusing on the respect of the person. (*L'Eveil de la conscience dans la civilisation médiévale* [Montréal: Institut d'Etudes Médiévales, 1969], pp. 26, 70). This explains how rigidity prevails in the Passion. Catherine dominates Maxence, for to her he is the living incarnation of evil to be combatted (See Paul Rousset, "La Croyance en la justice immanente à l'époque féodale," *Moyen Age,* 54 [1948], 225-248). The pagan character strikes a more sympathetic note than the heroine for the audience. The examination of all twelfth-century Passions shows how the martyr's exemplary behavior condemns without appeal the evil personality of his or her pagan

human as Laurence, and no specific humanization is to be found in the relationship between the female saint and Maxence.

Wace's *Marguerite* is a better example of the intrusion of pathos. [12] In many instances, the heroine is presented as a persecuted woman. The hagiographer chooses to underscore Margaret's state of helplessness so as to illustrate all the better the miraculous outcome of the story. Wace insists on the almost total isolation of his heroine, an orphan who lost her mother and was abandoned by her father. Unlike Catherine, Margaret does not come forward to question the pagan cult. It is Olybrius, the tyrant, who notices her beauty and forces her to declare that she is a Christian. Until this first encounter between Olybrius and Margaret, the young virgin lives outside Antioch with her nurse, who provides for her material and spiritual subsistence. The antithetical structure of the poem derives from the struggle between power and innocence, corruption and simplicity, the city and the country:

> Olimbrius un jor la vit,
> Berbis gardoit, ce dit l'escrit.
>
> *(Marguerite,* 85-86)

In these green pastures Marguerite symbolizes the arcadia of humanity, close to nature and to God. This lyric opening disappears at once when Olybrius unveils his plan:

> "Riche feme de toi ferai
> Et en mon lit te meterai."
>
> *(Marguerite,* 161-162)

Paganism here equals blindness and obstinacy, and the struggle between Olybrius and Margaret closely resembles the confrontation of Decius and Laurence, except that the greater weakness of the woman makes the pagan all the darker and the heroine compar-

---

tormentor. At the same time, and despite the poets' conscious effort to exalt the saint, the realistic traits which are part of the pagan's portrayal make it less allegorical and more interesting than the representation of the central hero.

[12] Elizabeth A. Francis, *Wace, La Vie de Sainte Marguerite* (Paris: Champion, 1932). Both the French and Latin versions are contained in this edition. See our Appendix.

atively more impressive. Tortures and evil temptations are overcome with the aid of the shield of protection bestowed by God.
Margaret's supplications move the crowd within the story as well
as the audience who listens to it:

> Tels i avoit, qui l'esgardoient,
> Qui por pitié de li ploroient,
> Por la paine qu'ele soffroit
> Et por le sanc que jus chaoit.
>
> (*Marguerite*, 197-200)

> Quant il voient de sa char tendre
> De totes pars le sanc espandre,
> Lor ex et lor chieres covroient,
> Car esgarder ne le pooient.
>
> (*Marguerite*, 255-258)

In the second quotation Olybrius is also subject to this emotive
reaction. But because he strives for domination, he does not cease
his tyranny, especially over a woman whose victory would signify
for him complete humiliation. During the tortures, Margaret is no
longer portrayed as a victim, but as a holy witness whose resistance
inspires numerous conversions in a crowd moved by such a dramatic scene:

> Plus de cinc mil s'i convertirent,
> Cinc mile homes i ot creans
> Sans les femes et les enfans.
>
> (*Marguerite*, 574-576)

Another episode, however, emphasizes the saint's human feebleness. When thrown in prison, Margaret experiences fear as she
must confront two successive apparitions of the Devil. A dragon
suddenly arises within the walls of her cell:

> Noirs ert et d'orible façon
> Fu ardant de son nes jetoit,
> Fun noir entor son col avoit,
> Barbe avoit d'or, de fer les dens,
> Les ioex ot vairs cunm a serpens.
>
> (*Marguerite*, 306-310)

The heroine does not attack the beast. Her only resource is to kneel and pray, a physical and internal attitude which shows how Margaret can only resort to a static and verbal struggle:

A la tere s'ajenoilla
Mains estendues, si ora.

(Marguerite, 317-318)

Margaret falls on her knees not only to pray but because fear momentarily overcomes her:

Paor ot la virge et pesance.

(Marguerite, 315)

The second apparition is that of the Devil himself. This time, Margaret shows no fear, but an unordinary self-control which inspires her to resort to action. The saint succeeds in mastering the Devil, and starts choking him under the miraculously strong pressure of her foot:

"Mais ton pié, que de sor moi as,
Fait un petitet relever
Que me puisse resalener."

(Marguerite, 406-408)

Each time the saint displays her capacities for heroic action, defeat is, for her male enemies, all the more bitter, as evidenced by Satan's final complaint:

"Las moi! Caitis maleüré,
Une virge m'a sormonté!"

(Marguerite, 447-448)

In his story, Wace intends to exalt the victory of virtue over all manifestations of evil. Virtue is here often demonstrated through the unequal combat which opposes a feeble woman and her tormentor. Apart from the last line of the poem, there is no occurrence of the word saint. *Pucele* (38), *damoisele* (105) and particularly *virge* are the qualifications attributed to Margaret. [13] The pagan

---

[13] This is not true of the Latin version in which Margaret is referred to as *sancta* or *beata*. The *Vita* describes the heroine's qualities as slightly

Olybrius is in turn described as concupiscent, conspicuous and contentious. The elements of pathos intensify the disproportionate dimensions of the two antagonists, a sign that internal greatness, not necessarily depicted in martial terms, may even coincide with terrestrial helplessness.

Regarding the literary success of this version, we disagree slightly with Francis' conclusions. She praises Wace's ability to adapt the Latin text with a preoccupation more intellectual than sentimental. [14] However, Wace adds lively details, which present a heroine more limited by her feminine weakness, therefore more dependent on pathetic interventions. This concession to pathos forbids seeing Wace as an intellectual hagiographer. On the contrary, his version places vernacular hagiography closer to romance. Within the texts studied in this chapter, *Marguerite* is the best example of the way a vernacular poet can popularize his Latin source, since pathos, in this case, transforms the struggle of the angel versus the devil into the confrontation of the beauty and the beast.

It seems, finally, that the literary level of the Passions never allows much mutual cognition between the saint and the pagan. In their verbal debate the misunderstanding stems from an irreducible blindness which impedes them from acknowledging the other's reality. Even the very pagans whose awareness of sainthood entails their conversion are not directed to this world but to the other. Two converted personages, in *Georges I,* reinforce the hero's effort. The empress is not frightened by martyrdom, and she chooses death over love. Confused by George's feint, the widow is also offended by her new faith in seeing how means are justified by the end. Both characters receive from conversion a strength of mind which dismisses any compromise with the world. Although anonymous, they play an important role in the description of the intercessive value of the saint, and their portrayal stresses how such disciples follow the hero's steps. They thus assume a continuity of the *fuga mundi* direction that excludes, in the Passions, any secularization since *le siècle* remains a burden, and heaven, the

---

more active than their French counterparts: "saint" suggests an energy that "virgin" does not convey.

[14] Francis, *op. cit.,* ix, x.

only worthy objective for these eager and new Christians. Haughtiness is the attitude observed by the saint and the convert as well, the latter not even being granted the title of saint.

The altruistic dimension of the savior-saint, incompatible with the general atmosphere of hostility which prevails in the Passions, is more likely to be seen in heroes belonging to later centuries and living in a then Christianized society.

CHAPTER V

THE SAINT AND THE SINNER

Telling the holy deeds of a saint is trying to present a mode
of life in which the individual has entirely consecrated his efforts
to the service of God. The vernacular hagiographers thus preach
the heroic merit of abnegation by choosing among the Latin legends
those which can best show their audience how to reform. Hermit-
saints and ascetics, pilgrims and martyrs are holy inasmuch as
their virtue, outstanding and above the common, receives its reward
in heaven. The edifying character of isolated holiness inspires the
public to admire these saints as intercessors between them and
God.

Sanctity, however, also refers to those men and women whose
unusual selflessness is manifested through charitable, or caritative
actions. When the vernacular legends praise outstanding individuals
of the past, it is sometimes in order to emphasize their generosity
in comparison with the decline in public morality. Several twelfth-
century Saints' Lives thus portray a hero whose merit is to have
helped others to return to God. Taking advantage of this opportunity to enumerate the many varieties of sins, the poets insist on the
intercessive function of sanctity, an attitude of compassion towards
the sinners, or at best, a communicated holiness. Apostleship, being
the matter of potential conversations and contrition, can then soften
the figure of the hero in so far as he displays emotions and concern
for his fellowmen.

In some instances, sin coincides with madness. Throughout the
poems, there are numerous examples of men possessed by the Devil.
Nicholas encounters such a madman:

> Uns hom plein de mal esperit
> Desqu'al mouster amenez fut.
> Fous ert, le sens aveit perdut.
> ...
> Del diable le delivrat.
>
> *(Nicolas,* 1520-1522; 1540)[1]

Sanctity equals sanity. The intercessive role of the saint is to interfere with the demonic power that menaces mankind. The sinner, in this respect, is only the sport of Fortune, since Satan exerts his influence as he wills. The saint, on the other hand, re-establishes order on earth and sainthood is associated with domination over evil. *Nicolas* relates another episode of natural disturbances during which Satan, under an almost manicheistic light, threatens to transform all water into fire:

> Contre nature de la mer
> Virent feu par tut alumer.
>
> *(Nicolas,* 427-428)

But Nicholas is not to be outdone. The miraculous oil that streams from his tomb illustrates how the combat between good and evil forecasts victory through allegorical images. Rightdoing appears more active here than in the case of the martyr, and the miraculous oil is also the spring for healing and benediction. Nicholas, however, displays no true compassion for others, which forbids one to speak of humanization. Faced with an evildoer, he reacts angrily and intimidates the sinner by announcing that various tortures will come unless he reforms:

> "Si vus ferai les oilz crever
> Et les poinz et les pez culper."
>
> *(Nicolas,* 705-706)

This particular saint is not made aware of the significance of apostleship.

---

[1] Einar Ronsjö, *La Vie de St. Nicolas par Wace: Poème religieux du XIIème siècle publié d'après tous les manuscrits. Etudes romanes de Lund,* n.º 5 (Lund: Gleerup and Munksgaard, 1942). See our Appendix.

Another aspect of sin is described by means of the reactions of the crowd in several of the narratives. In the hagiographers' mind, a gathering of people may easily be subject to hysteria. The rapid shift in mood, from admiration to anger, indicates how people, when assembled, lose their individuality and ability to reason. [2] There is an example of such a case in *Geneviève*. [3] In order to flatter the king, Valentin, the people of Paris depict Genevieve to him in an unfavourable light. When Saint Germain pays tribute to the saint, however, they eagerly acknowledge her virtue:

> Li pueples, qui apareilliez
> Est toz jorz des biens abessier
> Et des maus toz jorz essaucier,
> Dit par losenge et fait entendre
> Que sa bontez est assez mendre.
>
> *(Geneviève, 560-564)*

> Grant merveille ot sor tote rien
> Li pueples qui illuec estoit
> Del biau senblant qu'il li fesoit.
> Chascun d'els molt se merveilla
> De ce qu'einsint la salue.
>
> *(Geneviève, 604-608)*

All this takes place at the same time (*endementiers,* 579), and the Parisians already show what will subsequently be their traditional attribute of frivolity. There is even a trace of male chauvinism regarding the female saint. When Genevieve tries to sustain the Parisians' spirit at the announcement of Attila's invasion, their reaction is quite unexpected:

> De cest afaire qu'el lor dit
> Ont li borjois molt grant despit
> Et dient qu'el n'est pas veraie;
> . . .
> Fausse prophete en lui a une.
>
> *(Geneviève, 691-693; 695)*

---

[2] The people were ready to follow whoever knew how to move them. As Paul Rousset shows, knowledge comes from sensation. ("Recherches sur l'émotivité à l'époque romane," *Cahiers de Civilisation médiévale,* 2 [1959], 53-67).

[3] Lennart Bohm, ed., *La Vie de sainte Geneviève de Paris* (Upsala: 1955). See our Appendix.

The easiest way for them to discredit Genevieve is to accuse her of witchcraft. The crowd, stimulated by the dispute, hesitates between torturing her or simply stoning her. Thus, sin consists in despising the saint's strength in order to conceal one's own cowardice and fear.

The crowd's blindness is also mentioned at one point in *Edouard*. [4] It is clearly a sin committed out of madness and manifested through reprehensible laughter. Edward's people know the virtue of their saintly king. They are subject to his terrestrial domination and religious leadership as well. On many occasions they have acknowledged his prophetic power. When Edward carries a poor and ill man on his back inside the church, it is in their sight a comical action:

> Dunc veïsiez rei bien gabé
> E meint ris fait desordené.
> . . .
> Sa bunté e sa grant dulçur
> Jugierent en lui de folur.
> Ki k'en gabast ne ki k'en rist,
> Li reis AEdward sun curs parfist.
>
> (Edouard, 2395-2396; 2401-2404) [5]

Blindness and darkness are the elements used by the poets to describe the manifestation of sin. On a deeper level, they emphasize that the sinner becomes conscious of his acts. In *Brendan*, many episodes demonstrate that the members of the expedition are subject to such feeble reactions as those of fear, hunger, or discouragement. [6] Among them, one monk possesses greater fallibility. One night, Satan successfully tests his power of seduction on him:

> Cum endormit furent trestuit,
> Ast vos Sathan qui l'un seduit:

---

[4] Osten Södergärd, *La Vie d'Edouard le Confesseur, poème anglo-normand du XIIème siècle* (Upsala, 1948). See our Appendix.

[5] If laughter and madness are associated in this text with sin, they can at times be the attributes of sainthood as well. In the following chapter, we shall see how laughter and madness are the signs of divine joy and spiritual commitment.

[6] E. G. R. Waters, *The Anglo-Norman Voyages of Saint Brendan by Benedeit* (Oxford: Clarendon Press, 1928). See our Appendix.

> Mist l'en talent prendre an emblét
> Del or qu'il vit la ensemblét.
>
> (*Brendan,* 309-312)

The satanic effect takes the form of false brilliancy well adapted to the atmosphere of a voyage which aims toward visible goals. Indeed, the etymological meaning of the word Lucifer stresses the idea of light which Satan wants to produce, not by reflection of the divine, but from his own source. Light is represented by gold and the temptation focuses on the desire for immediate possession as if the traveller were tired of continual expectation:

> L'abes veilout, e bien vetheit
> Cum diables celui teneit,
> Cum lui tendeit un hanap de or.
> Plus riche n'at en nul tresor.
>
> (*Brendan,* 313-316)

Light is also opposed to the darkness of the night, and this contrast could be compared to the elements which surround Alexis' departure. But in the legend of Alexis, such a dramatization celebrates divine revelation whereas here it represents the diabolical way of seduction. In the midst of a peaceful night during which the voyagers enjoy a well deserved rest, being awake signifies a consciousness of right and wrong:

> Cil levet sus, prendre l'alat,
> E en repost tost l'enmalat:
> E puis que out fait le larecin,
> Revint dormir en sun reclin.
>
> (*Brendan,* 317-320)

At the same time, since he goes back to sleep, the robber does not show any sign of internal hesitation. He is guilty, but cannot be made responsible for his weakness. The witness of this action, Brendan, alone bears the awareness of the sin:

> Tut vit l'abes u reposout,
> Cum cil freres par nuit errout;
> Pur tenebres ne remaneit:
> Sanz candeile tut le vetheit,
> Quar quant ço Deus li volt mustrer,
> Sur ço ne stout cirge alumer.
>
> (*Brendan,* 321-326)

Thanks to this transfer of responsibility, the sinner is granted pardon and absolution, while the saint carries out his intercessive mission. It is only the saint who knows how to judge and to understand human nature.

Such an understanding is particularly revelatory in *Gilles,* when the saint encounters Charlemagne. [7] The king's guilt proceeds from his feeling of superiority over a man of lesser condition:

> "Or ne poez vus justiser
> Ne vostre quer humilier!
> Si vus conquerrez les granz terres
> E vus prenge ben de voz gueres,
> Ço est par Deu e nent par vus.
> Ne seiez ja si orguillus."
>
> *(Gilles,* 2885-2890)

> "Feble sen as e fol pensé,
> Ke tun mesfeit ne vols gehir.
> Quides tu vers Deu ren covrir?
> Ço ne poz tu faire vers mei."
>
> *(Gilles,* 3112-3115)

Shocked by Giles' audacity, Charlemagne confronts the saint in a very cutting dialogue. But rectitude overcomes arrogance. Because Giles is able to reveal his secret sin to him, Charlemagne, who otherwise puts the saint's authenticity in question, radically changes his attitude toward him. Before this conversion pride is associated with weakness, a paradoxical equation for depicting a royal personage. But divine humility — and even humiliation since Giles accepts Charlemagne's burst of anger — is victorious against terrestrial hierarchy, to the point of reversing values. It is now the king who implores Giles' attention, treating the hero as a heavenly messenger. Light drives away the darkness of the lie and of punishable secrecy. Charlemagne's pride was that he believed himself superior enough to claim the privilege of privacy. Giles' accomplishment consists in bringing the king unquestionable proof of his own superiority.

---

[7] Gaston Paris and Alphonse Bos, *La Vie de saint Gilles par Guillaume de Berneville, poème du XIIème siècle publié d'après le manuscrit unique de Florence* (Paris: Société des Anciens Textes Français, n.º 14, 1881). See our Appendix.

In *Edmond II* there is also a confrontation between the saint and the king. [8] Four characters incarnate sin in contrast to Edmund's virtue. The hero, being himself a king, could be in a position to wage an equal combat with them. But at the time of the Danish invasion, Edmund is dead. Jealous of his reputation, Lothebrok and his three sons decide to invade England. *Felunie* (1928), *sorcierie* (1934) and *ire* (1938) are the three attributes which explain why the Danish people, led by these sinners, are here feared for their misdeeds. Physically, Lothebrok ("Ruisel hainus [est] en franceis," 1888) waxes mean:

> Les denz aguisse e cruist e gruint,
> Frunce del neis, frunce del frunt,
> Roule des oilz; od quer enflé.
>
> *(Edmond II, 1965-1967)*

Their primitive form of revenge against the saintly king is to destroy the entire population, regardless of sex or age. They proceed in a very cowardly way. Landing at night, they kill from behind, torture and abuse women and virgins, and obtain their information through shameful force. [9] In contrast with such darkness, Edmund's body radiates light:

> Repleniz de bone manere,
> De la pardurable lumere.
>
> *(Edmond II, 2487-2488)*

Darkness and light again identify vice and virtue. [10]

---

[8] Hilding Kjellman, *La Vie seint Edmund le rei, poème anglo-normand du XIIème siècle par Denis Piramus* (Göteborg: Wettergren and Kerbor, 1935). See our Appendix.

[9] In the other version the felons' actions are even worse since they attack the infants, as described in a very touching quatrain:

> Ne nis ki sunt petit emfant,
> Ki sunt de lur mere laitant
> Ne lur pot estre nul guarant,
> K[e] il ne morent de lur brant.
>
> *(Edmond I, 261-264)*

Albert Nabert, *La Passiun de Seint Edmund. Ein anglonormannisches Gedicht aus dem 12. Jahrhundert* (Greifswald, 1915). See our Appendix.

[10] Ingar in *Edmond I* receives a satanic dimension when he tries to emulate God:

When witnessing a robbery, Brendan remains silent, an attitude which indicates a shift of responsibility as well as forgiveness. The robber's fate contradicts such an interpretation.[11] There is in *Edouard* a similar episode whose consequences enlighten both examples. One night, Edward observes a man who comes three times to steal small amounts of gold from the royal treasury. Edward keeps silent until he notices that his chamberlain intends to pursue the robber. At that point Edward unveils the secret and explains his reason for having left the man alone. Poverty, he explains, is a pitiful state: the man has stolen what he needed, and it is sufficient to forgive him and to forget. The hagiographer concludes:

> Mes jeo jug que cest digne fait
> Seit pur grant miracle retrait.
> . . .
> Plus deit estre de cest loé
> Ke des autres qu'il ad uvré.
>
> *(Edouard,* 1071-1072; 1079-1080)

Among all of Edward's miracles, this one is, from the poet's viewpoint, the greatest. The act of stealing material possessions cannot be associated with sin as long as the unequal repartition of wealth causes poverty. This is remarkable for two reasons: first, because necessity is not called greed; secondly, because Edward's openness to his people's need prevails over his gift for prophecies and his curative power. That recognition of poverty comes before the celebration of supernatural power is rare enough to be noticed as one exception within the usual position of vernacular hagiography.

Forgiveness is one characteristic of the saint's caritative functions. At times, the saint's compassion towards the sinner invades

---

Soleil e la clarté del cel
Les elemenz tut altre tel
A mei cunsentent en oël.

(Edmond I, 381-383)

[11] He disappears in the waters of Hell, as do the other two monks who have decided at the last moment to join the thirteen-member group. The fate of these monks, occurring in similarly dramatic circumstances, is one example of the negative aspect of the number three (See our Chapter III). It also tends to describe selection as a divine sign which cannot be achieved by human desire.

the hero in such a way that he identifies with the sinner, is moved to tears by his torments, and becomes unable to speak. In *Brendan,* the pilgrims discover the two islands of Hell, on which Judas is condemned to endure eternal pain:

> Dous enfers ad ci dejuste
> . . .
> L'uns est en munt e l'altre en val
> . . .
> Al un jurn munt, l'altre descent,
> N'est altre fin de mun turment.
>
> *(Brendan,* 1333, 1345, 1355-1356)

To summarize what has been said previously regarding arithmetical symbolism, duality is here a matter of evil division: unable to sleep, incessantly tortured, Judas begs for one night's rest. He once again strives for material ease, a weakness which resembles his former discouragement and, as the Scriptures relate, suicide. The repeated avoidance of awareness is in itself a guilty act. Judas cannot hope for rewards as long as he does not change his internal disposition. First greed, then cowardice and lassitude emphasize his sin. Brendan's reaction is particularly revealing of the reason, value and interest of repentance:

> Plurout Brandans a larges plurs
> D'iço que cist ad tanz dolurs.
>
> *(Brendan,* 1445-1446)

At last moved by the saint's display of pity, Judas perceives how his sin was one of selfishness. His principal weakness was paradoxically made of harshness. Repentance and conversion are here the result of commiseration. Thus tears have more psychological effect on the sinner than any sermon.

In the Passions, blood and water allegorically represent wrong and right. Here, water, symbolized by tears, is used to describe the relationship between the saint and the sinner. Contrition and compassion are closely associated in *Grégoire*: [12]

---

[12] Gerta Telger, *Die altfranzösische Gregoriuslegende nach der Londoner Handschrift, Arbeiten zür Romanischen Philologie,* n.º 5 (Paris: Droz, 1933). See our Appendix.

Quant il la veit e il la tient,
Dunc à primes li en sovient
A grant merveilles se repent
E si plure mult tendrement.

(Grégoire, 1891-1894)

With the mention of tears, the hagiographer shows that the fisherman is no longer sinful or blind. Water thus evokes the process of
pardon and remission. In *Geneviève* the mother, Gironde, has
been punished by God after she has kept the future saint from
going to church. One day she remembers the bishops' prediction
concerning her daughter and comes to hope in the intercessive
power of Genevieve. Gironde asks her daughter to fetch some water
and Genevieve goes toward the well where she weeps over her
mother's blindness:

Tendrement comence a plorer
Delez le puis desor la rive.
Pitiez les lermes li avive;
Del cuer as elz tot contremont
Jusqu'au menton lor voie font.

(Geneviève, 374-378)

The miraculous virtue of the water and tears effects the healing of
Gironde. The sinner realizes her fault when she remembers the
past and perceives her maternal injustice. Healing occurs through
saintly compassion. The daughter forgives the mother and establishes between them a new bond based on recognition of spiritual
superiority.

Humanization depends on the type of confrontation which places
the saint face to face with the pagan. If the conversion of a gathering
of pagans has little to do with true apostleship, it is because such
a phenomenon essentially occurs beyond logic and reason. But
between the saint and the sinner there is less distance and more
similarity. They both belong to the same religious world, the former
by choice, the latter despite his refusal of it. When the hero of a
legend becomes a saint through repentance, this distance is described in terms of interiority. The saintly accomplishment is then
perceived as a psychological movement by which the hagiographer
uses the literary value of time in his dynamic portrayal of the hero.

Two legends depict sin as an evil caricature of virtue. [13] In these poems sin does not derive from blindness or childishness, but from an evil deed committed with full or partial consciousness. [14] *Bon* relates how the saint, after many years of prayers addressed to the Virgin Mary, has received from her a cloak, an external sign of reward for his piety. [15] Bon's poverty appears all the more admirable as he is the bishop of Clermont, thus potentially destined to enjoy power and wealth. The apparition of the Virgin frightens a saint accustomed to his existence of retreat:

> Ne uoleit alter aprocier;
> De luinz estut, pur uerseiller.
> Ne quidout pas qu'il peust
> Aprocier l'alter, cum deust.
>
> (*Bon*, 49-52)

Adgar's version insists, by the enjambement of lines 51-52, on the saint's humility. Bon's attitude is similar to that of the publican of the parable. The Virgin approaches the saint and brings him a notoriety that does not change Bon's disposition of mind:

> Tut lur mustra par grant ducur,
> Par grant pitie, par grant amur.
> Vnkes n'i demena orguil;
> De pitie enplura de l'oil.
>
> (*Bon*, 143-146)

Compared to Bon's reaction of humility, his successor displays all indications of pride and thirst for glory. In his turn, he wants to be celebrated by his fellow men. He enters the church to spend, like

---

[13] Satan is, of course, the master of simulation. In the legend of Nicholas, for example, he deceives everyone and exerts his evil influence by assuming the features of a pious woman:

> Puis prist forme d'une moiller
> Que semblout de religion,
> De vesteüre et de façon.
>
> (*Nicolas*, 378-380)

[14] It should be noticed that the content of the legends of Bon and Hildefonse show no relation to their respective titles, apart from the notion of inverse imitation we shall now analyze.

[15] Carl Neuhaus, *Adgars Marienlegenden* (Heilbronn: Henninger, 1886), pp. 116-121. See our Appendix on *Bon*.

Bon, a night of prayer, a single night in his case, while Bon spent an entire lifetime. Here selfishness, there true devotion; here sleep, there vigilance. The opposition emphasizes the fact that the new bishop's apparent virtue is actually a sin. The following morning, since the sinner finds himself lying in his own bed, he is compelled to recognize his impiousness:

> Quant doux feiz li ert auenu,
> Pour aueit, dolent en fu.
>
> (*Bon,* 189-190)

The sinner's awareness arises only after two similar attempts at miracles. But the consequences are the same: the character recognizes having committed a foolish action by way of misguided imitation. To mime a human accomplishment instead of imitating the spirit of that accomplishment is to destroy any seed of sainthood. Two remarks must be made. First, Bon's successor does not receive a name, an anonymity which reinforces the symbolic significance of the saint's name. Secondly, the simulation of sainthood implies a scheme incompatible with the spirit of selflessness at all times characteristic of sainthood. The sinner is here culpable of sacrilege. Repentance is consequently a movement of internal conversion, a change of mind that is described as a silent contrition.

As a reward for his piety, the Virgin Mary honors Bon with a heavenly-made chasuble. This episode is not mentioned in the *Acta Sanctorum,* nor in the inventory of the cathedral of Clermont (end of the tenth century). G. Lozinski thus states that between the real existence of a Bon, bishop of Clermont from 858 to 872, and the Latin compilations of the eleventh and twelfth centuries, the saint became part of the Virgin's miracles tradition, probably around the year 1100. [16]

The legend of Bon is but a reproduction of that of Hildefonse, [17] according to a process of duplication so frequent in hagiography. The hero's name changes, the story remains basically the same,

---

[16] Grigorii L. Lozinski, *De Saint Bon, évêque de Clermont: Miracle versifié par Gautier de Coinci* (Helsinki: Annales Academiae Scientiarum Fennicae, 1938), p. 14.

[17] J. A. Herbert, "A New Manuscript of Adgar's Mary Legends," *Romania,* 32 (1903), 401-402. See our Appendix on Hildefonse.

convincing the audience to believe in the truth of a reiterated miracle. Virtue is produced by a life-long exercise in piety. In the context of these legends, the hagiographers suggest that virtue is the antonym of a quest for self-glorification, and the heroes' antagonists are guilty in that they imitate, not in spirit but to the letter, the material circumstances which had brought divine praise to their predecessors.

In *Ildefonse,* the new bishop feels the unfortunate urge to wear the miraculous chasuble and to sit on the saint's very chair. These objects, he claims, cannot be separated from the episcopal office. In his mind they undoubtedly predict for him many happy celebrations:

> "Evesque sui, cum il esteit,
> E ordené en tel endreit.
> Je l'userai tut ensement."
> *(Ildefonse,* 89-91)

He immediately dies, a dramatic event that depicts envy as the root of deadly evil whereas humility is a sure way to reach Paradise with the protection of the Virgin (109-112). The moral of the tale also indicates the merit of those who, like Adgar himself, devote their time and life to the propagation of the Marial cult. The chasuble motif illustrates in the portrayal of the sinner the dreadful result of twisted imitation. In *Ildefonse,* the sinner receives a name, Siagrius. Here the punishment is as fast as it is definitive. *Bon,* on the other hand, does not identify the sinner but insists on the movement of repentance which follows the sacrilege. Bon himself offers a tangible proof of humanization when he acknowledges, even though briefly, his human state of imperfection. It is clear for all listeners that greatness occurs in the midst of accepted weakness:

> Quant il ses pechiez recordout,
> En suspirant, de queor plurout.
> L'amur de la mere Deu chere
> Le fist plurer de grant maniere.
> *(Bon,* 45-48)

No mention is made of a particular sin which would explain why Bon feels that he belongs to the world of the repentant sinners. Weeping abundantly for himself, Bon knows his limitations and the spiritual poverty of the human condition. Studying the motif of repentance in medieval literature, J. C. Payen analyzes its theological impact and how the twelfth century has cultivated a moral of intention:

> Les textes littéraires ne mentent pas lorsqu'ils expriment une nouvelle conception de la responsabilité individuelle. [18]

Payen then examines such an awakening of consciousness among the monuments of epic, lyric, romance and didactic literatures. Although he mentions some twelfth-century Saints' Lives, namely *Alexis, Gilles* and *Marie l'Egyptienne,* it is interesting to note that he makes little use of vernacular hagiography.

The triumph of virtue over sin, presented in the hagiographic texts as rare and striking examples of edification, illustrates how the saint is spared from the moral lapses that threaten a weakened humanity. In the legends studied above, there is little or no contact between the saint and the sinner. If the portrayal of Bon associates sanctity and a certain recognition of man's spiritual feebleness, this humanization of the hero is not directly connected with the sinner's repentance. The two antagonistic elements remain apart, and the portrayals of sin and greatness are still divorced. In *Bon* and *Ildefonse,* such a moral division is intensified by the very structure of the texts: the first scene describes the circumstances of sainthood, while the second is staged after the hero's death, thus impeding any dialogues between the two main characters. Three other legends, in twelfth-century French hagiography, relate how imperfection and greatness may, if not co-exist, at least successively co-habit an individual. In these examples, the making of a saint is no longer antagonized by prior misconduct.

The legend of Gregory narrates the story of a repentant sinner, sanctified through psychological transformations. In the first sequence of the narrative, the hero's sin refers to several levels: sin of birth, of misunderstanding, of oedipal love. Only when he renounces his quest for identity does he fulfill his destiny. Speaking to Satan he says:

---

[18] Jean-Charles Payen, *Le Motif du repentir dans la littérature française médiévale* (Geneva: Droz, 1968), p. 75.

"Unkes ne fus del mal si liez,
Cum tu seras del bien iriez,
Quant tu veras les abstinences
E les dolentes penitences,
Ke io quid faire en ceste vïe."

(*Grégoire*, 1527-1531)

Contrition accompanied by seventeen years of penitence allows the saint to discover his true mission. Awareness of the self goes hand in hand in this case with recognition from others. The key to his chains is a proof for the Roman messengers, the sinful fisherman and the repentant sinner himself, that dedication to God is the sole identification worthy of a Christian.

Two twelfth-century versions recount the edifying story of Mary the Egyptian: [19]

Que nus pekiés n'est si pesant
Ne si horrible ne si grans
Dont Dex ne fache vrai pardon
Par foi et par confession
A ciax qui prendent penitance.

(*Marie I*, 15-19)

The intercessive role of the repentant sinner brings new hope to mankind. Sin is no longer reserved for evil men, it reaches everyone: the Apostles themselves, notes the hagiographer, have not been exempted from fallibility. The poem thus seems to reach a larger audience. It includes the whole of humanity under the common denominator of weakness, aiming at the same potential greatness:

Por chou ne me puis merveillier
D'un pecheor quant l'oi pechier,
Mais de celui est granz merveille
Qui tos tans dort et ne s'esveille
Et en sen ort pechié s'endort
Entreus que il vient a le mort.

(*Marie I*, 33-38)

---

[19] Peter F. Dembowski, *La Vie de Sainte Marie l'Egyptienne, versions en ancien et en moyen français* (Geneva: Droz, 1976). *Marie I* refers to Version "T", pp. 33-66, and *Marie II* to Version "W", pp. 153-158. See our Appendices.

The only impediment to salvation would therefore be to delay unnecessarily the act of contrition, in which case contrition would be equated to opportunism. The story of Mary the Egyptian demonstrates how repentance, occurring at the right time and with a sincerity of heart, can make sainthood accessible for former sinners. Mary has been duly baptized, but because of a neglected education, she falls into the temptations of lust. However, the hagiographer contradicts himself when evoking the pitiful spectacle of Mary's despairing parents. Neither their advice nor their effort to marry her to some honorable young man seems to attract Mary who, after twelve reprehensible years, finally leaves the family. The inverted *fuga mundi* carries her to Alexandria where she joyfully satisfies numerous young men:

> Ele estoit blance conme flour,
> Des jovenciax avoit l'amor.
> Tot i venoient au bordel
> Par se biauté li jovenchel.
>
> (*Marie I*, 113-116)

The triple aspect of her appetite — for drink, food and love (123) — is explained by an overall desire for pleasure and not for money. Mary's sin lies therefore in an internal disposition which makes the fault even worse, since it is not caused by the traditional carnal covetousness. It produces in the portrayal of the character a very powerful personage whose strength of body and mind takes the shape of reverse asceticism: [20]

> Tant par amoit a iaus border
> N'entendoit gaires al souper.
>
> (*Marie I*, 127-128)

It also presents a heroine who possesses all the apparent qualities for outstanding performance, except that she uses her will for an

---

[20] In Adgar's shorter version negative unselfishness is the mark of reverse asceticism. Mary despises money but her strength of will has nothing to do with generosity:

> Tuz receüt e nient pur aveir,
> Mais pur emplir sun fol voleir.
>
> (*Marie II*, 9-10)

opposite end. [21] Whereas, for example, Alexis and Brendan abandon
their familiar world and its facilities, it is in the name of a higher
mission. From a prosaic point of view such an attitude, although
mandatory in the process of ascetic sainthood, shows on their part
a strength of mind very similar to hardness of heart. Mary's destiny
is accomplished through an identical contempt of the weak. The
difference between sainthood and sinfulness is thus quite thin, for
these manifestations of *fuga* and *contemptus mundi* present Mary's
case as an exemplary existence which inspires a large number of
followers. Admiration has, of course, nothing to do with saintly
emulation. When Mary's suitors come to kill one another, such a
display of jealousy and sensual desire immediately condemns the
social function of the sinner:

> Ja cil qui iert por li navrés
> Par li ne fust seul regardés.
> Plus amoit o les sains joer
> Que les malades visiter.
>
> (*Marie I*, 145-148)

That Mary does not imitate any evil standard but borrows from
her own imagination what she considers a higher state of existence
emphasizes in her an intelligence comparable to that of Catherine.
The attraction Mary exerts on the male community is explained
on a strictly physical level.

Not only does Mary know what she wants, but once she gets
it, she is overcome by boredom. The fame that surrounds her is
not sufficient to fill her impulsive aspiration for superior ecstasy.
In the lyrical atmosphere of the tale, created by the seventy-line
long description of her romanesque beauty (149-216), comes a day
on which she wanders around the harbor, idle and perhaps lonely,
and sees a group of pilgrims:

> Che fu en mai, le mois d'esté,
> Qu'ele iert al mur de le cité

---

[21] This is not at all Adgar's viewpoint. In *Marie II* the woman seems to
be a sinner as long as she stays only a woman. Under the Virgin's protection
the saint has to renounce his or her attributes to be better able to assume the
role of intermediary. As long as she acts *de feminine fiebleté* (42), Mary is
automatically a sinner. As soon as she reacts out of emotive repentance, she
receives protection and strength.

Et esgarda aval au port
Ou soloit faire sen deport.

(Marie I, 217-220)

The courtly motif of the season (en mai) along with the successful use of the imperfect that describes Mary's walk as a daily habit, portray Mary as a lively character. [22] In contrast, the Latin text is a cold didactic narrative in which Mary is only a secondary figure subordinated to Zozima. In the French legend Mary is now the central character. The first vernacular version describes her in physical terms, without a definite disapproval on the part of the author, which in turn allows her inner motivations to rise beyond words and facts. [23] In this particular scene, her leisure tends to be the product of a tedium which entails a premonition of an ensuing anxiety that does not contradict, but rather, enhances the heroine's inner need for accomplishment.

The human dimension of the heroine's portrayal does not stem from simple lust. In the following lines the mere spectacle of young pilgrims playing and running on the shore appears to her an enjoyable scene:

Mais quant les aperchut Marie,
Ne puet muer qu'ele ne rie.

(Marie I, 233-234)

The source of her laughter is not clearly explained: it could be the disproportion between the virile exploits of the pilgrims and their childlike relaxation. The question she then asks one member of the group refutes this explanation. It becomes clear that Mary appreciates life in all its aspects. This detail adds to the verisimilitude of a heroine always aware of her human surroundings. At-

---

[22] The wheel of Fortune, still in favor of this attractive sinner, also forecasts that winter will come, that beauty will pass away. Fortune is then opposed to eschatology.

[23] Adgar's version, on the contrary, clearly denounces the sinner, not only because Mary's carnal thirst waxes foolish, but also through this condemnation:

Les avers, les larges, les pruz,
Tuz ama uelinement.

(Marie II, 18-19)

tracted by the cheerfulness which seems to characterize this group, Mary suddenly desires to follow them. Such a spontaneity, a gratuitous detail which enlivens the portrayal, bears no implicit disapproval on the part of the poet. Mary is not moved here by carnal desire, but by a thirst for novelty which propels her to travel every time she has exhausted all sources of ecstasy:

> "Car n'ai mais soing de ci ester.
> Aler vuel de ceste cité,
> Cho m'est vis, trop i ai esté."
>
> *(Marie I, 242-244)*

When the leader of the pilgrims hears Mary offering her body as payment for her passage, it is his turn to burst into laughter:

> Quant li preudom ot le folie,
> Ne puet muer qu'il ne s'en rie.
> Quant il oï le couvenent,
> Guerpist le, si s'en va riant.
>
> *(Marie I, 255-258)*

Since he does not try to answer with a sermon and offers no resistance to being amused, he too is described in credible terms. Entertained and not shocked by Mary's proposition, he is first immobilized so great is his hilarity. Then, returning to his companions, he still roars with laughter as he recounts the incident.

Distressed by the leader's reaction, says the tale, and most surely vexed, Mary does not lose her fixed determination nor her intuition for seduction. She succeeds in convincing the youngest members of the group, the very ones who were joyfully running on the beach, by eloquently presenting her alleged poverty, solitude and honesty. Whether in the presence of the Egyptian playboys of Alexandria or of the faithful Christians en route to Jerusalem, Mary plays with dexterity on their credulity. They accept her on the ship because they think they are responding to her appeal for charity. They also are unconsciously glad to welcome a very appealing *povre feme* (271). This interpretation points up the poet's craft and acknowledgment of human reality. The leader's laughter and the youngsters' credulity show how those Christians underestimate the power of feminine obstinacy.

The contrast between the pilgrims' virile assurance and Mary's scheme appears even more burlesque in the ensuing episode. During the first evening, after having rowed faithfully toward the Holy Land, the pilgrims endure a sleepless night. Even the leader succumbs to the most elementary temptation:

> Mais del dormir n'i ot nient,
> Car Marie si lor deffent.
> Lors les conmence a acoler,
> Aprés les prent a tastonner,
> A tous sengles aloit gesir
> Por chou que miex peüst plaisir.
>
> (*Marie I*, 295-300)

It is not so much the crafty action of the sinner as the stupidity of the faithful that seems to be emphasized here. Mary imposes her will, but no demoniacal light need interfere, and the four infinitives felicitously depict Mary's ardor, the silent progress of her ascendancy, and the lack of resistance she encounters on her way. The entire scene finally suggests the warm welcome Mary receives each time. Her ability and patience at her own skill, the degree of consciousness which makes every pilgrim both afraid and anxious to see his turn come, transform what could be a dramatic climax into a humorous situation:

> Por parfaire a tos ses delis
> Aloit le nuit par tous les lis.
> Cil le voloient de bon gré
> Qui en fisent lor volenté.
>
> (*Marie I*, 319-322)

Once in Jerusalem Mary is at first dismayed by solitude, and seeks every means to be in good company. She joins with every crowd, for carnal pleasure or for a devotional procession. It appears thus that Mary fears reclusion or isolation. Her sin in turn is lessened by this realistic observation. One day, when she cannot enter the church because of an invisible obstacle, pushed back by the knights, rejected by everyone, she plaintively weeps in a remote corner:

> Quant vit que nient ert de l'entree,
> En un angle s'es reculee.

Dont s'i conmenche a porpenser
Ke doit qu'el n'i pooit entrer.

(Marie I, 387-390)

Realizing the extent of her sin, but afraid of addressing herself
directly to God, she prays to the Virgin for protection:

Ne ja de lui ne partirai.
Toute guerpis je ceste vie
Et le malvaise legerie;

(Marie I, 440-442)

If the heroine is made so believable, it is not by the lengthy prayer
during which she recalls her life and makes her apology to the
Virgin, nor is it through the mysterious obstacle that forbids her to
enter the church and inspires her sudden awareness of sin. It is
rather through the way she has been portrayed, strong-minded and
yet insecure. A sign has made her recognize her error, a sign now
shows her the right path. Feeling protected and no longer alone,
she has enough strength to begin a *fuga mundi* movement on the
road toward sainthood.

The psychological credibility of the portrayal in *Marie I* is
lacking in the other version. According to Adgar, Mary's femininity
accounts for her sin. The first sequence of *Marie II*, describing the
circumstances of her moral weakness, fails to acknowledge any
other motivations than that of carnal appetite. There is no mention
of her thirst for novelty, no indication that she has an exuberant
nature. The second sequence, a monotonous record of Mary's
eremitic deeds, starts as suddenly as illogically. In that respect, the
structure of Adgar's version, resembling the bipartite scenes of *Bon*
and *Ildefonse*, intensifies the contradiction between vice and virtue.
If Mary finally reforms, it is through the unexpected intervention of
God. In *Marie I*, however, the poet hints at his heroine's internal
motivations, and indicates how, even during her prior misbehavior,
Mary's inner energy was a premonition of her future greatness.

A third French legend is devoted to the phenomenon of contrition, presenting a cycle of lapses and piety which is a realistic
observation of human fallibility. Theophile, a popular character

in medieval times, is the prototype of a sinner. [24] His story illustrates the way man is under the constant threat of Satan. At first a faithful believer, Theophile is on the road to perfection. Nothing in his conduct forecasts that he might weaken, and when he does, Theophile must atone at length for the forgiveness of his sin. Indeed, the struggle between good and evil takes place out of man's reach, and the hero is somewhat defenseless in the supernatural confrontation which opposes Satan and the Virgin Mary. But the hero's portrayal is consequently made closer to the public, who can identify with this lifelike picture of the human condition and is led in turn to hope for an identical redemption.

The saint is first described as a good and well educated believer whose devotion is concretized through true humility. When offered the archbishopric of Adane, he refuses, stating that:

> ... digne ne esteit
> D'itel honur, a tel endreit.
>
> (*Théophile*, 97-98)

His virtue is so well-known that the citizens insist upon having him as their bishop. Theophile then prays on his knees that such a burden not be placed upon him:

> "Cure n'aueit de tel honur;
> De cuer se reconuit pecheur."
>
> (*Théophile*, 109-110)

His tears and supplication finally persuade the crowd, and he keeps his charge until the cathedral clerics force the new bishop to dismiss Theophile. This does not affect he hero, but Satan becomes enraged to see that injustice has not yet caused anger to arise in Theophile's heart:

> El queor li mist grant felunie;
> De son uisdanz eut enuie
> E mist le en si fait errur,
> Ke milz amast mundain honur.
>
> (*Théophile*, 151-154)

---

[24] Carl Neuhaus, see note 15. *Théophile* is found on pp. 79-115. See our Appendix.

Here begins the segment of the poem that directly deals with the saint-sinner. Theophile cannot be made responsible for his sin, since it is the work of the devil. What is then the psychological credibility of the story? Perhaps to draw, behind these abstractions of tempters, a true picture of man's limitations. Surely the theatrical aspect of the conversations during which Theophile sells himself to the devil demonstrates that one sin leads to the next. Theophile first listens to Satan's perverse assistant, then follows him outside the city, and finally encounters Satan. In this scale of concessions, the saint no longer agrees to make the sign of the cross, and kneels at his tempter's feet while denying Mary, God and Christ, in that order. He consequently recovers his position in the church but illness paralyzes his mind and soul:

> Cum Theofle ert en poi de tens
> En tel orguil, en tel purpens,
> Pur sun chaitif reniement
> Liuerez a l'enfernal turment.
>
> (*Théophile*, 329-332)

It is interesting to note that the treatment of time takes two opposite directions when applied to the duration of good or evil. Virtue seems to be the product of a life-long effort, whereas vice worsens as soon as an errant intention crosses one's mind. Hence the lengthy lamentation uttered by the saint when he realizes the extent of his error. The error at the outset, since Satan has decided to seduce a believer, becomes a sin now that Theophile is conscious of his responsibility. God then considers and pities his good son:

> Deu, li glorius creatur,
> Ki ne uelt la mort de pecheur,
> Recorda la conuersiun
> Des biens, k'ainz feseit cest baron.
>
> (*Théophile*, 333-336)

The Virgin is the nucleus which gives to Adgar's work its unity. Here she appears as the sole intercessor between God and the sinner. Having wept over his misdeeds, Theophile decides to pray and fast, and awaits the Virgin's intervention. When she appears, she does not quite know what to do for him, fearing her Son's reaction:

"Jo ne uoil ueer, ne suffrir
Le coruz mun fiz, ne oir."

(*Théophile,* 563-564)

So Theophile must present his own defense, a plea in which he successively invokes the cases of Ninive, David, Peter and Justine before succeeding in moving his advocate to his favor. Now in joy, now in tears (791, 841, 861, 888), the saint finally gains both his pardon and his freedom. He feels the need to confess publicly in order to bring to the faithful new reasons for belief:

E l'euesque par les piez tint;
Chai s'en a ses piez de gre,
Cunta li coment il out erre.
Cunta li mult pitusement
Tut sun chaitif reniement.

(*Théophile,* 872-876)

When compared to his attitude before the devil's assistant, this prostration implies that humiliation is imperfect if not guided by pious intention, and also that contrition is incomplete without tears. The bishop knows how to interpret this miracle and claims:

"Tuit Crestien, uenez, uenez!
Cestes lermes saintes esguardez,
Ki Deu del ciel en pitie mouent,
Ki de son coruz pardun trouent!

(*Théophile,* 935-938)

Theophile is internally transformed. He not only recovers his good disposition but displays devotion, asceticism and charity, which lead him to a peaceful death and assure his redemption.

The threefold structure of this poem shows the hero, compared to Mary, to be a better example of a saint-sinner. Besides the allegorical intervention of Satan, evil is described as a constant threat against which no one is immune. In the first part, Theophile's humility runs counter to greed; in the second part, jealousy inspired by the devil transforms this humility into reprehensible silence; and in the third, repentance does not lead the hero to an outstanding performance. On the contrary, he now knows the limitations of man and avoids any situation which could tempt him to become a miracle worker and to enjoy an undeserved celebrity. In fact, Theophile does not act at any time: he merely reacts under the pressure of pride or shame. Such vulnerability to emotion implicitly describes the human condition as a state of unleashed passion that can work negatively or positively. The hagiographic message is perceived through the bishop's admonition that no one is ever sheltered from weakness unless under the Virgin's protection:

> "Refui de chaitifs, par fiance,
> Des erranz ueraie esperance,
> Refrigerie de chaitifs,
> Vie e salu a ses amis,
> Ki refreine la maleicun
> D'umaine nature a raisun,
> Ki est porte de pareis,
> Ki ure Deu pur nus chaitifs."
>
> (*Théophile*, 967-974)

The portrayal of Theophile alters the traditional concept of sainthood as heroic greatness. Events occur in a dramatic fashion, inasmuch as Theophile's destiny is assumed by supernatural characters. The saint himself has no active influence upon his fate: subject to demoniac or divine apparitions, he can only change his heart and pray that he be saved. Theatrically set, the limelight points to the true implements of the drama, and Theophile's own enlightenment is but a reflection of these opposing forces. Darkness symbolizes Theophile's state of uncertainty. The devil's assistant suddenly appears one night (175); he recommends that Theophilus call for help by night (197); he suggests that he follow his advice on a dark night (297), when they meet outside the city, in a theater lighted by several candles. The Virgin Mary intervenes during the fortieth night of Theophile's vigil (515); she brings him the devil's pact on the third night of his prayers (852). The source of light can be either detrimental or beneficial to the character's awareness. In this legend, it appears that sanctity is a slow, unsteady, internal perfecting of the individual.

There is in the legend of *Gilles* a comparable recognition of man's frailty. [25] The saint never allows himself to think he has defeated pride once and for all. Giles' quality of awareness is to know that man should never underestimate the dangers of failure. Theophile has good reasons to distrust his own mind; Giles, on the other hand, has no concrete proof that he might err. Such knowledge results in him from an innate understanding of human nature. In *Gilles* there is no allegorical representation of Satan. Evil is seen as a symbolic power that can destroy man as long as he acts on his own strength. Sin is not depicted as a deprivation or negation of good, but as the eventual consequence raised by self-assurance. Sainthood is no longer the automatic result of superhuman performance, but a life-long process of submission to God. Whereas Alexis or Brendan never question the value of their accomplishment, Giles suffers from a dual feeling of being called by God and being unworthy of such a call: [26]

> "Ki trop grant fès met sur con col
> Al departir se tent pur fol.
> Jo aveie grant fès levé,
> Meis or serrat amesuré.
> Je sui chargé de malveise herbe,
> Ço est d'orgoill e de superbe."
>
> (*Gilles*, 2095-2100)

---

[25] Piramus' version of the legend of Edmund also refers to the fragility of mankind in a few lines which summarize the secret of Edmund's success:

> Ne trop a destre enhalceant,
> Ne trop a senestre apuiant
> As vices, n'a l'inquité
> De l'humaine fragilité.
> Issi par reisun e dreiture,
> L'estreite line de mesure
> Tint.
>
> (*Edmond II*, 1835-1841)

Although never considered as a potential sinner, Edmund clearly perceives how thin is the boundary between righteousness and evil pride. His sense of measure is partly the cause for his triumph as king.

[26] The hagiographer follows Bernard of Clairvaux in that he considers humility the virtue enabling man to see himself in his true colors and to discover his worthlessness. See: Saint Bernard, *The Twelve Degrees of Humility*, trans. Barton R. R. Mills (London, 1929), p. 11.

Gires amat Deu e servi;
En oreisuns fud nuit e di;
Nen out en lui orguill neent.

(*Gilles*, 2309-2311)

According to the author, Guillaume de Berneville, Giles is indeed worthy of praise in that he does not deem himself a true mirror of Christ.

In so far as he himself imitates Christ's compassion towards the sinners, the saint exerts a caritative function in the world. The hagiographers seek to edify the faithful in recounting the glorious actions of the saints. Each time they address their prayers to the saint, or even when they merely invoke his name, the faithful may reduce a potential sojourn in Purgatory. The holy man's influence can also be felt before his death, through the miracles he performs, or because of his willingness to forgive even the wrongs done against him. When Giles is wounded by hunters, he pardons them in a Christlike manner:

Ki ceste vie funt escrire
E ki l'escutent e funt lire,
Ki l'escutent pur Deu amur
E en lur quers en unt tendrur,
Deus lur rende ben la merite
E de lur pechez seient quite
Par devant les pez nostre sire
Par l'oreisun del bon seint Gire!

(*Gilles*, 3773-3780)

"Ne sai ki tramist une sete,
Si m'ad aukes al cors blescé;
Meis Deus lui pardoinst le peché:
Il ne me saveit pas ici."

(*Gilles*, 2004-2007)

This episode marks the turning point of the story and the saint's return to the world. [27] Formerly a healer of body, now of soul, Giles abandons his eremitic mode of life in order to fulfill his vocation for apostleship.

---

[27] The injury actually occurs in line 1883 of a total of 3794 lines.

As Bernard of Clairvaux understood it, eremitism is a superior and more demanding way of preparing oneself for God. For those who had enough stamina to endure its hardships, Bernard recommended such a sojourn in isolation, before resuming once again the activities of the monastery. Eremitism is not to be opposed to cenobitism, nor should one dissociate contemplation and action, although vernacular hagiographers, in their effort to vulgarize these notions, tend to simplify and to present rigid distinctions. Hence a certain antithesis between isolated and communicated holiness. But the legend of Giles illustrates the benefits of combining the elements of retreat and communal life, as both experiences fulfill God's calling. Perfection is a state that occurs after death, because the renown of goodness is made known to all. Among the vernacular legends, some portrayals exemplify the way saintly humility refuses overconfidence. In these saints, perfecting is a slow and uneven process, virtue is both a duty and a reward for every Christian, and in that respect, no longer the sole attribute of an elite. Communicated holiness starts when the saint dispenses to the world the spiritual discoveries learned in isolation.

Chapter VI

THE SAINT AS MEDIATOR

Holy men and women celebrated by the twelfth-century French hagiographers are distant figures of a long-gone past, saints of Egypt, hermits isolated in fabulous deserts, martyrs belonging to the early centuries of Christendom, kings and bishops who labored to convert the Western world. To convince their audience of the veracity of sainthood, the poets amplify the heroic dimension of the saintly character, and the portrayal becomes a hyperbolic representation of virtue. Evil is pictured in colors that exaggerate man's criminal disposition, so that goodness appears all the more unique and impressive. The ascetic's frugality, unrealistic, improbable, strikes the audience by the very fact that such abstinence is unrivaled. Hermits and pilgrims defy the limitations of man's nature with an insurpassable stamina. The martyr's selflessness borders on suicide. All the saints' characteristics tend to portray them as larger than life, a magnification empowered by the very distance between models and the public. In terms of time and space, the saints are well removed from the social reality of the French-speaking countries of the twelfth century. The lesson to be drawn from such Lives is that, in a threatened world, outstanding individuals insure God's presence on earth and concur in the redemption of mankind. As intercessors, they assist whoever invokes them and thus remind the faithful of the merit of leading a devout life.

In these vernacular poems, the hero is more to be admired than to be imitated:[1] prologues and epilogues, summarizing the

---

[1] Imitation cannot be accomplished literally. This remark particularly applies to the case of saints as repentant sinners. The hagiographer of

matchless features of the saintly portrayal, instruct the audience that prayers will be granted when addressed to such a powerful personage. The intent of vernacular hagiographers seems to aim at increasing the elements of supernatural greatness, so as to ascertain the saint's superiority over the evil components of the world. This is not to say that the stories are bathed in unreality and void of substance. On the contrary, these poems abound with circumstantial details — exact enumeration of fasting days — and instruments of torture inflicted upon the hero, precise amounts of years spent on the road to sainthood — details whose very minuteness fails in the end to reproduce life. For the purpose is not to duplicate too familiar a world, a process that would reduce the level of wonder, but to conjure up an atmosphere of make-believe in which the improbable becomes possible. When the locations are foreign and the period remote, the oddity of the stories appears, if not normal, at least consequential, miraculous rather than unreal, a sign that the facts, prodigious as they are, deal with divine truth.

Inasmuch as the saint is given unordinary dimensions, and because of his unusual piety, his poise and wisdom, he is indeed the hero of the story, a leader who attracts around him a group of followers and admirers. The saint's superiority over his fellow men results in a distance anticipated and required by the logic of precedence: in the twelfth-century vernacular poems he alone receives the attribute of saint, he alone performs miracles and alters the course of events. As a consequence, moral greatness creates a remoteness which, stressing the heroic dimensions of the saint, also reduces his accessibility. Within the story, contacts between the saint and the crowd are kept to a minimum since holiness is defined as a flight from the world. Moreover, the reality of the saint is extraordinary and in constant conflict with the ordinary

---

Grégoire opens and closes his narrative with the same recommendation that his story should inspire a way to avoid mortal sins. He also realizes the unworkability of having to buy remission with seventeen years of reclusion:

> Jo . l sai mult bien trestut de fi
> Ke nul ce dels ki sunt ici,
> Ne pëust en mer tant ester
> Pur les suens pechiez amender
> Cum Gregorie fist, le bons hom.
>
> (*Grégoire*, 2053-2057)

reality of the audience. The road to sainthood is thus a solitary adventure, and the poets must first demonstrate the saint's heroic virtue before convincing the public of his powers as mediator. Saintly heroism refers to an internal fortitude whereby an individual disregards his own existence in the name of God. In celebrating the saint's spiritual achievement, the French poets disclose the concrete deeds which bring holiness into view. To reveal the saint's superiority, they oppose it to the many manifestations of weakness. Saintly heroes are thus enhanced by a comparison which not only reaffirms their supremacy but also underscores the general mediocrity of mankind. As a result, the hagiographic texts presents a hierarchical structure at the top of which the saints, isolated and superhuman, partake little of the human condition and remain untouched by the phenomenon of despondency. The heroes' strength is measured in concrete terms: with the exception of the repentant sinners, the saints rarely experience the discouragements of the common man, and the repentant sinners themselves, once secured in their determination to become virtuous, succeed amazingly in avoiding any occasions of relapse. Such moral resilience derives from the care with which the saints shun the worldly reality of vices and sins, and remoteness, essential to the preservation of virtue, limits in that respect the saints' direct interaction with others.

The process of celebration, however, attenuates the saints' isolation, for heroic greatness appeals to the crowd, within the story, and to future admirers as well. Forced to become a leader, despite his inner urge for solitude, the saint influences those who approach him. But most heroes of vernacular hagiography show their reluctance to participate in the affairs of the world. It is their role as saviors, however, which proves at once that the poets are dealing with holy men. Concrete deeds are also the poets' only means to illustrate in an irrefutable manner that the characters are indeed heroic, so ineffectual would a mere enumeration of their spiritual performances be. The moral leadership of the saintly heroes is thus evinced by their physical and social prestige, and through the tangible miracles accomplished before and after their death. Almost all the heroes of twelfth-century French hagiography are born noble, and most poets take note of their striking appearance, as if corporeal grace was an unquestioned sign of the saint's internal valor. [2] Prestige obliges the hero to assume a role of guidance, and in *Brendan*, the pilgrims are bound to their leader according to a traditional epic relationship which puts the vassals directly under sworn obedience: [3]

> Respundent lui comunalment
> Que ço enprist mult vassalment.
>
> *(Brendan, 113-114)*

In this legend, the saint actively participates in a quest that his fellow-pilgrims would be unable to achieve on their own. Brendan's role is one of protection, and his intervention tames a world altogether wild and threatening. The saint becomes heroic by virtue of his outstanding aptitude in bringing the journey to completion. His followers succeed in reaching Paradise but they do not receive the title of saint. And Brendan's subsequent admirers venerate him more for his concrete deeds than for his spiritual value.

Miracles, a material demonstration of holiness, are the usual feats which verify the saint's intercessive power. Since the heroes thus display their concern for mankind, miraculous deeds tend to evince the saint's social commitment. Compassion for the deprived is a way to portray the saint's participation in the world. In *Nicolas* the saint's intercession is manifested after, as well as before his death. [4] These miracles, attesting to the character's holiness, are

---

[2] See for example the portrayal of Edward:

> La grant bunté qu'al quer aveit
> En sun bel vult bien apareit.
> Del quer esteit parfit et sage,
> Bel out le cors, duz le visage.
>
> *(Edouard, 903-906)*

[3] E. G. R. Waters, *The Anglo-Norman Voyage of Saint Brendan by Benedeit* (Oxford: Clarendon Press, 1928). See our Appendix.

[4] Einar Ronsjö, *La Vie de Saint Nicolas par Wace: Poème religieux du XIIème siècle, publié d'après tous les manuscrits. Etudes romanes de Lund*, n.º 5 (Lund: Gleerup and Munksgaard, 1942). See our Appendix. M. Malkiel Jirmounsky ("Essai d'analyse des procédés littéraires de Wace," *Revue des Langues romanes*, 63 [1925-1926], 261-296), Margaret Houck (*Sources of the Roman de Brut of Wace* [University of California Publication in English, n.º 5, 1940-1944]), and Hans-Erich Keller ("Quelques réflexions sur la poésie hagiographique en ancien français: A propos de deux nouveaux

performed for the benefit of poor and rich, pagans and Christians, weak and strong, without distinction. Nicholas makes himself accessible to all, and especially to the helpless youths who endure innocently the adults' misdeeds, according to a legend which was to make him patron saint of children. The twelfth-century French version, however, does not portray Nicholas as a humanitarian hero: although he heals, helps or cures, Nicholas performs his miracles in an erratic manner, and there is no consistency other than mere chance in his interventions. Coming from a hieratic source of power to be adored and feared, Nicholas' remedial feats increase the disparity between greatness and commonness. His miracles are external, never spiritual, occurrences which are accomplished at random and bring relief on a strictly physical level. Although beneficial, these deeds display the saint's conspicuous magnanimity rather than his altruistic disposition. The very quantity of miracles is an attempt to assess concretely the extent of his individual ascendancy.

Miracles play a similar function in the story of Genevieve.[5] The audience is clearly informed of Genevieve's superiority. No obstacle hampers the influence of the heroine from asserting itself.[6] In healing a sick man, the saint even succeeds in accomplishing a miracle which other saints, previously invoked, had failed to produce:

> En maint leu mené l'avoit en,
> A maint saint et a mainte sainte.

---

manuscrits de la *Conception Nostre Dame* de Wace," *Vox Romanica*, 34 [1975], 94-123) show how Wace's style and technique are characterized by his use of an anecdotic structure. In his *Vie de Saint Nicolas*, the anecdotes are the numerous miracles which constitute most of the story. In our view, Wace's pedagogic intention suffers from such a fragmentation.

[5] Lennart Bohm, *La Vie de sainte Geneviève de Paris* (Upsala, 1955). See our Appendix.

[6] In one instance Genevieve chases the Devil in a crude fashion indeed:

> "Vils ordure, pulente et fainte,
> Issiez vos en tost par derriere!"
> . . .
> Sachiez ce ne fu pas l'oill
> Mes par desor la plus bas soill.
>
> (*Geneviève*, 2274-2275; 2281-2282)

Even Satan arouses no fear in the confident heroine.

Onques por ce ne fu esteinte
Sa dolor.

(*Geneviève*, 2828-2831)

Throughout the story, miraculous deeds, however trivial, demonstrate that the heroine masters the elemental forces of nature, as well as the maleficient influences of evil. Genevieve restores order and interferes with the causes of misfortune or misdeeds in a way which, at times, portrays the saint more as an avenger than as a mediator. One even notices occasional disproportions between sin and punishment: a woman, guilty of having stolen Genevieve's shoes, is made blind. This example serves as a warning that any marks of disrespect towards the saint are indeed sacrilegious. As a result, the saint belongs to another world, supernatural and divine, and sainthood is depicted as a case of clear, unequivocal, venerable exception.

Saintly heroism being the celebration of one man above the others, rare are the occasions of direct contact and interaction. In *Alexis I*, society exists only to be rejected, condemned or, at best, sermonized. [7] As if to identify even more clearly the central hero of his story, the poet of this Life does not name the characters of the mother and wife, although of prime importance at the outset of Alexis' journey. On the other hand, *Alexis II*, twice as long as the first, adds details which make both the hero and his family more realistic. [8] In this *Roumans* the women receive a name, and this late twelfth-century poem amplifies the wife's physical description so that, on the nuptial night, she is a character of flesh and blood whose presence the saint perceives:

Sains Alessins esgarda la pucele.
Assés i ardent candoiles et lanternes.
Mout la vit gente et couvoiteuse et bele.

(*Alexis II*, 124-126)

Whereas in the *Vie* Alexis never shows any pity for his family's sorrow — and such endurance is part of the saint's greatness in

---

[7] Christopher Storey, *La Vie de Saint Alexis* (Paris: Minard, 1968). Referred to as *Vie* and *Alexis I*. See our Appendix.

[8] Gaston Paris and L. Pannier, *La Vie de Saint Alexis* (Paris: Franck, 1872), pp. 222-260. Called here *Roumans* and *Alexis II*. See our Appendix.

this earlier, more austere version — the *Roumans* twice mentions his compassion for his faithful but grieving wife.[9] Between the two versions, the monolithic figure of the saint, here anchored in the beyond, there cast in a less abstract surrounding, becomes more human as some of his reactions appear lifelike.

Concession to realism thus seems to be one manifestation of change in the development of twelfth-century vernacular hagiography, reducing in the portrayal the urge for remoteness and the supernatural resistance to hardships, which traditionally depict saintly heroism. Vernacular Saints' Lives are works of vulgarization addressed to an audience of illiterate, unable to read Latin and untouched by the sophistications of theology. What can then be the actual impact of heroic sanctity upon a twelfth-century audience whose experience, on the whole, is to endure daily the harshness of poverty, ignorance and insecurity?[10] The majority of twelfth-century hagiographic texts praise ascetic and eremitic greatness and yet most members of their public are not powerful enough to afford the luxury of voluntary poverty. Fate imposes upon them a routine of vicissitudes, and social hierarchy does little to assist those who suffer. However, the same public valorizes the saintly portrayals offered as objects of veneration, as though fiction, more than verisimilitude, were the only proper medium in which to stage holiness. To act as mediator, to possess his intercessive power, the saint needs to be different, even at the expense of realism. He needs to excel at all levels, although such excellence might stiffen the portrayal as austerity works against all manifestations of human weakness.

---

[9] *Alexis II*, 335, 496.

[10] Wallace K. Ferguson summarizes this situation by wondering about the feelings of "the pious, sober, hardworking burgher" towards both secular and regular clergy. He may have regarded "the monks, especially such monks as he saw about him, as men who had not so much fled the pleasures and temptations of the world as escaped from its responsibilities.... The intellectual independence which education gave to laymen, together with the individualism fostered by a complex and changing society, might well have made men less ready to accept without question the absolute authority of the Church in matters of doctrine or the claim of the clergy to be the indispensable purveyors of the means of salvation." "The Church in a Changing World: A Contribution of the Interpretation of the Renaissance," *The Role of Religion in Modern European History* (New York, 1964), p. 26.

Vernacular hagiography remains singularly unaffected by the social and spiritual changes that marked the twelfth century. In the Church, isolation no longer appeared as the exclusive means for perfection. [11] The Councils of the period indicate that a new solicitude for the right of the individual was gradually emerging. Prior to 1072, the Church Councils were primarily concerned with the problems of heresy, simony and investiture, problems which were indeed crucial yet of a strictly ecclesiastical nature. It was only in 1114, that the Synods of Strigonia and Compostella reflected a recent interest in the welfare of the weaker members of the family and of the poor, respectively. [12] The Third Lateran Council in 1179 promoted even more clearly and extensively the concept of charity in favor of the indigent. [13] Thus the notion of good deeds emerges as a basic part of a truly Christian life, and saintly heroes of the century to come — Louis IX, Elizabeth of Hungary — embody the spirit of compassion which has come to coincide with the saintly ideal.

Since the saint is by situation led to act in the world, greatness may derive from the benevolent nature of his social services. The two saints mentioned above were socially eminent, hence their renown while still alive, and the value of their human kindness towards mankind. It is interesting to see whether saintly dignitaries who happen to be praised by twelfth-century French hagiographers might display a similar concern for the most humble of their subjects. Three of the Lives are Chronicles in which, to some extent, historicity plays a role in the portrayal of the central character. The poet of *Edmond I* inserts his hero into a long list of England's kings and shows his determining influence upon the fate of the

---

[11] A new definition of the term *vita apostolica* gradually emerges, as shown by M. D. Chenu in *La Théologie au XIIème siècle* (Paris: Vrin, 1957), p. 242. See also by the same author, *L'Eveil de la conscience dans la civilisation médiévale* (Montreal: Institut d'Etudes Médiévales, 1969), p. 79, and Etienne Delaruelle, "L'Idée de croisade dans la littérature clunisienne du XIème siècle et l'abbaye de Moissac," *Annales du Midi*, 75 (1963), 419-439.

[12] See Joannes Dominicus Mansi, *Sacrorum conciliorum* (Paris: Muguet, 1903), vol. XXI, 109 and 120.

[13] *Ibid.*, vol. XXII, 283-298; 324-326; 387-391.

country. [14] According to Piramus (*Edmond II*) the saint's greatness stems from his compassion toward the weak and the poor: [15]

> As vedues e as orfanins
> Fu pere pius e enterins,
> Franc e larges as bosoinus
> As povres e as sufreitus.
>
> (*Edmond II*, 1845-1848)

> Tuz jurs vesquirent de rapine.
> Tere ne cuntrée veisine
> N'ert pres d'els ou il a larun,
> N'eüsent feit envasïun.
>
> (*Edmond II*, 1907-1910)

If Edmund becomes the leader, it is not through divine selection, but because the barons have chosen him as the best among them. In the social hierarchy, the king is a necessary element of peace. He acts within the world whose harmony he wishes to preserve. Compared with this civic function of the saint, evil is described as the product of disorder:

> Kant la tere e le païs fu
> Si longement sanz chief segnur,
> Le poeple en est en grant errur,
> En grant crieme, en grant turment.
>
> (*Edmond II*, 1612-1615)

In the chronicle of *Edmond II*, holiness is not synonymous with isolation, and the king becomes a saint by virtue of his social participation which stabilizes the world and promotes both peace and religious expansion. Edmund's sanctity is perceived through the soothing influence he exerts on the historical evolution of his

---

[14] Albert Nabert, *La Passiun de Seint Edmond. Ein anglonormannisches Gedicht aus dem 12. Jahrhundert* (Greifswald, 1915). See our Appendix, Edmund I. Hilding Kjellman, *La Vie Seint Edmund le Rei, poème anglonormand du XIIème siècle par Denis Piramus* (Göteborg: Wettergren and Kerbor, 1935). See our Appendix, Edmund II.

[15] In *Edmond II*, the people convince Edmund to hide from the Danish because they need his leadership. In *Edmond I* the saint refuses to hide because he considers himself to be *unc pur chivaler* (501). The latter version therefore stresses that Edmund's greatness stems from his individual performance rather than from an altruistic achievement.

country. The poet praises a hero indeed involved in the affairs of
the social world, but fails to identify him as an individual. The
king himself is of less importance than the repercussions of his
kingship. As a result, the poet devotes only a few lines to suggest,
more than to demonstrate, Edmund's particular virtue, as if acknowledging his inability to characterize holiness:

> Li seint florist en ceste vie
> Cum l'arbre que fructefie,
> E gette e porte beles flurs,
> Dunt ist la tresdulce flairurs
> Bouche d'homme ne poet descrire.
>
> *(Edmond II,* 3299-3303)

Out of the 4033 lines, about one thousand apply to the saint
himself, sketching a character without any real substance or personalized qualities. Details are here to underscore the veracity of
the story through chronological anecdotes whereby the saint's biography fits history. Because of his desire to prove that the saint
really existed, the poet identifies his hero in a strictly documentary
manner. Behind historical facts the legendary dimension vanishes,
and so does the hyperbolic appeal of the saintly portrayal.

The life of Edward, also a chronicle, describes greatness in civic
terms. [16] Compared to Edmund, the king is more personalized in
that he shows an authentic inclination for answering God's call
in an eremitic fashion. Yet he lets his social obligation take
precedence. When the time comes for him to go on a pilgrimage
which he has vowed to accomplish, the people beg him not to
depart for fear that his absence would result in war. Edward
relinquishes his own aspiration:

> E tuz communement li prient
> Qu'il nes laist a tel duel murir
> Ne sun realme si perir
> Qu'il ne duinst a ses enemis
> Sa gent, sa tere e ses amis.
> Kar s'il de lui sul sunt guerpiz,
> D'eus serrunt mult tost envaïz.
>
> *(Edouard,* 1802-1808)

---

[16] Osten Södergärd, *La Vie d'Edouard le Confesseur, poème anglo-
normand du XIIème siècle* (Upsala, 1948). See our Appendix.

He strives to establish peace and equality within his kingdom, protects the poor, the sick and the weak, and never favors the rich:

> Unkes ne fist a povre utrage
> Pur plus riche de haut parage.
> *(Edouard,* 877-878)

He is also wearied by his own wealth, until he decides to give it away:

> La grant richeise qu'il aveit
> Pur sue pas ne la teneit
> ...
> De l'autrui prendre esteit huntus
> E de suen doner est joius.
> *(Edouard,* 891-892; 899-900)

Edward's function as mediator is closely associated with his altruistic disposition towards his people. In the poem, historical data do not hinder the caritative actions of the hero, as they did in both versions of *Edmond.* Sanctity is portrayed as a civic generosity at all times manifest, unordinary in a man of hierarchical dignity, yet too abstract for the sake of realism. Although venerable, magnanimity does not here call to mind the spirit of charity. And there are no specific anecdotes in the story which would exemplify concretely the actual contact between the hero and his fellow men, and which would thus clearly identify the occurences of interaction. Beneficial as they are, Edward's deeds are mentioned in a generalized fashion, a universality which, in the end, brings no life into the holy stereotype.

The chronicle of *Edouard* relates the life of a king whose actions took place in a distant time. What was then socially possible may be obsolete in the context of the twelfth century. However, there is a third vernacular chronicle which, venerating a contemporary personage, reduces the temporal distance between the model and the public. Murdered in 1170 and canonized two years later, Thomas Becket inspired many a Life both in Latin and in French. Two twelfth-century French versions, composed by Garnier de Pont-Sainte-Maxence and by Beneit, glorify the archbishop of Canterbury and praise this new martyr for his exceptional courage and integrity. [17] Obviously, the social and historical elements which surround any of the saints can affect the portrayal only if the poet uses them in a realistic way. In both *Edouard* and *Edmond*, historicity has no substantial impact on the humanization of the saints, as long as their deeds remain abstract and unspecified. The same is true with Beneit's version of the story of Becket. The poet feels free to expand all the traditional clichés whereby his hero is born noble and shows a moral fortitude which borders on austerity. Instead of the well-known bourgeois background to which Becket belonged, Beneit describes his hero's family as "one of the most noble in the city" (20), and Becket becomes the only son born in answer to his parents' prayers:

> Il esteit de Lundres né,
> Des plus nobles de la cité,
> Nus le creum,
> A joye de tut sun parenté.
> ...
> Kant il fu né de sa mere,
> Mult esteit joius sun pere,
> E par resun.
> Kar il n'aveit sorur ne frere.
>
> (*Becket II*, 19-22; 67-70)

Garnier makes a more serious attempt to relate, as it were, the exact account of Becket's progression towards martyrdom. Based on first-hand knowledge, his work incorporates letters of Becket and Henry II as well as royal edicts. Garnier's authentic effort to be veridical is nevertheless hampered at times by a comparable willingness to ascertain his hero's infallibility. In the struggle between ecclesiastical and royal power, all the wrongs are on Henry's side and the archbishop is always right. Impassioned and

---

[17] Börje Schlyter, *La Vie de Thomas Becket par Beneit: Poème anglonormand du XIIème siècle publié d'après tous les manuscrits, Etudes Romanes de Lund*, n.º 4 (Lund: Gleerup and Munksgaard, 1941). See our Appendix, *Becket II*. Emmanuel Walberg, *La Vie de Saint Thomas Becket par Guernes de Pont-Sainte-Maxence* (Paris: Champion, 1969). See our Appendix, *Becket I*.

partial, the poet expands his Latin sources by adding ominous qualifications which at once vilify the bad characters: [18]

> Mais cil quatre felun e li Deu enemi
> (Pur lur malvaise vie furent de Deu haï):
> Hue de Morevile, Willaumes de Traci
> E Reinalz li fiz Urs et li quarz altresi.
>
> *(Becket I,* 5121-5124)

He also resorts to traditional clichés in order to bring into relief the unusual destiny which awaits Becket. Several fabulous portents thus forecast the birth of a hero-to-be, a supernatural premonition whose effect indicates that God will protect the saint and consequently decreases Becket's individual accomplishment. Nevertheless, Garnier does not ennoble his hero's social origin, and Becket readily acknowledges his plebian parentage:

> "E se tu vols parler de mun povre lignage,
> Des citahains de Lundres fui nez, ne cel estage."
>
> *(Becket I,* 3411-3412)

Moreover, Garnier instructs his public — a relatively educated group of monks, compared to the more eclectic succession of admirers harangued by Beneit at the saint's tomb — that material poverty might indeed ease the preservation of virtue:

> Qui voldreit clerement a la raisun guarder,
> Mielz vient de basse gent e bon estre e munter
> Que de halte gent estre e en enfer aler.
>
> *(Becket I,* 3416-3418)

In *Becket I,* the portrayal of the saint is also humanized in that Becket experiences, like any ordinary man, anguish and fatigue. The hero shows a true concern for his family when, because of him, they have to endure the ordeal of exile:

> En teus essamples s'est granment reconfortez.
> Mais nepurquant mult ert el corage trublez,
> Quant essilliez esteit pur lui ses parentez.
>
> *(Becket I,* 2631-2633)

---

[18] The additions present a more vivid portrayal of the secondary characters who, contrary to Beneit's version, almost all receive a name in *Becket I.*

In a far off Edessa or in the remote corner of a Roman house, Alexis spends thirty-four years whose symbolic significance has a Christly orientation, yet does not concern himself over his parents' sorrow. In comparison, the story of Becket takes place in a concretized surrounding: the hero travels in the countries of France and England, and dies at the age of fifty-two, a number with no particular mystical connotation. What makes then a saint closer to the reality of the public is not so much historical facts — and Beneit's version exemplifies the way facts can be distorted and fictionalized — as it is psychological humanization. Spurious or not, the portrayal reflects and transcends the human condition to the sole extent of the poet's gift or readiness to combine realistic and supernatural elements. Thomas Becket is the only contemporary saint in twelfth-century vernacular hagiography. With Anselm of Canterbury, Francis of Assisi, and Louis IX of France, he reconciles worldly avoidance and involvement as all four personages, according to G. B. Ladner, "contributed to the Christian world order of the Middle Ages, though in a very real sense they were strangers in this world." [19] When mingled, isolated and communicated holiness is thus the true mark of sanctity, and in the four saints mentioned above "this doubleness of their character was an essential part of their greatness." [20] Any saintly portrayals are apt, regardless of external sources and facts, to embody this dual concept. When sanctity flourishes as an inalterable and immediate perfection, the hero is edifying yet inimitable. In the making of a saint, the poet's capacity for observing the phenomenon of maturation and perfecting both humanizes the dynamic dimension of the portrayal and valorizes the saint's role as mediator.

Identification between models and public occurs when the hero reacts in a way that makes him belong to mankind. In *Alexis II* and in Garnier's *Becket I,* both saints sympathize with the sufferings of others, and are themselves subject to anguish. These emotions contribute to the internal progression of the heroes without lessening their exceptional greatness. Through the experiences of ordeals, they realize that tribulations are an integral part of human

---

[19] G. B. Ladner, "Greatness in Medieval History," *Catholic Historical Review,* 50 (1964), 16.

[20] *Ibid.*

life and await the devout as well as the less fervent. Rare as they
are, their feelings of helplessness alter a heroism otherwise all too
inalterable. Sainthood is then the result of an outstanding courage
in the face of adversity. For the love of God, the hero assumes his
humanity and discovers that his inner self might be strengthened
through and despite the external factors of vulnerability. Such a
harmonious balance between human and divine dimensions, a sign
of maturity, instructs the public that they too can succeed in over-
coming their own feebleness. Virtue being thus the consequence
of transcended suffering, it becomes possible for all faithful to
strive for an identical poise.

The martyrs' endurance has little to do with this kind of accomplishment since the heroes of the twelfth-century French Passions rarely feel sensorial pain. They even display at times a peculiar
attitude of joy which, far from expressing their inner union with
God, mocks the pitiful attempt of the pagans who torture them:

> Dunc dist saint Lorenz en riant
> O simple vult, o bel semblant:
> "Deu, tei en puisse jeo loer
> Qui ci me deignas conforter."
>
> (*Laurent*, 890-893)[21]

Like Laurence, Catherine counters Maxence's efforts with derision,
a contempt which increases the definite separation of heaven and
earth. The examples of amusement, on the part of the martyrs,
demonstrate how the feeling of superiority lends itself to conde-
scending attitudes or provocation.

Such is not the case in *Brendan*. While the hero retains at all
times a sense of circumspection which helps bring the journey to
completion, he also shows an amazing understanding of human
nature. On several occasions, his fellow-travellers display a super-
stitious tendency to fear the unknown more than to entrust God.
After the awesome fight between the dragon and the griffin, Brendan starts praising God *mult halt, a voiz clere* (1041). The pilgrims
at once enjoin him to silence, for fear of disturbing the threatening

---

[21] Werner Söderhjelm, *De Saint Laurent, poème anglo-normand du
XIIème siècle, publié pour la première fois d'après le manuscrit unique de
Paris* (Paris: Welter, 1888). See our Appendix.

beast lying hidden beneath the sea. Brendan's reaction expresses the saint's paternal forgiveness of such a lack of spiritual confidence, a compassionate attitude which is sheer invention on the part of the French poet:

> Tunc abbas eos vituperans, et pro stultis reputans,
> chachinnavit.
>
> (*Navigatio*, p. 56)

> L'abes surist, e sis blasmat,
> Et pur mult fols les aasmat.
>
> (*Brendan*, 1053-1054)

As already noticed, Edward relinquishes his own desire to answer God's call in solitude so as to fulfill his civic duties. The choice is nevertheless painful for a saint undoubtedly annoyed by mundacity. Hence his secret sorrow at the time of his coronation:

> Vit seit meïsmes curuné
> E entent sa grant poësté,
> Si duta qu'il nen oust delit
> De la veine gloire qu'il vit.
>
> (*Edouard*, 3975-3978)

Edward is fully happy only when worldly reality does not interfere with his internal communion with God. At such times, an ineffable smile appears on the saint's face, radiating his inner joy to those around him:

> Od lie chiere, od duz senblant
> Leva ses oilz en surriant,
> Bele mesure en sun ris mist,
> Ja seit que grant joie veïst.
> Tuz ceus ki sun ris veü unt,
> Esmerveirlez forment se sunt.
>
> (*Edouard*, 1523-1528)

Saintly joy is the reward for transcended suffering. Joy is then of a divine nature, permanent and spiritual, compared to which terrestrial pleasures are but destined to perish and to keep the faithful away from God. The twelfth-century hagiographers are unanimous in the condemnation of worldly satisfactions, be they on the physical, material or psychological level. The poet of *Laurent* underscores the limitations of terrestrial happiness by recalling that all human possessions are doomed to destruction:

> Fous est qui en eveir sun cuer fiche,
> Car tuit muerent, povre et riche,
> Et li sages cumme li fols muert,
> A un vienent que qu'il demuert.
>
> (*Laurent*, 49-52)

The greatest foolishness of human nature is to devote one's life to the fugacious enjoyments of earth:

> Car le joie de ceste vie
> Est tote tornée a folie.
>
> (*Marie II*, 1249-1250)[22]

Madness is a frequent attribute used by the poets to describe the sinners' blindness concerning transitoriness.[23] The same attribute is applied to Laurence by a pagan contemptuous of the Christian belief, and praises in that context holy madness because it brings about eternal life. When Decius calls Laurence a *fol crestien* (559) and enjoins him to relinquish at once his *folie* (580), he inadvertently pays tribute to the saint. Religious madness — Erasmus' *stultitia* — suggests the spirit of inspired confidence in God with which Christ has redeemed mankind:

> Ipsum quoque Christum, quo stultitiae mortalium subeniret, cum esset sapientia Patris, tamen quodammodo stultum esse factum, cum hominis assumpta nature, habitu inventus est ut homo? quaemadmodum et peccatum factus est, ut peccatis mederetur. Neque alia ratione mederi voluit quam per stultitiam crucis, per Apostolos idiotas, ac pingues: quibus sedula stultitiam praecipit, a sapientia deterrens, cum eos ad puerorum, liliorum, sinapis, et passerculorum

---

[22] Peter F. Dembowski, *La Vie de Sainte Marie l'Egyptienne, versions en ancien et en moyen français* (Geneva: Droz, 1976), pp. 153-158. See our Appendix, *Marie II*.

[23] *Catherine*, 605; *Georges I*, 112 and 135; *Marie II*, 32.

exemplum provocat, rerum stupidarum ac sensu carentium, soloque naturae ductu, nulla arte, nulla sollicitudine, vitam agentium. [24]

Simplicity, more than ostensious superiority, reveals in the saintly portrayals an internal disposition to imitate Christ's humble way. The more he strives to surrender to God, the more able the saint becomes to radiate the ensuing joy brought about by complete self-denial.

In the character of Giles, the poet thus combines humility and gentleness. [25] Inspired by genuine devotion, Giles leads an ascetic existence. During his private dinner with Charlemagne, he spontaneously restrains from eating, hence inducing the king to remind him angrily of the virtue of sharing:

> "Dunt ne trovez vus en escrit
> Ço ke seinte escripture dit
> Ke nostre sire comanda
> A ses apostres e ruva,
> Kant il alouent preheschant,
> Ço k'um lur mettereit devant
> Receussent par charité?"
>
> (*Gilles*, 2709-2715)

A sad saint is a bad saint. [26] Giles reacts with humour and replaces with subtlety the proper order of reverence:

---

[24] Desiderius Erasmus, "Stultitiae Laus," *Opera Omnia,* vol. 4 (London, 1962), p. 498.

[25] Gaston Paris and Alphonse Bos, *La Vie de saint Gilles par Guillaume de Berneville, poème du XIIème siècle publié d'après le manuscrit unique de Florence* (Paris: Société des Anciens Textes Français, n.° 14, 1881). See our Appendix.

[26] When the French proverb says that "un saint triste est un triste saint," it summarizes the traditional idea that authentic sainthood is not exempt from basic human emotions. Susan Snyder, ("The Left Hand of God: Despair in Medieval and Renaissance Tradition," *Studies in the Renaissance,* 12 [1965], 18-59) states that "fear, joy, sorrow, love are seen as a kind of closed circuit, alternating between positive and negative" (pp. 36-37). *Tristitia* can then produce despair or virtue, as joy can mean enthusiasm or vanity. The manifestations of saintly joy prove how the quest for eternity does not always imply a contempt for the human condition. See: Philippe Delhaye, "Les Perspectives morales de Richard de Saint Victor," *Mélanges à René Crozet* (Poitiers: Société d'Etudes Médiévales, 1966), p. 860.

L'abbes Gires ad escuté
Içø ke Charlemaines dit;
Autre part si s'en turne e rit.
Il li demande belement:
"Sire," feit il, "cum lungement
Avez vus esté sermoner?
Vus savez mut ben preescher."

(*Gilles*, 2716-2722)

Similarly, Genevieve is described as overflowing with communicative glee. Humble, simple and sweet (25), she, like Becket, comes from a modest background. In the poem, there is no mention of divine selection, so that Genevieve's greatness rises from individual piety. Compared with the traditional idea that "on est saint: on ne le devient pas", summarized in the *Elucidarium,* the portrayals of Becket and Genevieve reflect an internal progression towards perfecting. [27] In describing his heroine's social origin, the poet notes on purpose that she was neither noble nor royal, in order to bring into relief Genevieve's simplicity:

Ne fu de contes ne de rois,
Ançois fu fille d'un borjois
La damoisele et de borjoise.

(*Geneviève*, 21-23)

No portrayal can be more appealing, no vision more comforting than the picture of this young, silent and smiling shepherdess whom two bishops are to heed. As they walk along the fields of Nanterre, St. Germain of Auxerre and St. Loup of Troyes, nonetheless preoccupied with the threatening problem of Arianism, notice her standing amidst her flock. Germain senses that hidden beneath these humble elements, lies a future saint, as he admires Genevieve's emanating serenity:

Quant il la voit, doçor et joie
El cuer li croist e monteploie.
Amener devant lui la roeve.

---

[27] Yves Lefèvre, *L'Elucidarium et les lucidaires* (Paris: Boccard, 1954), p. 338.

Cele qui est et fresche et noeve,
De Deu amer joianz et liee,
S'est de venir apareilliee.
                              (*Geneviève*, 117-122)

She is still very young when the bishops come to meet her, and
her spiritual maturity is all the more remarkable. Simplicity is here
synonymous with youth, in an attempt to show that sainthood and
maturation are internal and not contingent on age. From her
fifteenth birthday to her fiftieth, Genevieve observes a scrupulously
ascetic mode of life. Since she is ill, her fast and self-flagellation
could advance the day of her death. Hence her bishops' admonition:

"Genevieve," font li saint home,
"Vos portez trop greveuse some.
Vostre char trop affebloiez.
Nos vos prions que vos aiez
Merci de vos tant seulement
Que vivre puissiez longuement.
                              (*Geneviève*, 839-844)

Maturation in this case consists in acknowledging the danger of
excess.

With Gregory maturation is a question of discovering his true
identity. [28] He too is introduced at an early age, and the poet
describes in a felicitous scene the circumstances during which the
abbot of a monastery discovers the infant:

Quant l[i] abes vit le gent vadlet
Ki si ad fait le riselet,
Ambesdous [les] mains vers le ciel tent,
Deu en mercie del present.
                              (*Grégoire*, 685-688)

Although the period of Gregory's youth does not coincide with
spiritual maturity, it is an interesting episode in that it inspires
the poet to evoke with realism an age otherwise rarely represented

---

[28] Gerta Telger, *Die altfranzösische Gregoriuslegende nach der Londoner
Handschrift, Arbeiten zür romanischen Philologie*, n.º 5 (Paris: Droz, 1933).
See our Appendix.

in medieval literature, except when the authors intend to show how
the youth possesses the virile qualities of a hero-to-be. Evroul, for
instance, displays at seven an unusual precocity:

> Quant ala et parla assez
> Et out ja pres .vii. ans passez,
> Et entendit toute parole,
> Envoié l'en ont a l'escole;
> Et dieu tant de sens lui donna
> Que sens, avis et reson a.
>
> (*Evroul,* 121-126)[29]

In the same way, Giles is only seven when he performs his first
miracle. Having covered a sickly child with his own coat, the
saint causes his immediate cure. However, Giles receives the attribute of saint only later, in the course of a second miraculous
healing.[30] The witnesses easily recognize holiness in a mature man,
but fail to perceive it in a child. On this matter, normal children's
viewpoint corroborates their elders', and the playmates whom Giles
befriends show no appreciation for his meditative mood:

> Li vatletun de sun heé,
> Fiz as baruns de la cité,
> Le veneient sovent blamer
> K'il ne voleit o els juer.
> "Or veez," funt il, "juvencel:
> Gires vout estre sainterel.
> Li vileins dit en repruver:
> De jofne seint veil adverser
> Ne serrat mie tuz jurz tel:
> Mult ert unkor fel e cruel."
>
> (*Gilles,* 83-92)

Again object of ridicule when his barons blame as uncivil his
desire to relinquish his social duties (323), Giles' remains silent. In
the name of Christ, he endures the burden of living and the ordeal

---

[29] Ferdinand Danne, "Das altfranzösische Ebrulfusleben, eine Dictung aus
dem 12. Jahrhundert", *Romanische Forschungen,* 32 (1913), 748-893. See
our Appendix.

[30] See lines 1178, 1298, 1313, 1811, 2050, 2270, 2324, 2337, 2761, 2954
and 3280. These eleven attributes of *saint* occur only after Giles is recognized as a miracle-worker.

of humiliation according to the teaching of the New Testament. [31]
When abbot, on the eve of searching for a successor, Giles reminds
his monks that age cannot be an obstacle to election, for one is
worthy merely on grounds of internal qualities:

> "Meis entre vus si conseillez
> Ke de vus meisme eslisez
> Un ki sur vus ait la maistrie
> E ki maintenge l'abbeie;
> Si ne regardez a parage,
> N'a nule bealté, n'a aage:
> En bon començaill de juvente
> Pot l'um aver de ben atente;
> Pur aage nel refusez,
> Si vus le bien en lui savez."
>
> (*Gilles*, 3525-3534)

Mediator in so far as he radiates around him the spiritual discoveries that allow him to transcend his own humanity, Giles offers
to the world a concrete example of virtue and embodies the edifying
combination of isolated and communicated holiness. Of the twenty-
four Lives of twelfth-century French hagiography, the poet of Giles
comes the closest in portraying a saint of flesh and blood, both
uncommon and probable in his willingness to be and to do good.
Giles is a saint by virtue of both his heroic and his altruistic
dimensions. In him sainthood, never contemptuous or condescend-
ing, is exteriorized through concrete deeds whereby the saint dispenses indefatigably the sources of his inner peace.

By the end of the twelfth century, charity gradually took the
first place in the scale of virtues. As a recognition of the social
and dogmatic injustice regarding the involuntary indigent, new
religious orders updated the notion of *apostolica vita*. [32] Saint Francis of Assisi and Saint Dominic the Spaniard

> created a new kind of devotee, the friar, whose aim was
> not solitude or seclusion from the world, and whose oc-
> cupation was not primarily liturgical worship, but who

---

[31] *Gilles*, 183-187 and 3627-3630.

[32] David Knowles, *Christian Monasticism* (New York: Mc Graw-Hill,
1969), p. 108, and M.-H. Vicaire, *L"Imitation des apôtres: Moines, chanoines, mendiants* (*IVème-XIIIème siècles*) (Paris: Edition du Cerf, 1963).

went up and down the ways of men calling them to the
following of Christ and preaching Christian doctrine to
them. [33]

Although the portrayal of Giles seems to reflect substantially an
identical transformation in the saintly ideal, it would be presump-
tuous to assume that the poet has consciously chosen to celebrate
the virtue of humility rather than remoteness. What is certain, however, is that vernacular hagiographers, progressively and perhaps
intentionally, will portray the saint as a champion of the weak. The
cult of Saint Martin exemplifies this trend. Written at the end of
the sixth century, the *Vita Beati Martini* is inspired by numerous
pilgrimages to Tours where the faithful come in the sixth century
to request Martin's help against the evils of war, epidemics and
famine. According to D. Goubert, it is at the beginning of the
twelfth century that one witnesses a change in the devotion of
Saint Martin, a change which only affects "une infime minorité,
une élite morale et spirituelle," before reaching the totality of the
faithful. [34] What becomes the emblematic feature of the saint had
long been singularized in the artistic representations of Saint Martin,
"par excellence le saint de la charité, caractère qu'il doit sans doute
à la popularité et au pouvoir émotionnel de la scène du manteau." [35]
Between the figurative and the verbal exploitation of the famous
scene, there is a wide lapse perhaps explained by the delay with
which words, especially in the vernacular, come to express a deep-
rooted feeling. At any rate, the emotional power of charitable deeds
is largely employed in the thirteenth-century French version of the
legend of George. [36] The two twelfth-century *Passions* present a
militant saint whose greatness entails the Devil's immediate defeat,

---

[33] David Knowles, *op. cit.*, pp. 115-116.
[34] Danièle Goubert, "Recherche sur les pauvres et la pauvreté," *Centre de
Recherche et d'Histoire du Moyen Age*, 4 (1965-1966), 2.
[35] *Ibid.*
[36] John E. Matzke, *Les Oeuvres de Simund de Freine, publiées d'après
tous les textes manuscrits connus* (Paris: Société des Anciens Textes Français,
1909). See our Appendix, *Georges I*. Victor Luzarche, *La Vie de la Vierge
Marie, par Wace, suivie de la Vie de Saint Georges* (Tours: Bouserez, 1858).
See our Appendix, *Georges II. Histoire* refers to the edition of John E.
Matzke, "Contributions to the History of the Legend of Saint George,"
PMLA, 18 (1903), 158-171.

whereas the thirteenth-century *Histoire,* more in the atmosphere of romance, narrates the melodramatic victory of George against an awesome dragon. Both twelfth-century *Passions* clearly associate the idol of Apollo with a demoniac and bestial representation of evil. No real struggle occurs since the statue fearfully retreats before the saint's denouncing eyes. In the thirteenth-century *Histoire* evil is the first protagonist of the story:

> Une beste sauvage estoit,
> Qui toutes les gens devouroit.
> Moult par estoit laide et hideuse.
>
> (*Histoire,* 21-23)

This ugly beast attacks only children. The day comes when the people decide to offer a child a day in order to gain a transitory peace. But soon, only one youngster is left for this daily sacrifice, a young girl whose beauty equals her nobility. Strong are her parents' grief and her own fear when she finds herself alone on the road toward danger:

> Grant dueil furent pour leur enfant,
> Quand vindrent au departement.
> Quant elle fut en son chemin,
> Moult pensant ot le chief enclin.
>
> (*Histoire,* 51-54)

Now that the audience's emotions have been aroused, the hagiographer dramatizes in detail the imminent danger by showing on the horizon of the road the approach of this danger. In a very powerful passage, the scene is described through the young girl's eyes:

> Un homme a cheval vit venir,
> Bien cuida estre pres de mourir.
> En son cuer dist tout quoiement:
> "Ha, laisse, je voy le serpent."
>
> (*Histoire,* 55-58)

It is possible for the listener to feel the very texture of her young imagination, since there is no rational equation between the sight of a man, and the evocation of a snake. It is a very adroit way of presenting the hero. George, on his horse, is to encounter a

weak and beautiful girl. The effect of such a meeting, where the
hero is a fearless knight and the heroine a young child, defenseless
and on foot, is emphasized by the courteous tone of their dialogue,
typical of courtly romance. George is more than a valiant knight,
and the girl only a pagan lady:

> "Fille, vous estes sarinzine,
> Mais se vous voulez en Dieu croire,
> Le serpent ne vous puet mal faire."
>
> *(Histoire,* 74-76)

The hagiographer is now safe: he may continue his tale within
a tale, with the conventional dimension of the saint against the
sinner. But struggle here takes the form of polite exchange:

> "Sire, j'y croieray vraiement;
> Me puet il donc estre garant?"
> "Ouil voir, ma tres doulce amie;
> Menez m'y, et je vous en prie."
>
> *(Histoire,* 77-80)

Not only does he save the girl, thus gaining the admiration of
the townspeople, but he delivers them from the monster. This
happens so quickly that it is perhaps a sign of the hagiographer's
realization that it is time to come back to a more serious purpose:

> Lors la fery sans demourance
> Par le chief du fer de sa lance.
>
> *(Histoire,* 105-106)

In other versions the personage of the young girl is replaced by
the Virgin Mary, and George becomes the champion of innocence.

Identification between characters and listeners occurs in this
thirteenth-century poem on several levels. The hero himself is
attractive because he uses his power for the benefit of the weak:
still glorious, sainthood is also described in terms of altruistic
concern. George tames the wild elements of nature, thus displaying
a craft which might arouse dreams. As for the young girl, she is
the innocent victim of fate, yet saved at the last moment, a fantasy
indeed appealing to the imagination of the public. In this way
identification does not jeopardize the chances for the survival of

fiction. The saint's interaction with the world, efficient but not rigid, concrete without prosaism, prolongs in a romanticized way the dreamlike representation of sainthood which is the feature of twelfth-century vernacular hagiography. Four centuries later, Erasmus' sarcasms indicate how entertainment continues to be an integral part of public preaching, and how tales which concern the supernatural still continue to be popular:

> Postremo sic sculptus est hominis animus, ut longe magis fucis, quam veris capiatur. Cujus rei si quis experimentum expositum et obvium quaerat, conciones ac templa petat, in quibus si quid ferium narratur, dormitant, oscitant, nauseant omnes. Quod si clamator ille (lapsa sum, declamator dicere volebam) ita ut saepe faciunt, anilem aliquam fabellam exordiatur, expergiscuntur, eriguntur, inhiant omnes. Item si quis sit Divus fabulosior et Poeticus, quod si exemplum requiris, finge hujus generis Georgium aut Christophorum, aut Barbaram, videbitis hunc longe religiosius coli, quam Petrum, aut Paulum, aut ipsum etiam Christum. [37]

In all literary genres, heroism results from an identification between a set of outstanding values and its model. Vernacular hagiography complies with this general definition in mingling the terrestrial and the divine. The hagiographer's success depends on his talent for such a combination: when he gives preference to heaven his poem gains in doctrine what it loses in flavor. Yet the hero appears insipid if his earthly powers remain too automatic and rigid. The portrayal exudes credibility when it responds to the popular needs for hyperbole. The saintly hero is superhuman: he comes from here and nowhere, he reassures man that good excels evil, he wins without exhausting the possibility of further combats. In vernacular hagiography, fancy, magic and mystery, as long as they remain coherent and tangible, bring together dream and reality. Escaping the world is then a joint evasion.

---

[37] Erasmus, *op. cit.,* p. 450.

CONCLUSION

Along the six steps tentatively presented as six variations of the *fuga mundi* theme, the saint in vernacular hagiography resembles in many ways the epic or courtly hero of twelfth-century literature. Sometimes as impressive as Roland, sometimes indecisive like Lancelot, the saint is deeply involved in this world of action and hesitation. But he moves also in the beyond, either the menacing unknown of the Otherworld or the mysterious features of the Upperworld. His existence by definition presents the dual dimension of life, rooted as he is in the mortal condition, yet attracted by permanence. Born in the shadow of Latin hagiography, the vernacular Lives generate their own concept of sanctity, which stems from a paradoxical heroism: halfway between the chronicle and the novel, neither entirely predicatory nor fictional, and deserving of recognition. It reflects the genuine, authentic, refreshing needs of popular devotion and its unconditional belief in the supernatural, the divine and the magic. The story evolves between a pious sermon and a folk song, for the pleasure of an audience which can confer upon its favorite hero a nostalgic or utopian victory over reality.

In an imperfect world, prey to evil and witches, the holy witness guides his admirers on the proper road. He dismisses temptations and falseness, knows the magic words, interprets divine signs. His initial superiority begins with a movement of flight from all worldly vanity, aiming at poverty, solitude and silence, yet producing wealthy communities, gatherings and celebration. Popular veneration turns a remote place into a renowned terminal point for pilgrimages. There lies the true miracle of sainthood.

As the mentality evolved so did the folklore. Weary of regret-
ting or hoping for better times, the public began to show an
increasing interest in contemporary problems and personalities.
Although still paradoxical in its elements, sainthood is progressively granted to those who shared with the ordinary man the
tedious burden of life. In this perspective the mendicant friars
voiced an exemplary precept of abnegation and material humiliation. Their asceticism stemmed from this choice of living constantly
among, with, and for, the poor. Travelling in pairs, they wandered
from town to town, barefoot and sometimes rejected, in order to
witness the evangelical message. Because of their vows of avoiding
the rich and their desire to experience concretely the conditions
of the socially deprived, the Franciscans and Dominicans knew a
rapid if not solid welcome. Hardly thirty years later they were
attacked not only by the traditional orders but by the very ones
they intended to assist, the poor. Rutebeuf raises his fiercest voice
against them to disapprove the fact that the friars' mode of life
was threatening the real mendicants' survival. Moreover the movement settled down, becoming institutionalized and losing thereafter
its original value. Virtue had not yet found its ideal medium.

At the end of the twelfth century there is a re-examination of
holy heroism. Of the four ages of man, some hagiographers choose
youth to portray innocence and authenticity: greatness does not
exclusively belong to the sole stage of maturity, it is the result
of maturation. So it is with other genres of literature, as attested
by the evolution of the epic and a new interest in the role of the
child. With the growing popularity of the Nativity scene, figurative
and written arts exalt the weak and the compassionate. The same
Rutebeuf, whose imprecations are addressed to the hieratic figure
of Saint Louis and the hierarchical structure of the Church praises
without reserve those who display an unusual care for others. In his
poem about Saint Elizabeth of Hungary he glorifies the maternal
tenderness of a woman who, in the middle of the thirteenth century, protected and adopted orphan children. The saint and the
child, an odd couple for the twelfth century, become more and
more associated.

St. Vincent in the seventeenth century, Jean Baptiste Vianney
and Thérèse of Lisieux in the nineteenth and early twentieth centuries respectively embody a child-like spirit of humility. Recogniz-

ing in such persons an outstanding virtue, superhuman but not inhuman, people did not wait for an official edict to venerate them. Of the thousand names that figure in the Catholic list, the trend is presently to remove those which derive from legends. But no decree can alter the fortune of George, Christopher, Nicholas. A saint is real and authentic as long as he remains alive in the popular mind. Holiness is thus recognized before Rome's formal authentifications.

The values of asceticism, eremitism, even sainthood, are presently questioned by Catholics. Beyond the analysis, diagnosis, autopsy of these sophisticated inquirers, greatness keeps its intrinsic appeal when self-abnegation co-exists with altruism. As soon as humanitarian individuals are publicly eulogized, legend embellishes them. Religious or lay excellence — heroic deeds, feats of arms, athletic exploits — satisfies a hidden dream of mankind. Election, each time, is a revenge against platitude. Singularized because they avoid mediocrity and improve the average, the chosen have two functions: to dazzle and to enlighten the common man. Thus the process of consecration propels the world toward Paradise. All successful legends of twelfth-century vernacular hagiography value both time and perpetuity. Earth is heaven when illusion transforms reality.

APPENDICES

ALEXIS I

"Bons fut li secles al tens ancïenur"

This Life of St. Alexis has been the subject of more scholarly studies and editions than any other twelfth-century Saint's Life. It is impossible here to discuss all of them in detail; and it would be perhaps inappropriate, since traditional scholarship places the date of composition not in the early twelfth century but at mid-eleventh. For the purposes of this study, however, the date is of relative unimportance: *Alexis* remains the first full-fledged Saint's Life, the point of departure against which the hagiographic genre will define itself and the springboard for subsequent development of the image of saintliness.

It is generally accepted that the Life of St. Alexis is the fusion of two legends, that of the fifth-century Syriac Mar Riscia (Man of God),[1] and the Greco-Latin versions of St. John the Calybite (9th-13th centuries).[2] The fused version and its introduction to the Western world dates from the late tenth century. Sergius, archbishop of Damas, was exiled in 977, when he came to Rome. Surprised to learn that Alexis was unknown, he settled in the Church of St. Boniface on the Aventine in Rome and propagated the Greco-Syriac version, judiciously adding that the saint's relics were in the Church of St. Boniface.[3] This new Latin version was the most

---

[1] See A. Amiaud, *La Légende syriaque de Saint Alexis* (Paris: Bouillon, 1889).

[2] See Christopher Storey, *La Vie de Saint Alexis* (Paris: Minard, 1968), pp. 18-21, and C. E. Stebbins, "Les Origines de la légende de Saint Alexis," *Revue belge de Philologie et d'Histoire,* 51 (1973), 497-507.

[3] W. L. Duchesne, Les Légendes chrétiennes de l'Aventin," *Mélanges d'Archéologie et d'Histoire,* 10 (1890), 234-235. In this same article, Duchesne

widely known and is considered by most scholars to be the source of the OF versions. [4]

There are seven MSS of this Life:

1) L — Hildesheim, Godehardi Kirche, fol. 29-34. This is part of the St. Alban's Psalter, probably copied in England and presented to Christina of Markyate no later than 1123. It is considered to be the best MS, and the most faithful transcription of a lost original. [5]

2) A — Paris, Bibliothèque nationale, n. acq. fr. 4503 (formerly Ashburnham, Libri, 112), fol. 11v-19v. [6] Until recently this MS was considered inferior to L because it stops 15 stanzas before the end. H. Sckommodau maintains that A is a copy of the original and that stanzas 111-125 are an addition. [7] Howard S. Robertson shows through a careful thematic examination of the poem that stanzas 111-125 are no more than embroidery in the hagiographic convention and that they provide an illogical dénouement of human joy to what is otherwise a story of austere, human sadness. [8] Donald Maddox opts for a more diplomatic solution. His convincing demonstration proves that both L and A constitute a coherent but differing scribal interpretation of the legend. [9]

3) V — Vatican, Cod. Vat. lat. 5334, fol. 125v-126, 129-131.

4) P — Paris, Bibliothèque nationale, fr. 19525, fol. 26v-30.

---

states that no document whatsoever, martyrology, calendar or liturgy contains any mention of Alexis before the end of the tenth century (p. 240).

[4] In *Acta Sanctorum*, Jul. IV, 251-253. Recent German scholarship proposes another Latin rhythmical version as the probable source: Manfred Sprissler, *Das rhythmische Gedict "Pater deus ingenite" (11JH) und das altfranzösische Alexiuslied* (Munich: Aschendorff, 1966).

[5] For a description, see. C. Storey, *op. cit.,* pp. 24-26; Gaston Paris and L. Pannier, *La Vie de Saint Alexis* (Paris: Franck, 1872), pp. 2-3; and Francis Wormald, C. R. Dodwell and Otto Pächt, *The St. Albans Psalter* (London: The Warburg Institute, 1960), pp. 3-5 (by Wormald).

[6] For a description, see C. Storey, p. 28; Paris-Pannier, pp. 3-5.

[7] Hans Sckommodau, "Zum altfranzösischen Alexiuslied," *Zeitschrift für romanische Philologie,* 70 (1954), 161-203.

[8] Howard S. Robertson, *"La Vie de Saint Alexis*: Meaning and Manuscript A," *Studies in Philology,* 67 (1970), 419-438.

[9] Donald Maddox, "Pilgrimage Narrative and Meaning in Manuscripts L and A of the *Vie de Saint Alexis,*" *Romance Philology,* 27 (1973), 143-157.

5) S — Paris, Bibliothèque nationale, fr. 12471, fol. 51v-73. This is the sole MS of the Alexis II version which contains almost identical lines of L with lengthy interpolations. [10]

6) Ma — Paris, Bibliothèque nationale, fr. 1553, fol. 393v-400v.

7) Mb — Carlisle, Chapter Library (rhymed version of Ma).

The author remains anonymous in the eyes of modern critics, although Gaston Paris suggested in his 1872 edition that a certain Tedbalt of Vernon, chanoine of Rouen during the mid-eleventh century, could have been the author of the lost original (pp. 43-45).

The question of date is a delicate one. We shall abstain from taking sides and present simply a summary of the two views, for *Alexis* remains the point of departure for our study, regardless of which view is accepted.

Gaston Paris concludes on linguistic grounds that MS *L* is an Anglo-Norman copy of around 1150 of a Norman original composed in France around 1040, and that it pre-dates the Oxford Roland (pp. 29-43). It is now clear that the copy dates from 1119-1123, but the majority of scholars agree that it is only a copy, and that the lost original is of the mid-eleventh century, anterior to the Oxford Roland. [11]

Otto Pächt offers a different conclusion:

> Whether we investigate the cultural background of the new pictorial cycles or the origin of the hagiographical versions on which the French Alexis poem is based, or the iconographic and stylistic sources of the Alexis illustrations, the result is each time the same: invariably we are taken straight to Italy, while there is no trace whatsoever of a French intermediary stage. In other words, while there is proof that the Italian antecedents of the treatment of the Alexis story, as we have it in the Old French poem, were known in England and especially in the St. Albans milieu in the early 12th century, there is no sign of these sources having been available anywhere in France. This makes it extremely difficult to follow the historians of French liter-

---

[10] For a description see Paris-Pannier, pp. 199-221, and for an edition, pp. 222-260.

[11] C. Storey, pp. 24-26; M. D. Legge, *Anglo-Norman Literature and its Background* (Oxford: Clarendon Press, 1963), pp. 243-244.

ature in their dictum that the Hildesheim text represents a twelfth-century transcript of an eleventh century French poem, implying that this poem had been imported as a finished product from France into England. [12]

The linguistic argument of G. Paris has been strengthened in a study by Madeleine Tyssens, [13] prompted perhaps by a remark of O. Pächt. [14] She concludes after stylistic and lexical examination that the prologue is of a different hand than the poem.

Alexis has been extensively studied by literary critics and historians. In addition to those already mentioned, a few selected analyses and interpretations should be included here, in chronological order, to point out the highlights of Alexis scholarship.

In a seminal study, E. R. Curtius compares Alexis to Corneille's *Polyeucte*. [15] The Bollandist B. de Gaiffier points out that the central themes of Alexis in respect to marriage are commonplace and can be found in other Lives. [16] M. D. Legge recalls Goldschmidt's study of the St. Albans Psalter [17] and concludes that MS *L*: "was almost certainly written in or very soon after 1115." [18] E. W. Bulatkin publishes an ingenious interpretation based on numerical symbolism, lending credence to the assumption underlying all Saints' Lives that the saint models his life on that of Christ. [19] J. Györy underlines the rigid excesses of Alexis, comparing him to Roland, both reflections

---

[12] Otto Pächt, *op. cit.*, p. 142.

[13] Madeleine Tyssens, "Le Prologue de la *Vie de Saint Alexis* dans le manuscrit de Hildesheim," *Studi in onore di Italo Siciliano* (Florence, 1966), pp. 1165-1177.

[14] "One test has to my knowledge never been made: since the preamble as well as the translation from Pope Gregory's letter is supposed to be the work of the scribe who copied the 'chanson' in the St. Albans Psalter it ought to be possible to ascertain whether the 'Zeitstil' of its language is the same as that of the poem or not," p. 143, note 1.

[15] E. R. Curtius, "Zur Interpretation des Alexiusliedes," *Zeitschrift für romanische Philologie,* 56 (1936), 113-137.

[16] B. de Gaiffier, "INTACTAM SPONSARI RELINQUENS. A propos de la *Vie de Saint Alexis*," *Analecta Bollandiana,* 65 (1947), 157-195.

[17] A. Goldschmidt, *Der Albani-Psalter in Hildesheim* (Berlin, 1895).

[18] M. D. Legge, "Archaism and the Conquest," *Modern Language Review,* 51 (1956), 227-229.

[19] E. W. Bulatkin, "The Arithmetic Structure of the Old French *Vie de Saint Alexis*," *Publications of the Modern Language Association,* 74 (1959), 495-502.

of a firm social order. [20] P. R. Vincent stresses the dramatic impact which the family's lamentations, much expanded in OF, must have had on the audience. [21] Karl Uitti provides a superb miseau-point of Alexis scholarship to date, offers fine insight into the poem itself and suggests directions that future endeavors should take, thus giving focus to what had been fragmented, albeit insightful, contributions of scholars. [22] W. Ryding gives a structuralist view of the poem in his study of medieval narrative. [23] In a well documented work of erudition, Louise Gnädinger offers us one of the rare thematic interpretations of *Alexis*, discerning what part tradition and what part innovation belongs to the poem, within the context of the history of eremitism. [24]

A complete discussion of the iconography as found in the St. Albans Psalter has been done by Wormald, Dodwell and Pächt, [25] and Louis Réau has treated Alexis' iconography in general. [26]

The 625 decasyllabic lines, grouped in 5-line stanzas by assonance, relate the following story:

In the opening lines the poet expresses nostalgia for the lost ages when faith, Christian love and justice prevailed in the world (1-12). During this time, a rich nobleman, Euphemian, lived in Rome. He and his wife were childless for many years until God answered their prayers (13-28) and a son was born and baptized Alexis. The boy entered the emperor's service after finishing school

---

[20] Jean Györy, "Hagiographie hétérodoxe," *Acta Ethnographica Academiae Scientiarum Hungaricae*, 11 (1962), 375-390. The second half of the article treats the provençal *Chanson de Sainte Foy*.

[21] P. R. Vincent, "The Dramatic Aspect of the Old French *Vie de Saint Alexis*," *Studies in Philology*, 60 (1963), 525-541. The moving drama of the OF version in comparison to the *Vita* has been studied by Josef Merk, *Die literarische Gestaltung der altfranzösischen Heiligenleben bis Ende des 12. Jahrhunderts* (Affoltern am Albis: J. Weiss, 1946).

[22] Karl Uitti, "The Old French *Vie de Saint Alexis*: Paradigm, Legend, Meaning," *Romance Philology*, 20 (1966), 263-295.

[23] W. Ryding, *Structure in Medieval Narrative. De proprietatibus litterarum, Series Maior*, n.º 12 (Paris, 1971).

[24] Louise Gnädinger, *Eremitica. Studien zur altfranzösischen Heiligenvita des 12. und 13. Jahrhunderts. Beihefte zur Zeitschrift für romanische Philologie*, n.º 130 (Tübingen: Niemeyer, 1972). The chapter on Alexis covers pages 1-91.

[25] *Op. cit.*

[26] Louis Réau, *L'Iconographie des saints*, Vol. III, Pt. 1 of *L'Iconographie de l'art chrétien* (Paris: Presses universitaires de France, 1958), pp. 52-54.

(29-35). When Alexis reached maturity, Euphemian arranged a marriage for him with a count's daughter (36-50). On the wedding night, Alexis obeys his father's wishes and goes to his bride's chamber, feeling, however, threatened by impending sin. He speaks to her of the frailty and transience of this life compared to the durability and eternity of celestial truth (51-75). Then he flees by ship to Edessa, where he gives his belongings to the poor and becomes one of them (76-100).

In Rome, his parents and wife lament their loss and send messengers searching for Alexis. They find him in Edessa, but do not recognize him because of the physical change his life of self-imposed hardship has wrought in him (101-130). Alexis' wife and mother lament (131-155). For seventeen years Alexis serves his God, until an image appears calling him "Man of God," and bringing him fame and honor (156-185). Not wanting this burden, Alexis returns to Rome where, still a beggar, he asks his father to give him shelter under the staircase (186-225). Still unrecognized, he accepts only minimum nourishment for himself and distributes the rest to the poor (226-255). He continues his service to God for another seventeen years, a serene man even when his father's servants throw garbage at him and mistreat him (256-275). When he realizes he is near death, he sends for parchment and pen to write the story of his life.

A heavenly voice urges Pope Innocent and the emperors Arcadius and Honorius to fetch the man at Euphemian's house, the man who can save Rome from its sins (276-315). No one at Euphemian's house knows of the "Man of God"; the crowd led by the Pope and emperors is saddened and frightened that salvation is denied them. Alexis dies and his soul enters paradise. This news is brought to the crowd and Euphemian goes to Alexis but is unable to remove the parchment from his grasp (316-355). The pope and emperors pray and grieve for the "Man of God," and the parchment is released to the Pope (356-375).

Alexis' identity and life are revealed, which provokes a long lamentation from his father, replete with reproaches against his son who should have led a life that did not cause grief and agony to his family (376-420). The mother joins in this lament (421-465), and finally the wife too expresses her grief at the lack of joy in the world, and vows to serve God in the future (466-495).

The Pope reminds them that they should rejoice, and soon all of Rome rushes to Alexis' side. Prayers of thanks are raised to God for sending this holy man to expiate their sins (496-540). We are reminded that through penitence and a life of love and devotion to God we, too, may attain Paradise (541-560). [MS A ends at line 550.]

Alexis' body is placed in the church of St. Boniface, where the faithful come to pay their respects for seven days, after which he is buried, causing great sadness in the city (561-590). This saintly man has saved his family's souls by his presence. How blind we are to our sins until a person like Alexis reminds us of the path to truth and peace (591-625).

ALEXIS II

"Signour et dames, entendés un sermon"

This version of the legend is found in only one MS, Paris, Bibliothèque nationale, fr. 12471, fol. 51v-73, and can be found in the Paris-Pannier edition.[1] Since this MS contains the lines of MS *L* augmented by interpolations (printed in italics in the Paris-Pannier edition), it has been generally considered as a negligent copy of the Urtext rather than a different version in its own right. As a result, there have been no significant literary studies of this version.

Alexis II is composed in decasyllabic *laisses* of unequal length, grouped by assonance.

The second version of the Life of St. Alexis follows the same narrative as Alexis I with interpolated matter which accounts for its length: 1356 lines as opposed to 625 lines in the *L* manuscript.

The first eight lines contain a traditional opening: "Ladies and lords, listen to a sermon about St. Alexis who left his wife for God." The poem expands on the theme of the frailty and instability of mortal life, the infidelity of wife to husband, vassal to lord (14-18), focusing on the degradation of the present.

Alexis' father, Euphemian, was an honorable man who loved God, but Alexis was a better one because he devoted his life to God (23-46). The description of Alexis' mother, Bonne Eurée, daughter of Flourent, is more detailed in this version than in Alexis I. Alexis served the Emperor Octavian, who named him head chamberlain. This position made Alexis rich, and he shared

---

[1] G. Paris and L. Pannier, *La Vie de Saint Alexis* (Paris: Franck, 1872), pp. 222-260. For a description of the MS, see pp. 199-221. Our summary only gives line references to the interpolated material.

his wealth with his parents (73-83). Euphemian arranged a marriage for his son with Lesigne, daughter of Signouré (91); the wedding was celebrated in the Church of St. John Latran (97-99). All those present rejoiced. At the wedding supper Euphemian ordered Alexis to go to his wife (102-111) and Alexis went willingly (116). His parents prepared the wedding chamber with straw and gold and retired, locking the door behind them and posting two guards on duty (119-123).

Alexis looks at his wife and finds her "gente, couvoiteuse et bele" (126). He prays to the Lord to save him from the power of the devil and terrestrial life (131-138). He speaks to her of Christ, the Virgin Mary and the baptism in the Jordan (144-148), and cuts the wedding ring in two, so that in the future it can serve as a means of recognition. Lesigne, confused, asks him why he is leaving her, and he replies that the body rots in the earth, but the soul is happy with God. His wife listens and cannot stop crying. Alexis tells her to remarry if he hasn't returned within a year. She laments his harshness and the grief she will always feel, but hopes that he will return soon. When he declares that the greatest joy is in Paradise, she praises the worthiness of his reasons and, realizing she cannot make him yield, gives him her blessing. She asks Alexis if she may accompany him, but he refuses her to obey God (158-319), and escapes quietly. He walks to Rome. Looking at the city he is happy and with his face raised to the sky he prays to Christ. When he remembers his parents he begins to cry (321-336). The ship he boards sails to Jerusalem, where he prays at the holy sepulchre, and then fasts for two days and nights before going to the Jordan to bathe. He dares stay no longer in the company of Jews and travels to Edessa (341-356).

The family in Rome grieves (404, 405, 410, 412, 416, 418, 420-21, 423, 426, 428). Lesigne bemoans her loss and decides to serve God, for she "cannot do anything better" (430-434). She accuses herself of being evil, to explain Alexis' abandonment of her, and resolves to take God as a husband (440-450). Alexis converses with the two messengers sent to find him, but they do not recognize him for his clothes are tattered and worn (467-468); they recount to him his family's grief. Alexis breaks down in tears (470-500).

During mass one Christmas morning, the image resembling the Virgin announces that the man of God has left his family and possessions for the love of God (518-32). The cleric leaves the church to find Alexis; upon hearing that the holy man has spent seventeen years atoning for the sin of having been a knight and having married, the cleric falls to his knees (547-568). Alexis learns that the city fathers want to invest him as their bishop, and flees (574). Near Rome, he prays for God's help: his family would lead him astray, yet he wants to see them without being recognized. His prayer is granted. When Alexis leaves the ship he pauses to rest because he is very ill. Praying from his psalter, he is reminded of his parents and decides to speak with his father (602-656). He meets them returning from mass and speaks to them, begging them to let him live under their stairs in the name of their son (661-674). Euphemian consents and promises that he will never lack for food. The pilgrim thanks him, and tells him that he is a foreigner dedicated to God. He promises that Alexis will return, and the parents break down in tears. Troubled by their grief, Alexis prays for strength and puts all his faith in Christ (680-751). Lesigne brings the pilgrim food, and when Euphemian asks him his name, Alexis replies simply, "Christian," a name he hopes to keep, as his baptismal name has been lost in the evils of the world. He is so weak that his mother and wife fear he will die. They question him about himself and the mother notes resemblances between the pilgrim and her son. Alexis beckons her nearer and embraces her (752-881). His life of deprivation continues until, near death, he writes his story (914-926). In his final trance before death Alexis is visited by his wife. He asks to be buried in the church of St. Boniface and reveals his true story. He dies as she recognizes him. The servant announces the pilgrim's death to Euphemian (980-1034). St. Innocent, the Pope, arrives at the head of a procession, fearful of the letter grasped in the holy man's hand (1056-1066). When the Pope takes it, Lesigne, dressed in a hairshirt, is shamed; she cries when the letter's contents are revealed. Innocent reads a sermon on loyalty to one's spouse, citing the case of Alexis who confided not in his parents but in his wife. He presents Lesigne with the letter and she turns it over to St. Ambrose (1086-1127). When Alexis' half of the wedding ring is found, his identity is definitively established, and Lesigne faints (1133-1142). [Lines 1143-1356 do not differ radically from the L version, nor are there any significant additions in this final section.]

BON

"En Auuerne a une cite"

The only twelfth-century version of this saint's life is included in Adgar's *Miracles of the Virgin*. [1] The author, sometimes referred to as Willame Adgar (or simply Willame or Adgar) names himself in the prologue inserted between Miracles 1 and 2 in his collection, in such a way as to invite confusion:

> Mut uolenters me numerai:
> "Adgar" ai num; mais el i sai,
> Li plusur me apelent Willame;
> Bien le puent faire sanz blasme.
> Kar par cel nun fui primeseinet
> E puis par Adgar baptizet.
> Pur ceo par raisun m'est auis
> Ke enz es nuns n'ai rien mespris,
> Ne cil, ki Willame me claiment,
> Ore me apelgent quei ke milz aiment.
> (25-34)

He continues to say that he has taken the miracles he is translating from a book in St. Paul's Cathedral in London:

> S'il enquerent de l'essamplarie:
> Jo l'ai de saint Pol de l'almarie,
> De saint Pol, de la noble iglise,
> Ki en Lundres est bien asise.
> (39-42)

---

[1] Carl Neuhaus, *Marienlegenden* (Heilbronn: Henninger, 1886).

After Miracle 11 there is a second introduction stating that his original is in Latin and that his translation is for his friend Gregory. An epilogue follows Miracle 40 in which Adgar congratulates himself on reaching the end of St. Paul's book and names the compiler of it, "Mestre Albri." Neuhaus laments the fact that this book of Master Alberic had not yet been discovered. His edition of Adgar's *Miracles of the Virgin* is based on the then only extant MS: London, British Museum, Egerton 612,[2] and in his introduction he concentrates on delineating the Latin sources found in two MSS: Cleop. C. X. fol. 100r-143v, and Arundel 346, fol. 60r-73r.[3] Neither of these contains a life of St. Bon. Adolf Mussafia in his seminal study of marial literature and discussion of the relations between Adgar and other Mary-legends identifies the unknown Albri as the compiler of a yet to be found MS based on William of Malmebury's collection, preserved in a MS at Salisbury (Miracle 28).[4] The Salisbury MS is one of the principal sources for subsequent vernacular collections, along with Oxford, Balliol 240 and Cambridge, Mm 6, 15, and provides Adgar's source from Miracle 32 on.[5]

Hilding Kjellman outlines in great detail the manuscript tradition of the Mary-legends, their respective sources and interrelationships.[6] In his opinion Adgar's version of St. Bon, Miracle 18, marks the beginning of the dependance on William of Malmesbury. The edition in which he publishes the miracles preserved in the MS Old Royal 20B XIV of the British Museum and the corresponding versions in the MSS fr. 375 and 818 of the Bibliothèque Nationale

---

[2] See Catalogue of additions to the Manuscripts in the British Museum in the years 1836-40, London, 1843, p. 43, and A. M. Bouly de Lesdain, "Les Manuscrits didactiques antérieurs au XIVème siècle: Essai d'inventaire," *Bulletin de l'Institut de Recherche et d'Histoire des Textes*, n.º 14 (Paris, 1966). The Life of St. Bon is found in fol. 32-35, Miracle 18. This is referred to as the "Gregory" version. Subsequent MSS of Miracles by Adgar (not including Bon) are found in a fragment of Dulwich, Alleyne College 13, and British Museum, Add. 38664 (composed between 1175-80), referred to as the "Gracial" version. See Appendix on Hildefonse.

[3] These were published almost in their entirety by Neuhaus in *Die lateinischen Vorlagen zu den Adgar'schen Marienlegenden*, 2 vols. (Heilbronn: Henninger, 1886, 1890).

[4] Adolf Mussafia, *Studien zu den mittelalterlichen Marienlegenden* (Vienna: Tempsky, 1891), IV, 27.

[5] *Ibid.*

[6] Hilding Kjellman, *La Deuxième Collection anglo-normande des Miracles de la Sainte Vierge et son original latin* (Paris: Champion, 1922).

in Paris, makes known for the first time 17 sources identical to Adgar's, or almost. Thus Miracle 28 in the Salisbury MS recounts the same story as Egerton 18 and Oxford III b 2.[7]

Little is known about the author. Master Alberic was a canon of St. Paul's and witnessed documents dated 1162, 1160.[8] According to R. W. Southern, he was the first to compile all three collections of Latin legends:[9]

1) 40 stories formed by Anselm, abbot of St. Edmund's in 1120.

2) 14 stories by Dominic, prior of Evesham.

3) 55 stories by William of Malmesbury.

Alberic composed between 1148 and 1162. Adgar himself may have been the chaplain of St. Mary Magdalene, Bread Street, between 1162 and 1200.[10] His first version was composed between 1165-70, and the second between 1175-80.[11]

In 1938, Grigorii Lozinski published Gautier de Coinci's version of St. Bon and it is in his introduction that can be found a full discussion of the development of the legend.[12] St. Bon was bishop of Clermont, succeeding his brother, Saint Avit II. The Benedictine *Book of Saints* states that he was a Benedictine bishop, chancellor to King Sigebert III, governor of Provence and bishop of Clermont. After his service as bishop he retired to the Abbey of Manlieu and died in extreme old age (born 623, died Jan. 15, 710).[13]

Herbert, bishop of Norwich (1091-1119) claims that the chasuble of St. Bon was exhibited in Clermont-Ferrand during his life,[14]

---

[7] The text of the latter is found in Kjellman, *Ibid.*, p. 158.

[8] M. Gibbs, *Early Charters of St. Paul's Cathedral* (Camden Society, 3rd Series, lviii, 1939), numbers 217 and 245.

[9] R. W. Southern, "The Place of England in the Twelfth-Century Renaissance," *History*, 45 (1960), 201-216, and "The English Origins of the *Miracles of the Virgin*," *Medieval and Renaissance Studies*, 4 (1958), 176-216.

[10] M. D. Legge, *Anglo-Norman Literature and its Background* (Oxford: Clarendon Press, 1963), p. 190.

[11] *Ibid.*, pp. 188-90.

[12] G. Lozinski, "De Saint Bon, évêque de Clermont: Miracle versifié par Gautier de Coinci," *Annales Academiae Scientiarum Fennicae*, n.° B XL 1 (Helsinki, 1938).

[13] *The Book of Saints. A Dictionnary of Persons Canonized or Beatified by the Catholic Church*, ed. St. Augustine's Abbey (Ramsgate: Crowell, 1921).

[14] Gams, *Series episcoporum ecclesiae catholicae* (Ratisbonne, 1873), pp. 194-195.

whereas an inventory of the Treasures of the Cathedral at Clermont-Ferrand, dating from the end of the tenth century, makes no allusion to it. [15] Thus, concludes Lozinski, the formation of the legend oc-cured around the year 1100, the date of the earliest Latin version in which the miracle of the chasuble dominates. [16]

The legend of Hildefonse of Toledo became known in France early in the twelfth century and provides the essential structure of the Miracle. The legend of Bon appears to be a case of literary borrowing and transferral of miracles from one saint (Hildefonse) to another (Bon). [17]

Adgar's version of Bon, numbering 212 octosyllabic lines rhym-ing in couplets, has received scant attention from literary critics. [18]

The story is as follows:

In the town of Clermont in Auvergne, where the crusade was preached in 1095, there were two bishops named Bonitus and Sido-nius. I do not know who came first, but the two men were equally saintly (1-25). Bon was an extremely pious man, in the habit of spending both day and night in prayer and in lamentation of his sins, not daring to approach the altar (26-56). One night, as he prayed, a vision appeared to him: a long radiant procession of saints, prophets and patriarchs, with the Virgin Mary in the center. Bon was frightened and backed away, but the walls of the chapel retreated too (57-96). The Virgin ordered a mass to be sung, and the saints were discussing who could perform it, when Mary intervenes and asks Bon to say mass, because he was a saintly man, worthy of the task. Bon was frightened, but an angel dragged him to the

---

[15] Douet d'Arcq, "Inventaire du trésor de la cathédrale de Clermont-Ferrand," *Revue Archéologique,* 10 (1853), 160-174.

[16] Lozinski, pp. 13-14.

[17] *Ibid.,* p. 16.

[18] Uda Ebel discusses the development of the Miracle as a genre, and demonstrates the basic difference in Adgar's treatment as contrasted with the thirteenth-century version of Gautier de Coinci: Adgar's *Miracles* were based on the rational certainty of belief, whereas Gautier's relied on the certainty of salvation, founded upon the experience of belief. Thus Adgar's are shorter, less concrete in their development and were probably addressed to a simple, uneducated audience. (*Das altromanische Mirakel. Ursprung und Geschichte einer literarischen Gattung. Studia Romanica,* n.º 8 [Heidel-berg: Carl Winter Universitätsverlag, 1965]).

[19] Louis Réau, *L'Iconographie des saints,* Vol. III, Pt. 1 of *L'Iconographie de l'art chrétien* (Paris: Presses Universitaires de France), pp. 236-237.

altar, where he shook and trembled throughout the mass. Afterwards, he was led to the Virgin, who was so pleased with the mass that she gave him the magnificent mass-vestment of divine fabrication he had worn during the service (97-140). Bon deserved this glorious gift because he was never a proud man — if anyone doubts this miracle, they have only to ask the people of Clermont, or Herbert, Bishop of Norwich, who saw the vestment (141-166).

One of Bon's successors as bishop of Clermont wanted to receive a similarly magnificent gift, and imitated Bon. But every night he fell asleep in the middle of his prayers, and found himself in bed next morning, ignorant of how he got there. The Virgin helped him recognize his sin and he abandoned his desire for miracles. The Virgin intercedes for foolish sinners. Mary, help us in a similar manner (167-212).

BRENDAN

"Donna Aaliz la reïne"

The *Voyage of Saint Brendan* (1840 octosyllabic lines rhyming in pairs) is one of the earliest of the twelfth-century Lives. The author names himself in the Prologue: "Li apostoiles danz Benedeiz." [1] This single line has inspired much of the research that has been done on the identification of the author. E. G. R. Waters concludes that Benedeit was an Anglo-Norman monk (*"danz"*), reinforced by her interpretation of *apostoiles* as someone belonging to a monastery. [2] E. Walberg takes exception to this reading and proposes a different word order: "danz Benedeiz l'apostoile" (the original having been reversed to comply with the needs of the rhyme). [3] *L'apostoile* then becomes a sort of nickname, a hypothesis supported by lengthy documentation of similar occurences where nicknames became family names, e.g. Lepape, Lemoine, etc. This hypothesis seems probable and puts to rest the nagging doubts concerning the appellation of Pope for an author who obviously was not. Furthermore, *danz* was a term not strictly reserved for Benedictine monks, but was attributed as well to prelates and important laymen. [4]

Benedeit is writing for "Aaliz la reine" (l. 1), identified as Adeliza, daughter of Duke Godfrey of Louvain and second wife

---

[1] E. G. R. Waters, *The Anglo-Norman Voyage of Saint Brendan by Benedeit* (Oxford: Clarendon Press, 1928), l. 8.

[2] *Ibid.*, xxvi-xxvii.

[3] Emmanuel Walberg, "Sur le nom de l'auteur du *Voyage de Saint Brendan*," *Studia Neophilologica*, 12 (1939), 46-55.

[4] *Ibid.*, p. 48.

to Henry I, King of England (1100-35), also mentionned in line 5.[5] Their marriage took place in 1121, which leads Waters to the conclusion that the poem was written around that date. Another MS, however, names the poet's patroness Mahalt. R. L. G. Ritchie unfolds a strong argument in favor of Mahalt, identified as Maud, the same King's first wife, elder daughter of St. Margaret and Malcolm Canmore, a great niece of Edward The Confessor.[6] Maud would then be the first patroness, and the dedication would have been altered to suit the circumstances. This argument also dates the poem between 1106 and 1118, which would make *Brendan* the oldest twelfth-century Saint's Life, and the earliest poem written in octosyllabic rhyming couplets.

Brendan exists in five MSS:[7]

1) A.—British Museum, Cotton Vesp. B. x (1), fol. 1-11r.

2) B.—Paris, Bibliothèque Nationale, nouv. acq. fr. 4503, fol. 19v-42r.

3) C.—Oxford, Bodleian Library, Rawl. D 913 (formerly Rawl. misc. 1370), fol. 85.[8]

4) D.—York, Dean and Chapter Library, 16 K. 12, part 1, fol. 23-36r.

5) E.—Paris, Arsenal 3516 (formerly BLF 283), fol. 96r col. c-100v.

There are in addition four fragments corresponding to lines 794-893, 1169-1185 and 1188-1206 of Waters' edition, recently discovered by Françoise Vielliard.[9]

M. D. Legge explains the peculiarities of the meter (i.e. one-third of the lines are feminine, and for modern ears have only seven syllables) by the conjecture that *Brendan* was probably sung or chanted, hence the feminine 'e' given more stress.[10]

---

[5] Other MSS offer the forms Aeliz, Aliz.

[6] R. L. G. Ritchie, "The Date of the *Voyage de Saint Brendan*," *Medium Aevum*, 19 (1950), 64-66.

[7] For a description, see Waters, ix-xxii.

[8] This is the MS which names Mahalt.

[9] Françoise Vielliard, *Bibliotheca Bodmeriana. Manuscrits français du moyen age* (Geneva: Fondation Martin Bodmer, 1975), pp. 167-70.

[10] M. D. Legge, *Anglo-Norman Literature and its Background* (Oxford: Clarendon Press, 1963), pp. 14-17.

The Latin source of the poem is generally agreed to be the *Navigatio Sancti Brendani,* published conveniently in Waters' edition. He outlines in full detail the relation to and divergences from the *Navigatio* to the *Voyage.* [11] The legend was obviously a popular one as there exists at least 81 MSS in all corners of Europe. [12] The *Voyage* itself was later twice translated into Latin.

The origins and formation of the legend have been studied. [13] Wahlund provides us with the historical data concerning the saint. Brendan's fame in the Irish church rests on his holy behaviour as an abbot in the southwestern portion of the country. He was born in County Kerry's mountainous North in the village of Altraigi Caille near Tralee during the reign of Oengus mat Nat-fraech, King of Munster. The date normally accepted for his birth is 484. [14] Brendan was baptized by Erc of Atraige, who became the boy's confessor and raised him in the fear of God. There is some confusion as to Erc's identity, as the name was fairly common at that time. In 514, Brendan founded an abbey on what is now called the island of Tiree in Scotland. [15] About this time, during the first decade of the sixth century, Brendan was the abbot of the monastery of Llancarvan in Southern Wales. Proof of this is the baptism, by Brendan, between the years 510 and 520 of the child who became St. Macutus (St. Malo). Brendan adopted this boy as his spiritual son and raised him until he learned to speak and read. [16]

The basis for the belief in Brendan's sojourn in Brittany is the passage in the 16th chapter of *Vita Sancti Brendani* about the monastery of Ailech, founded by the saint. Many people have assumed

---

[11] Waters, lxxxi-cv.

[12] C. Steinweg in "Die handschriftlichen Gestaltungen der lateinischen *Navigatio Brendani,*" *Romanische Forschungen,* 7 (1891) lists 74, and 7 others are mentioned by C. Wahlund, *Die altfranzösische Prosaübersetzung von Brendans Meerfahrt, nach der Pariser Hdschr. Nat.-Bibl. fr. 1553* (Upsala, 1900; Slatkine Reprints, 1974), xxx.

[13] C. Wahlund, *Ibid.,* introduction, and C. Selmer, "The Beginnings of the Brendan Legend on the Continent," *Catholic Historical Review,* 29 (1943), 169-176.

[14] G. Schirmer, *Zur Brendanus-Legende* (Leipzig: Habilitationsschrift, 1888).

[15] Archbishop Ussher, *Works,* VI, 1654, *Index Chron.,* AN. DXIV, quoted by Wahlund, xii.

[16] Fr. Plaine, *Vie inédite de Saint Malo, écrite au IXème siècle par Bili* (Rennes: Arth. de la Broderie, 1804).

this monastery to be that of Aleth near Saint-Malo, who is often mentioned in conjunction with Brendan. According to the *Vita Sancti Macuti*, Malo was invited by Brendan to participate in the latter's sea voyage. In certain of the Latin MSS of the *Navigatio* Macutus is named specifically as Brendan's companion. There are geographical reminders of Brendan in Brittany: the grotto of St. Brendan in the rock of Césembre near St. Malo; in the Côtes du Nord, a town of several thousand inhabitants is still called St. Brendan.

In both the Irish *Betha Brenainn* and in the *Navigatio* there is mention of a month-long visit with St. Ende on the holy island of Aran. Adamnan's *Vita Sancti Columbae* reports a similar visit by Brendan, which must have taken place after 553, when Columba first came to the island of Hy. Brendan died on May 16, probably in 576. Another version places his death on November 28-29. Both the author of the *Vita* and Ussher agree that Brendan died in Enachdune (now Annaghdown on Lake Corrite, Galway County) at the convent he founded there, and of which his sister Brig was abbess. This same source places his grave at the convent of Cluainferta (now Clonfert on the Shannon, also in Galway) which he established c. 561.

One may safely assume that Brendan lived and worked primarily in Southwestern Ireland as several places bear his name: Brandon Hill, Mt. Brendan, Brandon's Well, etc. He is the patron saint of County Kerry and this, as well as the fact that his day is still celebrated is due to his significant activity in his homeland: conversions of heathen, miracles and the establishment of convents — and not at all to his legendary odyssey.

Selmer has also made another contribution to Brendan studies, providing a valuable bibliography which includes all vernacular versions and studies concerning these versions.[17] Louis Réau has studied the iconography, and J. Hillier Caulkins has shown how numerical and temporal notations are intimately connected to the cyclical concept of seasons and the liturgical calendar.[18]

---

[17] Carl Selmer, "The Vernacular Translations of the *Navigatio*: A Bibliographical Study," *Mediaeval Studies*, 18 (1956), 145-157.

[18] Louis Réau, *L'Iconographie des saints*, Vol. III, Pt. 1 of *L'Iconographie de l'art chrétien* (Paris: Presses Universitaires de France, 1956), pp. 241-242. J. Hillier Caulkins, "Les Notations numériques et temporelles dans la *Navigation de saint Brendan* de Benedeit," *Moyen Age*, 80 (1974), 245-260.

The story, as told in the *Voyage,* is as follows: The monk Benedeit translated the tale of Brendan into the vernacular for Queen Adeliza (1-18). Brendan was a noble who fled the world of earthly pleasure and temptation to become a monk. Contemplating one day, Brendan expressed the desire to visit Paradise before his death, consulting the hermit Barintus, whose disciple and godson Mernoc had already successfully completed his pilgrimage. He chose fourteen companions who prepared forty days' provisions for the voyage (19-184). As Brendan and his companions prepared to depart, three other monks asked to be included; Brendan accepted them despite his premonitions of the evil and temptation they would bring. They sail westward for fifteen days until the wind dies. Encouraged by Brendan they row on. God sends them a good wind which brings them within sight of land, whose rough terrain hinders their landing for three days. When they finally disembark, they discover an uninhabited but well-provisioned city. Brendan warns his companions against excess, but they satisfy their appetites nevertheless. During the night, while the others are sleeping, Brendan sees one of the three monks, inspired by Satan, stealing a goblet. Before departure four days later, Brendan requests that no one abscond with anything from the city, and the guilty monk repents and dies; his soul goes to Paradise (185-354).

They reach another port where a messenger brings them all the necessary provisions. They sail on from here for approximately a year until they reach the Island of Sheep, where they land easily and stay to celebrate Easter. Another messenger appears mysteriously with food and drink. He advises them to sail to a nearby island. They soon regret this advice for the island is really a great fish. They depart, reaching eventually the Island of Birds. One bird explains to Brendan that they are fallen angels. Following a restful night, the travellers stock the ship for the second year (355-622).

Six months later land is sighted, the Isle of Ailbe; they find two fountains there, one clear and one cloudy. An old man runs up to the monks, frightening them. He leads them to his abbey, which houses many treasures. The abbot recounts to them the founding of the abbey eighty years previously. He foresees that Brendan will die in his homeland during Epiphany. The next stop brings them to an intoxicating spring full of fish; although Brendan preaches moderation, the monks all become drunk. They set sail for the Great Fish where they intend to celebrate Easter again, and on the way stop to visit the Island of Birds again. Heading West once more, the travellers witness a battle of sea-serpents (623-968).

Tired and hungry, they are attacked by a griffin, but a dragon sent by God rescues them and Brendan tries to assuage his companions' fears. Eventually they reach the huge pillar jutting out of the sea that marks the entrance to Hell. They continue undaunted through flames and smoke under God's protection. They approach a smoking mountain where the second monk jumps overboard and cries out his remorse before being engulfed by the flames (969-1214).

They encounter Judas, who is hanging on to a pillar and begging for Christ's mercy. Brendan makes the sign of the cross over him and asks why he suffers such great torture. Judas recounts his story and then outlines, day by day, the eternal torment to which he is subjected, provoking tears from Brendan (1215-1498). Leaving Hell, they discover that one monk has mysteriously disappeared, bringing their number back to the original fifteen. Their next encounter is with Paul the hermit, who lives in the woods, is brought fish by an otter and gets his water from a nearby fountain. He knows all about Brendan and that he has been travelling for seven years. The group revisits former stops and celebrates Easter on the Great Fish again. Heading eastward, they sail for forty days before reaching the fog-cloaked entrance to Paradise. The mountain is made of gold, and the surrounding walls are studded with precious stones. The beautiful and abundant fruits and flowers in the garden emit a wonderful odor. This is the land of plenty, where there is no heat or cold, no hunger or thirst, and no suffering. Angels appear to tell Brendan to return home: three months later he arrives in Ireland and spreads the good news about Paradise before dying (1499-1840).

CATHERINE

"Cil ki le bien seit e entent"

The Life of Saint Catherine of Alexandria, written in the last
third of the twelfth century by Clemence, a nun at the Benedictine
abbey of Barking, comprises 2700 octosyllabic lines rhyming in
couplets.[1] It was first edited in 1894 by J. U. Jarník,[2] and after
the discovery of a third manuscript was recently edited by William
Macbain in 1964.[3] It is preserved in three MSS:

1) The oldest A.—Paris, Bibliothèque Nationale, n. acq. fr.
4503;[4]

2) W.—Welbeck iCi from the Duke of Portland's collection, on
loan to the British Museum;[5]

---

[1] For details on date and authorship, see William Macbain, *The Life of
Saint Catherine. Anglo-Norman Text Society,* n.º 18 (Oxford, 1964), xxiv-
xxvi, and his article, "The Literary Apprenticeship of Clemence of Barking,"
*Journal of the Australasian Universities Language and Literature Associa-
tion,* 9 (1958), 3-22. Macbain's edition received a favorable review by
C. Camproux in *Revue des Langues romanes,* 108 (1966), 220, and a mixed
review by Léon Geschière, "Un passage obscur de la *Vie de Sainte Catherine,*" in *Festschrift Wartburg zum 80. Geburstag, 18 mai, 1968* (Tübingen:
Niemeyer, 1968), I, pp. 343-358, and by J. Monfrin in *Zeitschrift für romanische Philologie,* 83 (1967), 132-135.
[2] J. U. Jarník, *Dvé verse starofrancouské legendy o sv. Kateriné Alexandrinské* (Prague, 1894).
[3] Macbain, *op. cit.*
[4] For a detailed description of this MS see E. G. R. Waters, *The Anglo-
Normand Voyage of St. Brendan by Benedeit* (Oxford: Clarendon Press,
1928) and Macbain's edition.
[5] See A. Strong, *A Catalogue of Letters and Other Historical Documents
Exhibited in the Library of Welbeck Abbey* (London, 1903); O. Södergärd,

3) P.—Paris, Bibliothèque Nationale, fr. 23112;[6]

The origins of the Saint Catherine legend remain dubious, despite some attempts to elucidate them,[7] and the question of her relics raises similar difficulties.[8]

Clemence of Barking's version accounts for three of the eight rhymed versions of the legend in Old French written before 1500. Only one of these[9] has been considered a source. The Latin Vulgata version of mid eleventh century is of greater importance as a source[10] since the author retains the essential idea of this version in translating and amending it.

The history of the development of the legend has been fully treated, most recently by Giovanni Bronzini, who also has edited the Greek and Latin versions and discussed their interrelationships.[11] Louis Réau has treated Catherine's iconography.[12]

The story as told by Clemence is the following:

He who possesses the wisdom of Christ's example should make it known to others. I would thus like to translate this from the

---

La Vie Seinte Audrée, poème anglo-normand du XIIème siècle (Upsala, 1955), p. 37ff.

[6] Macbain erroneously refers to a description in Notices et Extraits des Manuscrits de la Bibliothèque Nationale, 35 (1896).

[7] E. Einenckel, The Life of Saint Katherine (London, 1884), a short account of her life found in the Basilian menology dating from the second half of the ninth century; J. Rendel Harris, "A New Christian Apology," Bulletin of the John Rylands Library, 7, 8 and 9 (1923-25), sees John of Damascus as the author of both the St. Catherine legend and Barlaam and Josaphat, a Christian romance; J. A. Robinson, "The Passion of Saint Catherine and the Romance of Barlaam and Josaphat," Journal of Theological Studies, 25 (1924).

[8] R. Fawtier, "Les Reliques rouennaises de sainte Catherine d'Alexandrie," Analecta Bollandiana, 41 (1923), 357-368.

[9] A frament of 200 lines, MS French 6 of the John Rylands Library in Manchester. See E. C. Fawtier-Jones, "Les Vies de sainte Catherine d'Alexandrie," Romania, 56 (1930), 80-104. See also M. D. Legge, Anglo-Norman Literature and its Background (Oxford: Clarendon Press, 1963), pp. 66-72.

[10] K. Manger, Die französischen Bearbeitungen der Legende der h. Katharina von Alexandrien (Tübingen: Niemeyer, 1901).

[11] Giovanni Bronzini, La leggenda di S. Caterina d'Alessandria. Passioni greche e latine. Atti della accad. naz. dei Lincei, Memorie, cl. di Scienze morale, stor. et filol., Ser. 8, Vol. 9, Fasc. 2 (Rome, 1960), 254-416.

[12] Louis Réau, L'Iconographie des saints, Vol. III, Pt. 1 of L'Iconographie de l'art chrétien (Paris: Presses Universitaires de France, 1958), pp. 262-272.

Latin although it has already been done, because times have changed (1-50).

There was an emperor of great vigor named Constantine, the son of Constantius and Helen, who ruled in Rome many years ago. He conquered Maxence who had wanted to steal his throne, and chased him to Alexandria, where Maxence ruled for thirty-five years, causing much trouble for the Christians. On a certain day, Maxence ordered the entire population to congregate in front of the temple to hear his will: 130 Christians were sacrificed to the gods (51-132).

In this city lived a beautiful and noble girl, Catherine, only daughter of a king. She was well educated and very devout and pure. Upon her father's death, she became queen and ruled wisely. She saw the agony of the Christians being put to death by Maxence and prayed to be able to face him. She went directly to the temple and up to the tyrant. Catherine insists that one must believe in God, whereupon Maxence states that it is a false religion, and that her good education is marred by this belief in God. Catherine tells him that she belongs to God and they argue, trying to convince each other of the correctness of their respective religions (133-322).

Maxence calls his counsellors and one evil cleric promises the emperor that he knows how to change Catherine's mind. Catherine is imprisoned and prays to Christ, and again demonstrates her faith and knowledge to the tyrant. She prays to God, who makes her a gift of wise speech to help her against her enemies, and sends an angel to comfort her. The angel announces that she can triumph over her enemies by martyrdom (323-584).

Catherine is taken from her cell for her dialectical battle with the fifty rhetoricians. They mock her as insane and give her the right to speak first, intending to tear her arguments apart when it is their turn. She propounds her philosophy that God cannot be God and man, cites miracles and Plato's prophecy, describes God's wisdom and love of the poor, and the immortality one finds through Christianity. In the end the fifty are convinced by her wisdom and the truth she speaks. Maxence flies into a rage and decides to burn them (585-1119).

One valiant man declares that the fifty now believe in Christ and want to be baptized. Catherine comforts them and tells them they will be baptized in blood. On the thirteenth day of November they are martyred, but God does not want them to suffer and performs a miracle: those thrown into the flames do not burn. The people in the crowd marvel at God's bounty and are converted to Christianity through the power of this miracle (1120-1238).

Maxence praises Catherine's beauty and proposes to marry her if she renounces her God. He describes the wonderful things she will own as his wife and promises her anything else she wants. She mocks him and replies that she does not want her tombstone to read: here lies Catherine, who abandoned God. She scorns his honor and promises, and tells him that he will have to abandon his false gods. Her only husband is Jesus, her life and honor, her delight and comfort. Maxence feels dishonored by her refusal and condemns her to be beheaded. This offer she accepts, laughingly. Maxence has her beaten and thrown in prison, and she willingly accepts her punishment (1239-1476).

Refusing to eat or drink, she is visited by an angel who comforts her. One day Maxence is absent, and his queen, curious about Catherine, decides to see her. She is touched by tales of her beauty and youth, as well as her persistent refusal to eat or drink. She tells Porphire, Maxence's chief of staff, a dream she had in which Catherine gave her the crown of Christ. The queen is obsessed with the idea of seeing Catherine, and Porphire tells her of the martyrdom of the fifty. Catherine tells the queen and Porphire that their visit is an answer to her prayer. She wants them to follow the right path and prays that they be converted (1477-1616).

The angels tell her that when she has won her battle, she will return to Christ. Catherine warns the queen that Maxence's love is fragile and unenduring. To Porphire she explains the changeability and instability of terrestrial life, and the heavenly city and afterlife one finds in Christianity. She speaks to them at length of the Virgin and Christian love. Both the queen and Porphire are now ready to die for God if He wishes it. When they leave Catherine, several knights ask Porphire where he has been, and he launches into a description of Christianity, heaven and Catherine's goodness, until all 200 are converted (1617-1832).

Catherine eats nothing but the celestial bread brought by God's dove. God himself appears to her in her cell with a company of angels and a choir of virgins to comfort her. When the emperor returns, he visits Catherine and is struck by her beauty, which he had hoped starvation would tarnish. He accuses her of sorcery but she tells him firmly that he can kill her body, but that her soul is immortal. She warns him of the vengeance God will take on him if he does not believe in Him. Maxence grinds his teeth in anger and has her beaten. People take pity on her and urge her to renounce her faith to save her life. Her death, she replies, assures her of life, whereas theirs do not. Many of these people, hearing her words, embrace Christianity, but keep it a secret from the emperor to save themselves from torture. Cursateis, a cruel provost of the palace, promises Maxence that after a certain torture he has in mind for her, Catherine will abandon her faith. He describes the wheel. Catherine is shown the wheel and told what will happen to her, but she is not afraid and prays for the destruction of the wheel. An angel appears to her and the wheel does not turn, but is burned by lightning, killing 4000 people, and causing panic and conversion among the pagan onlookers (1833-2154). The queen attempts to prove by this that Christian faith is stronger than the pagan. Maxence is furious that she has been enchanted by the evil Christians and decides to kill her along with other converts if she does not change her mind. He declares his love for her. The queen goes to Catherine for help, is tortured and put to death on the twenty-third day of November. Porphire buries her, with honor, secretly at night. Everyone mourns her death. Porphire tells Maxence that the queen has been buried, and reproaches him for his cruelty, accusing him of being in the devil's power. Maxence, alone, feels abandoned by all; even his last friend, Porphire, has left him. He tells himself that it is Porphire's counsel that killed his queen and on the twenty-fourth of May, Porphire and his 200 knights, who declared themselves Christians, are executed (2155-2468).

Maxence goes to Catherine and asks her again to abandon her faith, which has led so many to death. He assures her again that if she changes religion he will marry her, and if not she will die. She answers that in death, she will be born, and that she awaits her true husband. Angry, Maxence finally commands that she be beheaded outside the city. All are saddened by her fate, but she consoles them and asks if she may pray. A voice welcomes her to heaven. She is decapitated on November 25, her blood turns into milk, and the angels carry her to Mount Sinai. Oil flows from her tomb, healing the sick who come to her (2469-2638).

We should all love God as she did. May she intercede for us. My name is Clemence, I am a nun at Barking, and I translated this work for the love of the Lord who will reign forever (2639-2700).

EDMUND I

"Ore entendez la passiun"

The anonymous author of *La Passiun de Seint Edmund* composed his legend in Anglo-Norman monorhymed octosyllabic couplets numbering 1696. The only available edition is by Albert Nabert[1] who dates the poem at the second half of the twelfth century. M. D. Legge feels that he is perhaps underestimating the age and places its composition before 1150.[2]

This version is contained in one MS: 435 of Caius and Gonville College, Cambridge.[3]

The legend of Saint Edmund has historical roots. In 856 he became king of East Anglia (region corresponding roughly to present-day Suffolk), was recaptured by the invading Danes and died on November 20, 870. Grant Loomis summarizes all references to Edmund until 1433 and traces the development of the legend.[4] Popular imagination accounts for the embellishment of scanty facts.[5]

---

[1] Albert Nabert, *La Passiun de Seint Edmund. Ein anglonormannisches Gedicht aus dem 12. Jahrhundert* (Greifswald, 1915). A yet unpublished new edition is on deposit in the Cambridge University Library, a doctoral dissertation by C. W. J. Higson.

[2] M. D. Legge, *Anglo-Norman Literature and its Background* (Oxford: Clarendon Press, 1963).

[3] For a description of the MS see Paul Meyer, in *Romania*, 36 (1915), 532.

[4] Grant Loomis, "The Growth of the Saint Edmund Legend," *Harvard Studies and Notes in Philology and Literature*, 4 (1932), 83-113. See also Irene P. McKeehan, "Saint Edmund of East Anglia: The Development of a Romantic Legend," *University of Colorado Studies*, 15 (1925), 13-74.

[5] Many documents relating to Edmund and to his shrine can be found in Thomas Arnold, *Memorials of St. Edmund's Abbey*, 3 vols. (London: Rolls Series, 1890-1896).

The Latin source of this version is generally accepted to be the first literary treatment of the legend, *Vita et passio Sancti Eadmundi* by Abbo of Fleury.[6] It was composed barely a century after the martyrdom of the saint and dedicated to Dunstan (925?-988), Archbishop of Canterbury.[7]

To date there has been no literary critical study of this version. Louis Réau has treated Edmund's iconography.[8] The story is as follows:

Listen to the passion of saint Edmund, a powerful king who, by his service to the Lord, redeemed us from damnation. Three days after his death he was resurrected, rose up like Christ, and went to Paradise (1-48). His country was Brittany, which is now known as England. His entourage guarded him poorly and he was chased from his land (49-68). In Germany, three peoples assembled to attack, they invaded and divided the country into three parts, renaming it England. In Eastanglia the Saxons lived peacefully and prosperously within their protective walls, surrounded by the bounteous sea and land (69-152).

Edmund led a Christian and law-abiding life. As king he was kind to widows, orphans and the poor (153-198). The Devil, jealous of all things religious, incited Ingar, King of Northumbria, and his companion Ubbe who had killed Saint Oswald, to commit crimes. They laid wast the surrounding countryside. They sailed for Eastanglia, killing Christians along the way (199-256), sparing no one. They asked to see King Edmund, but the people avoided a direct answer, saying Edmund might be resting in the country. Ingar sent a messenger to the king, who feared no mortal and was ferocious in battle, demanding obedience. The alternative was death (257-428). Edmund, saddened by this news, asked his bishop for advice. The bishop urged him to hide, but Edmund deemed this cowardly and preferred to die rather than leave his country so shamefully. Dead or alive, he would be God's servant, and recalled

---

[6] Published in Migne, *PL*, CXXXIX, 507-520. The Bollandists have not yet reached Edmund's feast day of November 20 in *Acta Sanctorum*.

[7] M. E. Porter and J. H. Baltzell, "The Old French Lives of Saint Edmund King of East Anglia," *Romanic Review*, 45 (1954), 81-88.

[8] Louis Réau, *L'Iconographie des saints*, Vol. III, Pt. 1 of *L'Iconographie de l'art chrétien* (Paris: Presses Universitaires de France, 1958), pp. 410-411.

his lifelong dedication to Christianity (429-558). Edmund sent back the messenger, calling Ingar the son of the Devil and announcing that he will receive the pagan unarmed to prove his readiness for martyrdom (559-704). Ingar's men brought Edmund before him, as Christ was led before Pilate. They tortured, beat and mocked him. He was tied to a tree and pierced with arrows, then decapitated. The angels carry his soul to Paradise (705-864).

Ingar ordered the head thrown into thorny bushes, and then departed. The Eastanglians grieved, and searched the woods for Edmund's head. They called out, and it answered them three times, first in English, then in French: "Here, here, here!" The people joined the head and body together before burial in a chapel (865-1084). Edmund's curative powers became renowned throughout Eastanglia. The people of the city of Boedricsworth decided to move the tomb. His friends are astounded to find that his body has not decomposed and that his head and body have grown back together (1085-1152).

Oswen, a devout woman, speaks often with Edmund, notices a crimson streak which symbolizes his martyrdom, and decides that his fame would increase if this were known (1153-1200). The bishop of the diocese is the highly respected Saint Theodore. Some of the people plan to destroy the church in which the martyr is interred, but his power thwarts the attempt. They can enter the next morning only when the faithful come to pray, and evil leaves the intruders as they become true believers. A messenger recounts this miracle to Saint Theodore, who when he sees it, recognizes it as God's will. In his anger, Theodore orders all the men in the church to be hanged. The condemned pray for mercy and as the prophet Joram had changed those who wanted to kill the King in Samaria, so the supplication causes Theodore to repent. All prayed so intensely to Saint Edmund that their sins were absolved (1201-1424). The bishop washes Edmund and dresses him in royal robes before placing him in a beautiful sepulcher. He then serves the saint for the rest of his life.

The rich and powerful Lefstan comes to the church and asks that the tomb be opened for him to view the saint's body. The guardian does not dare refuse. When Lefstan sees Edmund, his evil intentions and pride cause the Devil to enter his body, and he loses his senses. He is carried to his wise old father, who is grief-stricken by his son's state, but satisfied by divine justice. This is how Christ revenges Saint Edmund (1425-1540).

Saint Gregory has told us how other saints were revenged in Rome. Those who did not serve Saint Laurence found sudden death. We should honor martyrs.

I know that the saint suffered physical torture, but his soul is comforted. Christ will join Edmund's body and soul together on the Judgement Day, but until then they will remain separated. Edmund was chaste all his life, and like others who keep their virginity, he can be close to God. We sinners who are not virgins can find hope and comfort in Christ our Saviour, and in Saint Edmund through prayer. Let us purge our bodies through penitence so as not to be separated from him. Isaiah said: those who wrong a saint will never know God. That is what we fear, so we pray to our Lord for strength to obey his commandments, and always to serve Him well (1541-1696).

EDMUND II

"Mult ai usé cum[e] pechere"

The *Life of Saint Edmund*,[1] composed by Denis Piramus has been the subject of much interest, not as much for the inherent qualities of the poem itself, but because of the mention of Marie de France (l. 35). Attempts to pinpoint biographical information about Denis himself have led to several hypotheses. Henry Haxo[2] identifies Denis with Magister Dionisius, a prominent rival of Samson who was elected abbot of St. Edmund's Bury in 1182. Kjellman remains, however, unconvinced by this theory. All that is certain is that he was a monk of St. Edmund's.[3]

The different dates of composition attributed to the *Life* reflect differing linguistic and historical arguments. The mention of Marie de France offers a *terminus a quo* of 1160. The language and "impure rhyme" of the poet places the *terminus ad quem* at 1200. For lack of more specific information, Kjellman's linguistic analysis appears to be the most convincing, i.e. around 1170.

There is only one surviving MS (British Museum, Cotton Domitian A. xi, fol. 1-24), written in England in the thirteenth century.[4] The Life of St. Edmund is followed by Garnier de Pont-Ste-

---

[1] Hilding Kjellman, *La Vie seint Edmund le Rei, poème anglo-normand du XIIème siècle par Denis Piramus* (Göteborg: Wettergren and Kerbor, 1935).

[2] Henry Haxo, "Denis Piramus: La Vie Seint Edmunt," *Modern Philology*, 12 (1914), 345-366 and 13 (1915), 559-583.

[3] M. D. Legge, *Anglo-Norman Literature and its Background* (Oxford: Clarendon Press, 1963), p. 83.

[4] Studied by Paul Meyer, in *Romania*, 22 (1893), 170.

Maxence's Life of Thomas Beckett (MS D of Walberg's edition). According to Josef Merk,[5] the probable Latin sources are:[6]

1) ll. 128-368: Geoffrey of Monmouth's *Historia Regum Britanniae.*

2) ll. 369-432, 2054-3260: *Passio Sancti Edmundi* of Abbo of Fleury.

3) ll. 433-1788: Galfridus de Fontibus' *De Infantia Sancti Eadmundi.*

4) ll. 1789-2018: numbers 2 and 3 of this list.

5) ll. 3261-4033: Hermanus the Archdeacon's *Liber de Miraculis Sancti Eadmundi.* [7]

The lines not accounted for in Merk's study, he attributes to Denis' originality.

Denis has embroidered the historical facts quite generously with fabrication and legend. The continental origin of Edmund, King Offe, and the sea voyage all belong to the realm of fiction. The episode about the Viking Lodbrok contains a grain of truth, but the degree of historicity and/or legend remains unsettled. The Viking invasions correspond to the years 866-70. Charles The Bald was already dead during the siege of Paris (885-89). Thus Denis bends chronology to suit his needs. The list of successors is exact: Edward (901-24), Athelstan (925-40), Edmund I (940-46), Eadred (946-55), Edwi The Handsome (955-59), Edgar The Peaceful (959-75), Edward The Martyr (975-78), Ethelred II, The Redeless (978-1016). The plotting vassals existed; however the two best known of the period are not mentioned (Elfric and Edric Streona).

The 4,033 octosyllabic lines, rhyming in couplets, tell the following story:

I have committed great sins by writing lyric poetry, but I shall no longer be trapped by the devil. My name is Denis Piramus. May God help me to repent (1-24). The poetry that pleases lords and

[5] Josef Merk, *Die literarische Gestaltung der altfranzösischen Heiligenleben bis Ende des 12. Jahrhunderts* (Affoltern am Albis: J. Weiss, 1946).

[6] All published in *Memorials of St. Edmund's Abbey* by Thomas Arnold (London: Rolls Series, 1890-1896).

[7] Both Kjellman and Haxo arrive at different correspondances but refer to the same Latin versions.

ladies resembles fables and lies. Even the beloved Marie de France recounts falsehoods to please her public. My story will delight you too, but it is not a dream: it happened in our time and is true (25-78). I shall tell you about the childhood and miracle-working of St. Edmund. He is a good example for all: kings, counts and Christians.

He was from Saxony, of royal lineage, and became king of East Anglia (79-120). You may wonder why England was divided in three, so I shall tell you. (A brief history of England follows.) When Brutus was king, England was called Brittany. Then followed Vortigern, Uterpendragon, Arthur and Cadwaldre, during whose reign there was a famine. The people fled to little Britanny, where king Alan generously harbored them (121-68). The Angles, the Saxons, and the Jutes eyed England, allied themselves for an invasion and conquered it. They work the land well and crops are plentiful. The Britons in exile are saddened and angered by this conquest of their homeland and return to claim it (169-288). A battle ensues at the end of which the Britons are forced to take refuge in Wales. Vortigern, who had also been routed by Horsa and Hengist, welcomes and honors them. This explains why the Welsh and Britons hate the English, and also why there are three languages and three kings (289-398). The eastern region is East Anglia, which is further divided into three counties: Norfolk, Suffolk and Essex. The Saxons reproduced and the once ravaged lang grows fertile. The second king of East Anglia was a wise old Christian named Offe. As he had no heirs, he decided to go on a pilgrimage to Jerusalem to find out who should inherit his throne. He was royally hosted by his cousin on his way east. His nephew, Edmund, was designated to serve him. Edmund was a beautiful child, well-educated and well-loved (399-502). Offe is struck by the child's wisdom. He continues his pilgrimage, which saddens Edmund; Offe gives him a ring in memory of his service. Edmund's father jokes with him, saying that he is no longer the father, and that Edmund prefers Offe. He then gives Edmund to Offe as a son, and Offe promises to treat him as his own (503-610). Offe behaves piously in Jerusalem, but on the return trip he is stricken by illness. On the verge of death he calls his barons together and asks them to take a ring and letter to Edmund, and also requests that they accept his nephew as their king. Offe dies peacefully after confession. He is the incarnation of faith, hope

and charity (611-754). This particular Offe of whom I speak is not
the one betrayed by Ayelbrict, nor the good Saxon king who abandoned everything to become a monk. The East Anglians mourn
Offe's death, and so do his cousin, the king of Saxony, and his son.
Offe's barons announce his last wish that Edmund be king of East
Anglia, but the father refuses (755-934). After much pleading, the
confused king asks his knights for advice. His eldest and wisest
counselor recommends sending three ships laden with rich presents
to the people of East Anglia, who will then adore Edmund; the
king will be king of Saxony and of East Anglia through his son.
As the two countries are not far from each other, frequent visits
would be possible. But the king still refuses to be separated from
Edmund (935-1110). A Roman widow, now a nun, had received the
gift of prophecy from God, and during one of the king's pilgrimages
to Rome before Edmund's birth, she had spoken with him. They
became good friends since she was wise; gossips whispered that
they were lovers. He remembers her prophetic gift, and the day
she had noticed rays of light miraculously shining out of his feet
(1111-1224). She tells him how she has prayed for him to follow
God, and a bishop interprets the flame as a divine sign that Edmund
should be King of East Anglia and enlarge his father's realm, just
as the flame and sunbeam shine in four directions. The king finally
agrees and has three ships laden with treasures and 240 knights
prepared to escort Edmund to East Anglia. On the fourth day of
the voyage, a wind endangers them, but is calmed through Edmund's
prayers. Edmund prays when they land in the fertile country. Travelling on horseback, he comes upon beautiful fountains whose
waters possess curative powers (1225-1540). After the coronation,
Edmund spends his time in a chapel. His barons lead him to
Attleborough where he remains for a year, learning the art of go-
verning. Offe's death resulted in disputes about his kingdom among
his vassals, and the people, without a leader, turned to crime. The
senechal announces the promise given to Offe to crown Edmund
king and offers two convincing reasons to do so: the child's goodness and the anger of the father that would be incurred if Edmund
were not chosen. The bishop approves and Edmund is crowned in
Bures by bishop Hubert in front of all his people (1541-1788). The
new king displays all the civic virtues and his actions are always
tempered by reason and a sense of measure. He exudes an aura of

sanctity which makes a neighboring lord, Lodbrok, jealous. He and his tree evil sons, Ingar, Hubbe and Bern live in Denmark, hated by all (1789-1948). Lodbrok incites his sons' jealousy by recounting Edmund's power. They set sail with 1000 ships, with the intention of avenging their honor and killing the king and his people. Under Ingar's leadership they disembark at night and slaughter sleeping people. They torture some to learn of Edmund's whereabouts in Hailedun (1949-2202). Ingar sends a messenger to Edmund demanding his wealth and his kingdom. He is given the ultimatum of surrendering or seeing his people killed unless he denies his faith. Edmund weeps and asks his bishop for help, since he refuses to abandon his religion. Edmund tells the messenger that he should be killed, but that he will spare him in imitation of Christ. Ingar is angered and immediately swoops in and captures the king, who is tied to a tree and tortured. His body is so full of arrows that it looks like a porcupine. When Edmund still does not abandon his faith, the invaders decapitate him, and a divine light shines from his body (2203-2522). He suffered to save us, as Christ did. Before leaving, Ingar throws the head into some bushes, which causes consternation among the East Anglians who cannot find it for a proper burial. They search the woods in vain until the head speaks, proof of God's affection for Edmond. A second miracle is manifested when they find a wolf guarding the head. When the wolf realizes that their intentions are good, it behaves gently and returns to the forest (2523-2810). The head is buried with the body and the two parts are miraculously joined as in life. Edmund's remains repose in a little hut in the forest. The sick, blind, deaf and crippled come to him to be cured. The body is finally moved to Beodricksworth (present-day Bury-St-Edmund's), where a chapel, inn and church have been built to commemorate the martyr's death. There is a joyous procession on the day the body is transferred, and it is found to be perfectly preserved (2811-3034). A nun named Oswen takes care of the body, and in reward is granted a very long life. Robbers planning to pillage Edmund's tomb come during the night, but all their attempts fail. The morning worshippers catch the thieves in the act, because the bellringer had been miraculously kept from ringing for the morning service. The bishop Theodred has them executed and then repents of his violence. By fasting and praying he becomes worthy of washing and dressing Edmund's body. I have translated this adventure into French. May God grant me the grace to continue telling of miracles. The world was created 5000 years ago, and St. Edmund was martyred in 870 (3035-3318). East Anglia was then without a king. In Westsex a good Christian king named Eadred avenged Edmund's death in a five-year war against Ingar. The villainous Danes were forced to flee to Normandy, where Charles The Bald repelled them. They wandered from land to land, robbing and killing, until they returned to England to find that Eadred's brother, Alure (Alfred The Great), is king. Edmund's powers annihilate the invaders with famine and pestilence, bringing peace to the country. Pope Martin rewards Alure with a part of the Holy Cross, which is guarded and honored in England to this day. Alure's successors were Edward, Athelston, Edmund, Ealured. Edwi, Edgar and Aielred who had the life of St. Edmund written down (3319-3390).

Lefstan, vicount of the region in which Edmund is buried, exploits the poor. When one woman laments her lot to Edmund, Lefstan becomes furious and sends his men to seize her. Others pray to Edmund for help and he throws Lefstan to the devil. Thus there were two miracles: the woman was saved from death and Lefstan died mad in a ditch outside of town (3391-3696). God showed his love for Edmund another time when an ambitious king, Sven, set out from Denmark to conquer other lands. The good Ulfketel routs the Danish forces after killing hundreds. He gives thanks to Edmund for his help. Another king, the cowardly Aildred, refused to bear arms. He envied four brave knights who sent to Sven to complain of their unjust treatment and to seek revenge. Sven returns to avenge his defeat under Ulfketel, who is determined to destroy him this time (3697-4033). (The manuscript stops here.)

EDWARD

"Al loënge le creatur"

One of two important Lives in verse produced in the Abbey of Barking, the *Life of Edward The Confessor* is based on the *Vita S. Edwardi Regis et Confessoris* by Ailred of Rievaulx, written in commemoration of the transferral of the relics of St. Edward in 1163.[1] The *terminus ad quem* of 1170 has been favored by Södergard based on the friendly attitude of the author toward Henry II.[2] Legge believes it was composed nearer 1163, before the outbreak of the quarrel with the Church at Clarendon in 1164.[3] MacBain studied the vocabulary and syntax of the poem, comparing it to the *Life of St. Catherine,* and found striking similarities in the language, style and subject matter.[4] He has suggested that *Edouard* might be an earlier work by Clemence of Barking and *Catherine* a more mature one.

The life was evidently a popular one, given the number of versions and MSS in different languages.[5] This OF version is found in 3 MSS, none of which is complete:

---

[1] Migne, *Patrologia Latina,* CXCV, col. 739.

[2] Osten Södergard, *La Vie d'Edouard le Confesseur, poème anglonormand du XIIème siècle* (Upsala, 1948).

[3] M. D. Legge, *Anglo-Norman Literature and its Background* (Oxford: Clarendon Press, 1963).

[4] William MacBain, "The Literary Apprenticeship of Clemence of Barking," *Journal of the Australasian Universities Language and Literature Association,* 9 (1958), 3-22.

[5] For a list see Södergard, pp. 37-46.

1) W.—Welbeck Abbey 1C1, fol. 55c-85c (4,239 lines). [6]
2) V.—Vatican, Reg. Lat. 489, fol. 1a-35b (5,222 lines). [7]
3) P.—Paris, Bibliothèque Nationale, fr. 1416, fol. 157a-181b
(ll. 69-4,482). [8]

There is also a short fragment of 240 lines, identical to MS W
except for the prologue. [9] The final collated version as published by
Södergard comprises 6,685 octosyllabic lines, as usual rhyming in
pairs.

The development of the legend has been treated by R. Fritz. [10]
No literary study other than those mentioned has been done on
the *Life* to date. Louis Réau has treated its iconography. [11]

A narrative summary of the story follows.

I apologize for my poor French: I have never been to France
to learn it. I undertake this work for the glory of God and hope
that it will please Edward, beloved of God. The saint scorned
riches and received God's grace. That is my hope also (1-68).
Edelred, king of England, married Emma, the daughter of the Duke
of Normandy (69-142). Shortly after the birth of their second son,
the Danes started their invasion and the English asked their king
to pick a successor. Edelred asked them which they preferred, and
the country was divided between those who wanted Edmund and
those who chose Alvred. God made known his choice, and fidelity
was sworn to the unborn child (143-266). Edward, the future king,
dedicated himself to God. Shortly after his birth the Danes invaded
again, forcing King Edelred to lead his family to Normandy.
Edward was a joy to all who knew him: he treated the poor as

---

[6] Described by A. Strong, *A Catalogue of Letters and Other Historical Documents Exhibited in the Library of Welbeck Abbey* (London, 1903).

[7] Described by E. Langlois, in *Notices et Extraits des Manuscrits de la Bibliothèque Nationale*, Vol. 33, Pt. 2 (1906), 10.

[8] Thomas Arnold pointed out that these lines had been substituted for lines 14763-74 of Wace's *Brut* in a MS of that text; see his edition, *Le Roman de Brut de Wace*, 2 vols. (Paris: Société des Anciens Textes Français, 1938-40).

[9] A. T. Baker discovered it, and announced its publication, but the MS has since disappeared ("Fragment of an Anglo-Norman Life of Edward the Confessor," *Modern Language Review*, 3 [1907-1908], 374-375).

[10] R. Fritz, *Uber Verfasser und Quellen der altfranzösischen Estoire de Seint Aedward le Rei* (Heidelberg: Marcus Zöller, 1910).

[11] Louis Réau, *L'Iconographie des Saints*, Vol. III, Pt. 1 of *L'Iconographie de l'art chrétien* (Paris: Presses Universitaires de France, 1958), pp. 411-413.

his equal, and adapted himself to his companions (267-354). England
was still at war against the Danes. The bishop of Winchester,
Brihwald, had a vision of St. Peter choosing a king. When he
requested an explanation, Peter told him that the people's sins were
being punished and that eventually God would choose a man to
banish their enemies and restore justice to the realm (355-510).
When Brihwald urged the English to repent they did not believe
his vision, and at the king's death the majority of the population
surrendered to Knut, thereby violating their oath. Edmund was
given to the Danes, and Alvred was captured and killed when he
came to England to see his mother. Edward prayed God for help.
After Knut's death, the English asked Edward to return. He restored
peace and faith in his kingdom, and his worth was recognized by
neighboring rulers (511-850). Edward championed the poor, shared
his wealth with the needy and was never proud or unjust. The
king's virtues were not diminished by his power and wealth, nor
did he regret the loss of his riches (851-978). The king's entourage
urged him to marry and beget an heir. Edward feared that a marriage would offend God. However, as he was afraid to reveal his
chastity, he agreed to marry, all the while praying to God to
preserve his virginity. He declared himself willing to marry any
woman as long as she was worthy of him in birth, character and
wisdom. Edith, daughter of the treacherous and powerful Count
Godwin, was such a pure woman. She was much admired for her
education and devotion to good deeds. Her father (who had betrayed Alvred) hoped to secure a pardon by marrying her to Edward,
and urged his friends to counsel Edward in her favor. Edward
agreed, and he begged his wife not to betray God by a worldly
love, to which she agreed happily. The two enjoyed a friendship
devoid of all sin or desire. God rewarded Edward with the power
of prophecy (979-1462). Edward's first vision was at his coronation
ceremony at Easter, in which he saw the Danes preparing another
attack, but their king slipped into the sea and drowned (1463-1640).
Edward had promised God to make a pilgrimage to St. Peter's if
he were allowed to regain his throne, and now he wished to fulfill
this promise. His people would not let him depart, fearing invasion,
or an accident that would kill him. The envoy he sent to the Pope
returned with a dispensation: Pope Leo ordered him to build a
church honoring St. Peter and to give away his wealth to the poor

(1641-2018). To reassure Edward, St. Peter appeared to a man who lived undergound (to escape sin), and revealed what had happened in Rome. This hermit had the story written and sent to the king. It caused much joy (2019-2204). A cripple came to Edward to be cured, for God had foretold that if the king carried him to the altar of Westminster, he would be cured. It happened as God had predicted (2205-2480). Edward devoted all of his care to Kent, because of the miracle that had occurred there at the church of St. Peter (2481-2696). The king sent another envoy to the Pope, asking if he had accomplished his mission, begging Nicholas to renew the grace bestowed on him by Leo, and to pray for England's safety (2697-2800). Nicholas did all of this. In order to dedicate himself completely to God, Edward handed the government of the country to some of his princes (2801-2960). In Westminster one day, Jesus appeared to Edward and to Count Lievrich. They agreed never to speak of the vision, but the count had it written down, and after Edward's death the letter was found (2961-3074). After this miracle Edward's healing power increased: he cured a woman of scrofula and barrenness; he cured several blind people by letting them wash with his towel and water (3075-3692). His gift of prophecy demonstrated itself in the case of Harold and Tostig, Godwin's sons. He foretold (after watching them fight) that their hate would grow until Harold banished his brother; later he would kill him, but expiate his sin (3693-3766). The king was well aware of Godwin's sins and treacheries. At a feast to which all the lords were invited, a steward tripped but righted himself, his feet helping each other (Godwin remarked) as brothers normally help each other. King Edward's veiled remark about his brother not being able to aid him because Godwin had not allowed it, upset the latter so deeply that, to prove his innocence, he asked God to let him swallow the morsel he was chewing. It stuck in his throat and he choked to death (3767-3932). At his coronation, Edward had a vision in which plague and famine and pagan invasions attacked the Christians. His listeners asked the bishop of Ephèse to verify it, which he did, and the prophecy was fulfilled (3933-4164).

   Edward was aging, and although his soul was strong, his body was weakening. He had particularly revered two saints: Peter and John, and he finally decided that he preferred Peter. One day John appeared before him disguised as a pilgrim begging for alms, and, having no money, Edward gave him his own ring (4165-4476). When Edward realized he was dying he gave all his money to the poor and the orphans. He had wanted to consecrate his church at Westminster, but because of Christmas, he had to wait a few days. At the ceremony he hid his agony and donated his riches to the church. During the consecration mass, he was so weak that Edith had to support him (4477-4638). The queen, who never left his side, and intimate friends surrounded his deathbed. After two days of unconsciousness the king sat up and implored God to be merciful with his people. He told them of his last vision: Peter and John had announced the punishment of his people. There was no hope of salvation for them, because they feared nothing. The saints described a miraculous event after which the English could hope for some mercy. This prophecy was also fulfilled in the conquest of 1066 (4639-4912). Edward's last requests were the protection and honoring of Edith, and good treatment for his Norman companions. He asked that he be buried in his church of St. Peter. At his death on January 5, 1066, he had ruled 23 years, six months and twenty-seven days; the grief was terrible (4913-5275). The author intervenes to say that this Life was written in Barking (5276-5335). Many miracle-cures of cripples and the blind were worked after his death (5336-5501). Edward's gift of prophecy was demonstrated again during the war between Tostig and Harold: the saint appeared to Harold of England and told him how to conquer his foes, which he did. This fulfilled Edward's prophecy, made when he saw the brothers fighting (5502-5601). Two more miracles involving a blind man and Saint Ulstan were worked by St. Edward (5602-5949).

Several members of the clergy at Westminster wondered about the state of Edward's body, and finally it was decided to examine it. The king's clothes and body were as beautiful as at his death 36 years before (5950-6071). The poem closes with descriptions of Edward's further miracle-cures of paralytics and those suffering from fevers (6072-6685).

EVROUL

"Li haut conseil et l'ordenance"

Evroul is one of the lesser known saints whose popularity was limited to the specific region of Normandy. Remains of the cloister St. Evroult d'Ouche near Argentan (Orne) can be visited today. His feast day is December 29,[1] and mention of him can be found in the oldest missel of the diocese of Lisieux. This *Life* exists in only one MS: Paris, Bibliothèque Nationale, fr. 19867, and has been edited but once.[2] The Latin source is the second part of Orderic Vitalis' *Historia Ecclesiastica* written between 1131-41. Of the twelve Latin MSS, the poet of the OF version probably had before his eyes two of them: Lat. 5506 and Lat. 10913.[3]

King Henry is mentioned in line 4255, and Danne identifies him as Henry I, second son of William The Conqueror, who visited St. Evroul's in 1113. He dates the *Life* in the second half of the twelfth century.[4]

From the tone of the work, Danne concludes that the author was probably an educated monk of St. Evroul's. He remains anonymous: all that is known is that he was a Norman. He must not have lived after 1214, the year in which the relics were transported to the cloister, a fact the author would have mentioned had he been alive.

---

[1] Therefore the Bollandists have not yet treated the *Lives* of this saint.

[2] Ferdinand Danne, "Das altfranzösische Ebrulfusleben, eine Dictung aus dem 12. Jahrhundert", *Romanische Forschungen*, 32 (1913), 748-893.

[3] *Ibid.*, introduction.

[4] Langfors places it immediately after 1150 (*Romania*, 46 [1915-17], 102-103).

The 4,397 octosyllabic lines rhyming in pairs recount the following story:

By example, Evroul proves God's mercy and provides us with
proof that the weak and sinful may be saved (1-38). Evroul was
a luminary, destined to follow God from birth. His father was from
Bayeux and loved by all. Evroul was born in answer to his prayers
(39-120). The child led a life of simplicity until age fifteen (121-78).
Clotaire, King of France, sent for Evroul, having heard of his
goodness, and asked him to be his counsellor. The saint refuses this
worldly honor (179-234). His parents urge him to marry a rich
neighbor's daughter. After the ceremony Evroul is torn between
his marital duty and his desire to remain chaste according to St.
Paul's words. After many months of inner turmoil he finally speaks
to his wife, who feels relieved for she suffers from the same internal
struggle (235-424). Evroul outlines the glories of a celestial life and
the temporary joys of this world. The wife accepts his wishes and
asks only that he teach her how to obey (425-538). Evroul suggests
that they leave this world devoid of charity. They give their wealth
to the poor, she enters a convent and he becomes a monk at the
Abbey of Deux Jumeaux (539-680). The Abbey was named after
two twin infants who had died before baptism. Evroul was such
a successful monk in demand by the knights of the area, that he
wants to leave for the desert to flee the honors of this world. His
example inspires others to follow him (681-828). They leave for
Montfort and settle in the Ouche Forest near some water. In answer
to their prayers an angel appears to tell them where to build their
church. A thief whose hideout is in the forest, tries to persuade
Evroul that the land is barren and fit only for his sort. Evroul
answers that he is not afraid of those who kill bodies, and that his
mission is to save souls. He speaks of the power of forgiveness and
urges the robber to repent. He is converted, falls to his knees
and becomes a monk, proving that the forest is a place for saintly
hermits and monks, not thieves (829-1104). This was the first in a
long line: others of the band became monks, some laborors; all
were good Christians. They build a church where Evroul continues
to be an example of patience, abstinence and prayer. Now you
know enough of his life. It is time to tell of his miracles (1105-1210).

One day, against the wishes of the monk in charge of food,
Evroul insists that he give the last piece of bread to a poor man.

The monk runs after the man, gives him the bread, whereupon the man drives his staff into the ground, giving rise to a fountain. The water has curative powers which attract sufferers from far and wide. Beranger inherited this land and waxes angry, for the pilgrims ruin his crops en route to the fountain. The miraculous cures cease as long as Beranger or his heirs lay claim to the land (1211-1340).

But let's return to the story. When the monk had given the bread to the poor man, a merchant arrives and donates meat to the abbey. Attracted by the wealth of the religious community, two thieves plan a robbery. Evroul devines their intention, speaks to them in a forgiving tone and they renounce evil to become monks in the abbey. Evroul continues to be an example for all. His fame spreads as does his establishment, now numbering fifteen whose names I have forgotten (1341-1572).

His fame reached the ears of King Childebert who wishes to remove the relics with him. But the relics remain solidly in the ground, immovable until the Queen confesses her sins and promises to build another church. She fulfills her promise and for many years in another part of the forest, near Charenton, there was a beautiful marble chapel dedicated to the Virgin Mary. Later it fell into ruins. "Viel" tells of these things. One man took away a piece of the marble, hid it for his private devotion and told only his godson Marc of the whereabouts. Two monks possessed by the devil kill each other and Marc relates the story. Evroul pursues the devil and pushes him into an oven. Some women preparing to bake bread are distressed, but Evroul tells them to put the loaves in front of the oven where they are miraculously cooked without flame. That is how the place received its name: Eschaufour. Then Evroul ressuscitates the two monks, hears their confession and buries them (1573-1916).

One day after mass a candle was left burning. It soon consumed the book containing the written account of miracles. That is why we only know what legend and memory have given us. After twenty-two years at Deux Jumeaux, Evroul calls his flock together exhorting them to fight against the devil. Once, a monk, Aubert, dies without confession or communion. Evroul brings him to life so that he may die in peace. The devil redoubles his effort and 78 monks die. On Christmas a good and diligent administrator of the abbey dies and Evroul brings him back to life. He spends the rest of his life praying and working. Evroul receives anyone, rich or poor, nobles and pilgrims. He cures the sick (1917-2264).

One day a wealthy noble lady suffering from a fever arrives, drawn by the renown of Evroul. She is cured. A poor sick man comes too, so weak he must crawl, and he, too, is cured. After 24 years Evroul knew his time to die had come. He calls his companions together and asks that they always be sober, chaste and humble, and to avoid pride. He died on the fourth day of Calends in January. One of his dear friends, a humble devoted monk, laments his parting and dies of grief. They are buried side by side. Evroul is with the heavenly Father. May we abandon our sins with his help. Here ends the life of saint Evroul "in galico." (2265-2604).

(Lines 2605-3424 recount the battle between the Danes and the French. Evroul plays only a minor part in this section: his abbey becomes a refuge for one of the camps, his relics are part of the booty seized by the enemy, and the abbey is abandoned).

(Lines 3425-4397 tell how a priest returns to Evroul's abbey where he served God. A peasant's bull discovers the altar. The peasant and his family remained there for the rest of their lives. Others happen upon the abbey later, and little by little the church is restored, and the relics returned. Miracles attributed to Evroul's relics continue. Thus ends the account of the miracles of St. Evroul).

GENEVIEVE

"La dame de Valois me prie"

The *Life of Saint Genevieve* was written upon the request of the "dame de Valois" by a certain Renaut who names himself at the end of the poem:

> Renauz qui ceste vie dit
> Ne puet trover plus en escrit.
> Sachiez bien qu'il vos a conté
> De l'estoire la verité,
> Ce qu'il en escrit en trova. [1]

The only fact he provides us is that he is a "clerc." Attempts to identify Renaut and the *dame de Valois* have produced varying results. L. Bohm presents a mise-au-point of the various findings and develops his argument in favor of identifying the *dame de Valois* as Eleanor de Vermandois. [2] This places the *terminus a quo* at 1182 or 1183, the year she became a Valois, and the *terminus ad quem* at 1214, the year of her death. Renaut had previously been identified as Renaut de Marizy, prior at Ste. Genevieve's in 1296, chancelor in 1306, mentioned in *Gallia Christiana*. [3] According to Gröber, Renaut would also be the author of *La Vie de Saint Jehan Bouche d'or*. [4] The editor of this Life, however, shows this

---

[1] Lennart Bohm, *La Vie de sainte Geneviève de Paris* (Upsala, 1955), lines 3575-79.

[2] *Ibid.,* pp. 50-62.

[3] Petit, *Charles de Valois,* p. 228. *Gallia Christiana*, VII p. 748. Cited by Bohm.

[4] G. Gröber, *Grundiss der romanischen Philologie*, Vol. II, Pt. 1, p. 924.

to be erroneous. [5] Renaut is not an unusual name and Bohm finds references to other Renauts in necrologies pre-dating the late 13th century. There is nothing in his argument, however, which permits us to identify definitely the author of the poem. Based on historical and linguistic criteria, he establishes the date of composition around the year 1200.

This late 12th-century version is found in three MSS:

1) A.—Paris, Bibliothèque nationale, lat. 5667, fol. 35r-95v. (Barrois 179). [6]

2) B.—Paris, Bibliothèque nationale, fr. 13508, fol. 1r-27r. [7]

3) C.—Paris, Bibliothèque Ste. Geneviève, 1283, fol. 80r-113r.

Renaut often refers to a source. The Latin versions were the subject of a study by Charles Kohler. [8] He classified the 29 MSS into four families, the latter containing 14 MSS. The 12th-century vernacular version has its source in this fourth family of MSS, but no single MS is identical to Renaut's version. Bohm discusses the Latin sources at length and gives a table of concordance, showing that the order of episodes has been treated very freely, and that it is impossible to discern one single Latin MS as the definitive source.

Patron saint of Paris, Genevieve was born in Nanterre, c. 420 and died in Paris, c. 500. The idea that she was a shepherdess is probably a contamination by the legend of Saint Margaret. Evidence suggests that she was of a noble family. The iconography of the saint has been detailed by Louis Réau. [9]

As is the case with most 12th-century saints' Lives, *Geneviève* is written in octosyllabic verse, rhyming in couplets. It has been the

---

[5] Dirickx van der Straeten, *La Vie de Saint Jehan Bouche d'Or et la Vie de Sainte Dieudonnée, sa mère* (Liège: Vaillant-Carmanne, 1931), p. 21.

[6] For a description see L. Delisle, *Catalogue des Manuscrits des fonds Libri et Barrois* (Paris: Bibliothèque Nationale, nd), p. 207.

[7] *Catalogue général des Manuscrits, Bibliothèque Nationale, Ancien supplément français*, Vol. III, p. 67.

[8] C. Kohler, *Etude critique sur le texte de la vie latine de Sainte Geneviève de Paris, avec deux textes de cette vie. Bibliothèque de l'Ecole des Hautes Etudes*, n.º 48 (Paris: Vieweg, 1881).

[9] Louis Réau, *L'Iconographie des Saints*, Vol. III, Pt. 3 of *L'Iconographie de l'art chrétien* (Paris, Presses universitaires de France, 1958), pp. 563-568.

subject of no literary treatment. The 3,632 lines tell the following story:

I have translated into French the Latin history of the life of Saint Genevieve at the command of the *dame de Valois,* so as to make it accessible to all (1-20). Genevieve's family belonged to the bourgeoisie of Nanterre. St. Germain of Auxerre and St. Loup of Troyes, aroused by the heresy in England voyaged there to fight it. On their way they passed through Nanterre. In the crowd that surrounded them, Germain noticed Genevieve and sensed her divine election. He asked Genevieve if she would dedicate herself to God, and the child promised immediately. When the saints leave town they give her a coin stamped with the cross, and exhort her to lead a true Christian life (21-300). Genevieve's first miracle occurred when God, in anger at Genevieve's mother for making her daughter stay home from church, blinded her as punishment. Twenty-one months later Genevieve restores her mother's sight by washing her eyes in water she had drawn and blessed. When it came time to take the veil, Genevieve went to Chartres with two older friends. Contrary to custom, Genevieve, the youngest, was initiated first (301-474).

After her parents' death she moved to Paris where she was struck by a malady and paralyzed. An angel, however, bore her to Heaven and Hell so that she could understand both. St. Germain passed through Paris shortly thereafter, and learning of Genevieve's presence he went to visit her and pay his respects. To the astounded Parisians, Germain explained his revelation of her vocation in Nanterre (475-639). News of the Hun invasion reached Paris and the people wanted to abandon the city for safer places. Genevieve's exhortations to trust in God were not only ignored, many Parisians looked on her as a false prophetess and pondered how to get rid of her. An archdeacon from Auxerre who had heard about Genevieve from Germain, was passing through Paris at this time. When he heard that the people were planning to kill her he announced that one should listen to her prophecies as she was one of God's chosen. He evoked other saints who had preserved the city in order to calm their fears, and convince them of Genevieve's power (640-800).

Genevieve led a life of prayer and mortification, eating but twice a week, and then only bread and water. She followed this regimen until the age of fifty when the bishops, frightened by her physical weakness, ordered her to eat more (801-900). She performed several miracles in connection with the construction of the Chapel of St. Denis. Once she filled an empty pitcher with water and it was full until the end of the building, although everyone drank from it every day (901-1130). Walking to the chapel through a storm one night, the candle in her companion's hand was extinguished; but when Genevieve took it, it started burning, and did so until they reached the church. She cured the sick and lame as Jesus had done (1131-1292).

A pagan king had imprisonned some Christians in Paris whom Genevieve decided to save. Because she could not leave the city (the gates were locked), she prayed God to help her reach the king so she could plead with him. She succeeded in securing his mercy. Upon request from her maidservant, who admired Genevieve's pure life, the saint helped her escape from her fiancé and reach a convent where she found a life of abstinence and chastity (1293-1494). Genevieve performed many such miracles, exorcising devils, resurrecting the dead, healing paralytics and those whom God punished for their sins towards her or Him (1495-1770). For her goodness and purity, Genevieve was much praised and honored, but she continued her humble and virtuous life (1771-2152). As her fame as a healer spread, more and more people came to her for help (2153-2490).

Genevieve was in Orleans at the time of the election of the new bishop. St. Ivultres (Evurce), learning she was there, hurried to meet her. A white dove landed on his shoulder during the ceremony in the church of St. Martin, and the people accepted him as God's chosen. God advised Ivultres that only Genevieve could keep the demons out of the church (2491-2604). Genevieve died on January third at the age of 80, and was buried outside the city on a hill that has been known since as Mount St. Genevieve (2605-2650).

I regret being unable to recount all of the miracles which Genevieve worked after her death, but I promise to tell faithfully all those I have found written down. A deaf-mute was cured when he reached Genevieve's tomb and two paralytics were likewise cured. Most of her miracles are of two types: the deliverance of those possessed by demons, and the healing of those afflicted with some malady or other physical handicap (2651-2758). During the first Norman attack on Paris, Genevieve's bones were removed to Athis and then to the greater safety of Draveil (2759-3064). They were returned to the church when the danger had passed. In 1129 an epidemic struck Paris and neither the Virgin nor the other saints could cure the more than 100 afflicted. When the bones of St. Genevieve were brought into the city all of the sick, excepting three heathen, were cured (3065-3115). During subsequent Norman attacks, the relics were carried first to Draveil and then later to Marizy where they remained for five years (3116-3574).

I assure you that I have not omitted anything. I hope that the *Dame de Valois* will be pleased with the work she ordered, and that God will not forget me (3575-3632).

GEORGE I

"Sages est qui sen escrit"

The *Life of St. George* by Simund de Freine offers a unique
example in twelfth-century versification, by virtue of being written
in seven syllables, rhyming in pairs. The author names himself in
an acrostic, "Simund de Freine me fist," found in the opening lines
of both his *Georgs* and the *Roman de Philosophie*. [1]

John Matzke has done a thorough study of the development of
the legend and has established the scant information known about
the author. [2] From references to Simund in two Latin poems addressed by him to Giraldus Cambrensis, [3] Matzke concludes that
Simund was a canon at the Cathedral of Hereford in Wales, that
he was born before 1147 and was still living in 1216. Matzke's
linguistic analysis places the date of composition at the end of
the twelfth century, posterior to the *Roman de Philosophie*, and
probably inspired by the third Crusade under Richard the Lion-
hearted (1189-93). George was hailed as the special guardian saint
of the English knights during this crusade and in 1222, on his

---

[1] John E. Matzke, *Les Oeuvres de Simund de Freine, publiées d'après
tous les textes manuscrits connus* (Paris: Société des Anciens Textes Français, 1909).

[2] Matzke, *Ibid.*, xi; "The Anglo-Norman Poet Simund de Freine,"
Transactions and Proceedings of the American Philological Association, 33
(1902), xc; and "Contributions to the History of the Legend of Saint George,
with Special Reference to the Sources of the French, German and Anglo-
Saxon Metrical Versions," *Publications of the Modern Language Association*, 17 (1902), 464-535, and 18 (1903), 99-171.

[3] *Geraldi Cambrensis Opera*, Rolls Series, I, p. 382. Cited by Matzke.

feast day of April 23, he was proclaimed patron saint of England. [4]

In his very careful and complete study of the development of the legend of St. George, Matzke provides a detailed analysis of all extant versions in all languages, pointing out the uniqueness of each and/or the indebtedness of each. A summary of his findings follows and the reader is referred to his article in two parts if further information is desired.

The most widely spread Latin version known during the Middle Ages was the aprocryphal version, called O. [5] The Bollandists' treatment can be found in *Acta Sanctorum*, Apr. III, 101-65. In 494, Pope Gelasius termed the account apocryphal, and the story was changed: the name of Diocletian was introduced to connect the death of the saint with the tenth persecution of the Christians; the tortures he suffered, and the miracles he wrought were both reduced.

Simund's source remains unknown, since the order of events differ from that in O, and some features are absent from O. The Greek form had apparently no influence on Simund's version. A detailed comparison of the Coptic, [6] Syriac, [7] and Arabic [8] versions shows that they all derive from a common source.

The appearance of the dragon, which is today so readily associated with George, stems from the *Legenda Aurea*, and is therefore not found in the twelfth-century versions.

Simund's version is preserved in two MSS:

1)—Paris, Bibliothèque nationale, fr. 902, fol. 108v-117v.

2)—Dublin, Trinity College, C. 4. 2, fol. 46b-52.

Matzke knew only the first when he published his edition. Marius Esposito thought it would be useful to see if the Dublin MS, that

---

[4] *Ibid.*, pp. 147-155.

[5] Wilhelm Arndt, *Berichte über die Verhandlungen der K. sächs. Gesellschaft der Wissenschaften zu Leipzig* (Phil.-Hist. Klasse, 1875), pp. 43-70.

[6] E. A. Wallis Budge, *The Martyrdom and Miracles of Saint George of Cappadocia. The Coptic Text Edited with an English Translation* (London, 1885).

[7] Dillman, "Uber die apokryphischen Märtyrer-geschichten des Cyriacus mit Julitta und des Georgius," *Sitzb. d. k. preuss. Acad. d. Wiss. zu Berlin* (Phil.-Hist. Klasse, 1887), p. 339ff. Cited by Matzke.

[8] Known to Matzke only through an account given in Dillman, *Ibid.*

he first brought to the attention of scholars, could allow corrections in the readings of the Paris MS, which is rather faulty. [9]

At the date of this writing no literary criticism has appeared. [10] The story, as told by Simund in 1,711 lines, is the following:

I shall tell you the story of St. George who was martyred for defending his faith in God. Dacien, emperor of Rome, calls a council to determine what measures to take against the Christians. Thirty-two kings attend and decide to torture all those who confess to being Christians. A young Christian knight from Cappadocia appears: George affirms his intention to confess his faith before Dacien and to request that the emperor cease the persecutions (1-158). The two engage in a discussion of the merits of their respective gods. George promises to believe in the "true God" and when Dacien embraces him for joy, the saint again professes his faith in the Trinity. Angered, Dacien orders the tortures to begin (159-429).

George is placed on a bench. Weights of iron and lead are attached to his feet, a fire is lighted beneath him, he is pierced with lances, and poison is poured into his wounds, but all this does not affect him. He is whipped and salt is put on his open wounds. Blood flows from his feet like water from a fountain. He still feels no pain. He is taken to prison where God appears to him, tells him to be courageous for he will suffer greatly, and that he will die three times, but the fourth will bring him to paradise (430-498).

The following day he again undergoes tortures. He dies and his body is thrown into a well. God and the archangel Michel appear in a cloud and an earthquake is felt. George resuscitates and goes straight to Dacien who cannot believe his eyes (499-568).

A pagan, Magnacius, states that he is ready to believe in God, provided George can change fourteen thrones into fruit-bearing trees. George accomplishes the miracle and Magnacius is baptized along with more than one hundred others (569-94).

---

[9] M. Esposito, "Inventaire des anciens manuscrits français des bibliothèques de Dublin," *Revue des Bibliothèques,* 24 (1914), 185-198.

[10] Other than the studies of Matzke and others mentioned, there is a short article by J. Archer, "Sur un calembour méconnu de Simund de Freine," *Zeitschrift für romanische Philologie,* 34 (1910), 211-212, and a short section in M. D. Legge, *Anglo-Norman Literature and its Background* (Oxford: Clarendon Press, 1963).

Dacien sends for a magician, Anastasius, who displays his powers by cutting a bull in two and then rejoining the parts. He prepares a poison which George drinks, suffering no discomfort. Anastasius is converted, executed, and carried to heaven (595-647).

The tortures continue: sixty nails are driven into George's head, it is cut in two, he is thrown in a caldron of boiling tar. When the body is completely dissolved, St. Michel comes to put it back together, Christ blesses it and George resuscitates again. Those who witness this miracle are converted. George strikes the ground with his foot and a fountain surges forth. He uses the water to baptize five hundred persons. They parade before the emperor, confessing their new faith. Dacien thinks that George is a magician (648-725).

George is taken to the house of a poor widow. When he asks for bread she has none to give him. In conversation, he discovers her belief in Apollo, which accounts for her poverty. While she leaves to borrow bread, George enlarges her hut, fills the table with meat and drink. At her return she is astonished, believes George to be a god and falls at his feet. She speaks of her son who is deaf, mute, blind and crippled. If George can cure him, she promises that both will convert. He cures the son, but leaves him crippled, saying that she will understand why later (726-828).

A woman comes to lament the death of her bull. George comforts her and revives the animal (829-63).

Dacien arrives and is surprised by the new appearance of the hut. George tells him that it is the result of the powers of the true God. Dacien promises him riches if he will make a sacrifice to Apollo. George feigns acceptance. The widow reproaches him for denying his faith. George is so delighted with her fervor that he makes her son walk. He goes to the temple of Apollo where 2,500 people accompany him. He addresses the idol, forces it to show its hideous face and to confess that it has no power. George strikes the ground, the earth opens up and swallows the idol. Then he breaks the other statues. Dacien, at a new height of anger, orders new tortures (864-1121).

Torches are applied to George's body until it is reduced to ashes. What remains is taken to the top of a mountain to feed the crows. But God had promised to resuscitate him three times and He keeps his promise. Many who witnessed the miracle convert (1122-67).

Dacien heats two iron boots which he puts on the martyr. George feels nothing. The emperor then throws him into a ditch full of wild animals who do not harm the saint (1168-1215).

When the queen Alexandrine sees this miracle she is converted. Dacien tries to reason with her, but she remains firm. In her turn, she is hung by her hair and tortured. George baptizes her with rain which falls at his command. She is put to death, and her soul is received in paradise (1216-1364).

Dacien says he will pardon George provided he can resuscitate the dead. A tomb is opened, disclosing only some ashes. After a long prayer, five men, nine women and three children are brought to life. They kneel before George and beg him not to return them to the torments they have just known. One of them, Joel, tells how he worshipped Apollo more than 200 years ago, and describes the hell he has known since. George baptizes them and they go to paradise (1365-1526).

Dacien becomes so angry that his belt breaks and he falls from his chair. He again orders the death of the saint who is decapitated after a lengthy prayer. Angels carry his soul to heaven. The noblemen of the city bury George at night in a church where many miracles have occurred since (1527-1685).

Dacien and his faithful entourage are annihilated by heavenly flames and go to hell (1686-1711).

GEORGE II

"Bel gent, qui venuz este ensemble"

A poem in octosyllabic verse dating from approximately the same period as *Georges I* [1] has been published but once. [2] Luzarche attributed this version to Wace, but this has been found to be an erroneous attribution. [3] Although, according to Matzke, [4] Weber's material was insufficient for him to reach valid conclusions, the attribution to Wace remains unsubstantiated. The source and the author are unknown. It is found in only one MS: Tours 927, fol. 47. [5]

Luzarche's edition is not readily available nor easy to use, since the lines are not numbered. It is, however, the only edition of this version. The differences between *Georges I* and *II* have been detailed by Matzke. [6] The brevity of the pseudo-Wace version (478 lines) deletes many details found in *Georges I*, as can be ascertained by the following summary:

I have come to tell you the story of Saint George the martyr. He was a Christian knight of noble lineage. During his life Dacien

---

[1] Holger Petersen, "Une Vie inédite de Saint George," *Neuphilologische Mitteilungen*, 28 (1926), 1-7.

[2] V. Luzarche, *La Vie de la Vierge Marie, par Wace, suivie de la Vie de Saint Georges* (Tours: Bouserez, 1858).

[3] C. Weber, "Uber die Sprache und Quelle des altfrz. hl. Georg.," *Zeitschrift für romanische Philologie*, 5 (1881), 498-520.

[4] John E. Matzke, "Contributions to the History of the Legend of Saint George, with Special Reference to the Sources of the French, German and Anglo-Saxon Metrical Versions," *Publications of the Modern Language Association*, 18 (1903), 112-115.

[5] For a description, see L. Delisle, "Notices," *Romania*, 2 (1873), 91-95.

[6] Matzke, *op. cit.*, 112-115.

was emperor, and he hated God and the Christians. In his desire to wage war on Christ he announces his intention to torture all Christians who keep their faith, and describes the various methods of torture. In Cappadocia George hears of this and goes to Militaine to confront Dacien. He is surprised to find the worship of idols, and tells Dacien of his own God. The emperor promises him wealth and succession to the throne if he abandons his faith. George retorts that worldly riches are ephemeral. Dacien is moved by the saint's beauty and says he would be grieved if he had to put him to death (1-88). George reminds him that his only grief should be his own pagan faith. Dacien then decides to make an example of George and laughs diabolically, while George is tortured and put to death. Dacien asks: "Where is your god now?" The earth moves, George is brought back to life, and asks: "Where are your torments?" Dacien waxes angry. George goes to the home of a poor widow where he fills her table with food and cures her deaf-mute son (89-160).

When Dacien learns of this, he accuses George of trickery. To prove his faith George accepts the challenge of making barren trees bear fruit. Many who saw this miracle were converted, but Dacien persists in not believing, attributing the miracle to the devil. George feigns acquiescence to a sacrificial ceremony to the false idols, only to mock them. In a conversation with Apollo George becomes angry and destroys the idols. This rekindles Dacien's anger and the torture recommences. God extinguishes the fire and the queen is converted. She requests martyrdom and Dacien pleas with her. The worldly comfort he offers does not convince her and she is put to death. She asks George to baptize her before her death, which he does with dew brought by an angel (161-302).

Her soul is taken to heaven. Dacien puts George to another test: he must resuscitate the dead from an ancient tomb. He does and one of them, Jobel, says that they had been dead for 200 years, during which time they had suffered the tortures of hell. He requests baptism for all. George makes the sign of the cross on the ground and a fountain springs up, washing them of their sins. Dacien again angered promises vengeance. George prays once more for the forgiveness of all sinners, and a celestial voice calls for George to come. George waits no longer and goes to paradise in great joy. You have heard of the saintly life of Saint George. May God give you health and joy and hear your prayers (303-478).

GILES

"D'un dulz escrit orrez la sume"

The Life of St. Giles presents a unique phenomenon in twelfth-century hagiography. The author, Guillaume de Berneville, treats his Latin source in the usual manner (amplifications taken whole cloth from his imagination, addition of dialogue in the mouth of the characters, description of characters and analysis of their sentiments, and adaptation of the *Vita* to contemporary tastes). In this case, however, the *Vita Sancti Egidii* is a legendary fabrication with no historical basis. E. C. Jones has done a fascinating study in how this particular legend was born.[1] He demonstrates that the most primitive Latin version[2] was written to give prestige to a monastery in the Flavian Valley during the tenth century. The persistence of the cult is explained in part by the date of his feast day, September 1, thus coinciding with seasonal celebrations such as harvests and the opening of the hunting season. Traditionally Giles has been considered an agrarian saint, patron saint of the woods, shepherds, and protector of the land.

The episode which has interested most scholars concerns Charlemagne's sin. According to Guillaume, Giles is called to Orleans to hear Charlemagne's confession. The king refuses to tell all and the saint prays for him. An angel descends with a letter, informing Giles of the details. The reader is never advised of the nature of Charlemagne's sin in this version or in the *Vita*. Among later

---

[1] E. C. Jones, *Saint Gilles. Essai d'histoire littéraire* (Paris: Champion, 1914).

[2] *Acta Sanctorum,* Sept. I, 299-303, called P by Jones.

references to the emperor's sin, the *Karlamagnus-Saga* (thirteenth century) elucidates: the emperor had incest with his sister and the product of this union was none other than Roland.[3] Baudoin de Gaiffier and Rita Lejeune discuss at length all literary treatments of Charlemagne's sin pointing out differences and resemblances.[4] For Jones, the insertion of such an episode, specific or not in its details, reflects a theological preoccupation of the Church at that time, namely mandatory confession.[5]

Once the *Vita* was written, others followed: at least nine complete and several abridged versions in Latin, which form the focus of Jones' study. There are in addition a number of "translations" into the vernacular:

1) the Anglo-Norman version of Guillaume de Berneville (1170).

2) a fourteenth-century version by Jean de Vignay.

3) an English version by Caxton.

4) an abridged version found in MSS: Bibliothèque Nationale fr. 988 and Lille, 451.

5) a poem by Lydgate.

6) an Italian version of the early fourteenth century.

7) Chronique of Philippe Mousket (early thirteenth century).

In other works Giles is mentioned or plays a major role:

Song of Roland (l. 2096)[6]
Elie de Saint-Gilles
Aiol
Raoul de Cambrai (second part)

---

[3] Gaston Paris, *L'Histoire poétique de Charlemagne* (Paris: Franck, 1863), pp. 378-82.

[4] B. de Gaiffier, "La Légende de Charlemagne, le péché de l'empereur et son pardon," in *Recueil de Travaux Offerts à M. Clovis Brunel* (Paris: Société de l'Ecole des Chartes, 1955), I, p. 490ff. Giles' role is discussed pp. 496-503; and Rita Lejeune, "Le Péché de Charlemagne et la *Chanson de Roland*," *Studia Philologica, Homenaje ofrecido a Dámaso Alonso* (Madrid, 1961), II, pp. 339-371.

[5] For a full discussion of this doctrine, see H. C. Lea, *A History of Auricular Confession and Indulgences in the Latin Church*, 3 vols. (London, 1896).

[6] Joseph Bédier traces the evolution of this theme through the epic in *Légendes épiques* (Paris, 1908-1913), III, p. 357ff.

Tristan de Nanteuil
Parise la Duchesse. [7]

His fame spread as well into the North and to Central Europe. [8] It was, however, displaced, as Aiguemortes became a more important port city in the thirteenth century.

Guillaume de Berneville's version has been published but once. [9] The only MS available at the time is the more complete: Florence, Laurentienne, Conventi Soppressi, 99, fol. 111r-145r. [10] A fragment was published by Louis Brandis which corresponds to lines 2975-3057 of the Paris-Bos edition. [11] Much of the historicity of Giles as presented by Paris has been refuted by Jones. The Latin source is the *Acta Sanctorum* version, [12] which Paris compares to the Old French version of Guillaume. [13]

All we know of the author is that he was "chanoine". [14] Relying on linguistic data and the literary references Guillaume makes, Paris concludes that the author was Norman in origin, of an English family, and that his work dates from 1170 at the earliest. Louis Réau has treated Giles' iconography. [15]

The 3,794 octosyllabic lines rhyming in pairs tell the following story:

I shall tell you the story of a nobleman who left his land and his friends to live among the animals. He was from Greece. Giles was his name. His parents were Theodorus and Pelagia. At seven,

---

[7] These are all discussed in Jones, *op. cit.*, pp. 62-92.

[8] Abbé Ernest Rembry, *Saint Gilles, sa vie, ses reliques, son culte dans la Belgique et le nord de la France*, 2 vols. (Bruges: Gailliard, 1881).

[9] Gaston Paris and Alphonse Bos, *La Vie de saint Gilles par Guillaume de Berneville, poème du XIIème siècle publié d'après le manuscrit unique de Florence* (Paris: Société des Anciens Textes Français, n.° 14, 1881).

[10] For a description see Paris-Bos, *Ibid.*, ii-xiv.

[11] L. Brandin, "Un Fragment de la *Vie de saint Gilles* en vers français," *Romania*, 33 (1904), 94-98.

[12] See footnote 2.

[13] Paris-Bos, *op. cit.*, xxxvi-xlvi. See also Joseph Merk, *Die literarische Gestaltung der altfranzösischen Heiligenleben bis Ende des 12. Jahrhunderts* (Affoltern am Albis: J. Weiss, 1946).

[14] M. D. Legge, *Anglo-Normand Literature and its Background* (Oxford: Clarendon Press, 1963).

[15] Louis Réau, *L'Iconographie des saints*, Vol. III, Pt. 2 of *L'Iconographie de l'art chrétien* (Paris: Presses Universitaires de France, 1958), pp. 593-597.

Giles was a charming blond boy, honest and devoted to God. Other children made fun of him, for he did not want to play. His joy was in the spiritual world (1-98). On his way to school one day, he meets a sickly, crippled child. Giles is moved to tears and gives him his coat. The child is immediately cured. The acclamation of the crowd provokes suffering in Giles. His father questions him about his coat, and the boy launches into a long sermon on charity and fear of chastisement. His father is pleased by such wisdom and buys him an even better coat (99-252).

At the death of his parents, Giles distributes his inheritance among the poor and needy. His barons become upset and urge him to marry to assure continuity of the line. Giles admits he loves a young damsel but asks for delay until St. Martin's Day. Once in church, a man suffering from a snake bite asks for Giles' help. The saint weeps and prays for him and he is cured. This miracle occasions other requests. Overwhelmed, Giles turns to God in prayer, and asks forgiveness for his sins. He decides to go to Rome, but before leaving has a banquet prepared. He feigns joy while all eat and drink merrily. While they sleep, he slips away in the night (253-640).

Anyone who might look for him will find his search to be in vain. The next morning his absence is discovered and everyone grieves. Giles goes to the sea and a ship arrives in answer to his prayer. He embarks with the merchants, after calming a tempest, and sails peacefully towards Rumania. The fifth day at sea they set sight of an island where a hermit greets them, and tells them his story. They take their leave and continue to Marseilles where Giles parts company (641-1058).

Giles leaves the city to look for the bishop Cesaire. Travelling through a forest he finds lodging with a widow, Theocrita, whose mother is sick. Giles intercedes and she is cured. He stays two years and continues to work miracles. Fame is a burden and Giles flees to the forest where he encounters the hermit, Veredimius, living high on a rock. They stay together two years, living a saintly life. One day four men come to ask Giles to cure one of them who had been sick for seven years. Giles remains humble and refers them to Veredimius, but they insist on Giles' intervention. The saint prays, weeps and the sick man is cured. Not wanting to outshine the hermit, Giles leaves in search of solitude (1059-1454).

He finds a cave with a fountain nearby. He stays there three years, seeing no one, and eating only roots. God sends a beautiful doe who gives the saint milk. Flovent, a powerful king at that time, goes on a hunt and pursues the doe almost to the cave. Night falls and the search begins the next day, still to no avail. Flovent asks the bishop for advice and the bishop decides to accompany him. The dogs again find the scent, the doe seeks refuge with Giles, and the saint receives the arrow meant for the doe. They bandage his wounds and Giles tells them his story. Ashamed of having wounded a man of God, Flovent proposes his help, but Giles refuses, wishing to remain solitary. He asks that Flovent build an abbey with his wealth, and the king accepts, providing Giles direct it. Giles is forced to accept the leadership and the church is built (1455-2248).

I can find no more mention of the doe who served him so well. The church is richly adorned and Giles continues to serve God. Charlemagne hears of him and sends messengers to bring him to Orleans. Giles prays for guidance, and asks counsel of his fellow monks. They fear for his health, but give him leave to go. Giles tells his life story again. Charlemagne serves him a sumptuous meal which Giles does not eat. The emperor scolds him and Giles retorts with humor. The next morning after mass, Charlemagne wants to confess to Giles, who comforts him by reciting the sins of the apostles. Charlemagne clains his sin is so great that he cannot confess it. Giles accuses him of being too proud, stays twenty days trying to convince him that his sin will be forgiven. During his stay he cured a man possessed by the devil. Giles continues to pray for Charlemagne and then an angel appears, invisible to all but Giles, bearing a letter explaining the sin. Giles confronts Charlemagne with the knowledge of his sin and assures him of forgiveness. Charlemagne is radiant with joy, and showers gifts on Giles before the saint returns to his abbey. On his return trip, his old wound reopens. He receives treatment and tells of his trip (2249-3276).

He leads a life of an ascetic and decides to go to Rome to solicit recognition for the abbey. The pope receives him, approves the priviledge, and gives him two wooden doors engraved in gold and silver. Giles is troubled since they are too heavy for him to transport. God intervenes and sends them up the Tiber to the port where the abbey is located. Giles feels death near and calls his monks together to choose a new abbot. Giles invokes God in a lengthy prayer and dies. St. Michel carried his soul to heaven (3277-3718).

Now listen to another miracle: this place became a pilgrimage site. Whoever listens to this story can be remitted of sins through Giles' intercession (3719-3794).

GREGORY

The *Life of St. Gregory* is preserved in two versions called A and B. A is still awaiting a critical edition which would take into account all three MSS of this version.[1] However, the two versions differ but slightly: A tends to amplify the basic schema of B. Mario Roques felt that the variations could be included in a single edition.[2] Gerta Telger has produced a valuable critical edition of version B, and it is upon this edition that our study has been based.[3] She outlines the MSS grouping as follows:

1) A_1.—Tours, Bibliothèque municipale, 927.[4]
2) A_2.—Paris, Arsenal, 3516.
3) A_3.—Paris, Bibliothèque nationale, fr. 1545.
4) B_1.—London, British Museum, Egerton 612.
5) B_2.—Paris, Arsenal, 3527.
6) B_3.—Cambrai, Bibliothèque municipale, 812.[5]

---

[1] *La Vie du Pape Grégoire le Grand,* edited by Victor Luzarche (Tours, 1857) was based on A_1 and B_2, with the latter supplying the lacunae of the Tours MS.

[2] M. Roques, "Notes pour l'édition de la *Vie de Saint Grégoire* en ancien français," *Romania,* 77 (1956), 1-25.

[3] G. Telger, *Die altfranzösische Gregoriuslegende nach der Londoner Handschrift Arbeiten zür Romanische Philologie,* n.° 5 (Paris: Droz, 1933).

[4] For a description of all MSS but B_3 see W. Miehle, *Das Verhältnis der Handschriften des altfranzösischen Gregorius,* Diss. (Halle, 1886). Roques (see note 8) disagrees with Miehle's groupings.

[5] Gerd Kraus discusses this MS at length in *Die Handschrift von Cambrai der altfranzösischen Vie de Saint Grégoire,* Diss. (Halle, 1932), as well as group A. Roques again disproves these findings.

The authors of both versions remain anonymous. H. Bieling assumes from the handwriting that B_1, considered the oldest, was written either at the end of the twelfth or the beginning of the thirteenth century. [6] K. Kuchenbäcker establishes the date of composition at the second half of the twelfth century, based on a study of the language. [7] Luzarche puts the date of version A at the first half of the thirteenth century, and no further studies have elucidated this problem. [8]

The legend is wide-spread, but scholars have not yet found any written source. A. H. Krappe concludes: "The legend of St. Gregory is Byzantine or Oriental in origin, dating from the sixth or perhaps fifth century of the Christan era." [9] There are obvious similarities to the Oedipus myth, if only the incest between mother and son. [10] We know of no literary treatment of the legend. Louis Réau has treated its iconography. [11]

Version B_1 comprises 2,078 octosyllabic lines rhyming in pairs. The story is the following (the differences in A and additions of B_2 and B_3 are indicated in parenthesis):

The life recounted here is replete with horrible sins. I tell it to keep others from sin and to combat despair, for divine mercy is assured to the repentent sinner, as is proven by this story of Gregory, who thought the work of the devil was the fruit of incest and who committed incest himself (1-62).

In Aquitaine there lived a count whose wife gave him a son and a daughter, both of incredulous beauty. The mother died, then the count fell sick. Sensing that his end was near, he called his children

---

[6] H. Bieling, *Ein Beitrag zur Uberlieferung des Gregorlegende. Altfranzösischen Bibliothek*, n.º 9 (Berlin, 1874).

[7] K. Kuchenbäcker, *Uber die Sprache des altfranzösischen Gregor B*, Diss. (Halle, 1886).

[8] Mario Roques in his article "Sur deux particularités métriques de la *Vie de Saint Grégoire* en ancien français," *Romania*, 48 (1929), 41-59, concludes that B is anterior to A.

[9] Alexander Haggerty Krappe, "La Légende de Saint Grégoire," *Moyen Age*, 46 (1936), 161-177.

[10] The two have been considered sufficiently different to be classified separately, Aarne-Thompson, *Types of the Folk-tale. Folklore Fellows Communications*, n.º 74 (Helsingfors, 1928), numbers 931 and 933.

[11] Louis Réau, *L'Iconographie des saints*, Vol. III, Pt. 2 of *L'Iconographie de l'art chrétien* (Paris: Presses Universitaires de France, 1958), pp. 609-616.

to his side, summoned his barons and in front of these witnesses entrusted the girl to the care of her brother (62-128).

Both youngsters were fond of each other and their friendship was so perfect that the devil thought he could take advantage of the situation. The young man becomes a prey to an ardent passion, and one night rapes his sister. She remains silent for fear of scandal. Thus Gregory was conceived (129-192).

When the young woman learns of her pregnancy, she tells her brother. Both profoundly stricken with a sense of grief, they seek counsel from a wise knight, an old friend of their father (193-262).

When he learns of their distress, he advises the young count to expiate his sin by a pilgrimage to the Holy Sepulture. He, on the other hand, will keep the young woman with him in his castle and will never divulge anything which could bring shame to her. The young count summons his barons, tells them of his projected pilgrimage and requests that they remain faithful to his sister should he not return from the Holy Land (263-342).

When the baby is born, the mother resolves to send it away because of its impure origin. She wraps it in expensive cloth and places it in a cradle with gold and silver. On tablets she inscribes the story of her sin, a prayer that the child should be raised and educated in such a way as to expiate his sinful origin, and the recommendation that he read these tablets often to remember the crime which weighs upon him. She puts the tablets in the cradle and the cradle in a small barrel. Against their wishes, her protectors take it to a boat which they send off guided only by God and the sea. The young countess is chagrined. A messenger arrives to say that her brother has died and that she should come back to her estate. There she becomes the coveted object of neighboring princes. She refuses all requests for marriage out of penitence (343-596).

The child is found by two fishermen from an abbey. The barrel opens and the child appears laughing. The abbot is pleased with this gift from Heaven, gives the silver to the poorer of the two fishermen, and the child to the other who was wealthy but with no children. The latter will pretend to be the child's grandfather. The abbot himself keeps the gold, the tablets and the cloth (597-766).

The child is baptized and given the name of Gregory. He is raised by his 'grandfather' and educated by the abbot. Af fifteen Gregory inspires the admiration of everyone because of his wisdom, beauty and gentleness. The wife of the first fisherman, piqued by curiosity, managed to learn the story of incest. One day while playing (*pelota*) Gregory strikes the fisherman's son who runs whining to his mother. In retaliation she tells Gregory that in reality he is an abandoned child. Gregory asks the abbot for permission to flee this shame. He wants to become a knight and travel the world to discover the secret of his birth. The abbot shows him the tablets and requests that he stay in the service of God. Gregory refuses and leaves (767-1037).

The devil takes him to the country of his mother where he is retained as soldier. The enemy has just laid siege on the city. [12] Gregory distinguishes himself in battle, and is acclaimed by the people who want him to marry the countess and become the defendor of the country. The countess accepts and they are wed. Gregory hides the tablets in a secret place where he can read them every day and lament the sin of his birth. His wife/mother discovers them and reveals the horror of the two-fold sin to Gregory. He comforts her, puts faith in God, gives her strict rules to obey and leaves seeking expiation (1038-1630).

He is dressed as a mendicant, taking with him only the tablets. On the third day he seeks asylum in the house of a fisherman, who mocks Gregory for his lack of apparent asceticism. Gregory delights in this scorn for it is the beginning of his penitence. When he refuses to eat other than bread and water, the fisherman again remonstrates him, indicating that a true hermit should live far from the world. He knows a perfect place: a barren rock lost at sea where no one dares go. If Gregory wishes he will show him the way and even attach him with chains. Gregory accepts these mocking proposals with joy. The next day Gregory forgets the tablets in his haste. The fisherman chains him to the rock, locks the chain and throws the key into the sea. The penitent stays there alone, exposed to sun and storm for seventeen years. His only nourishment is the rain which falls into a nearby hole (1631-1812).

Then the pope dies in Rome. An angel descends to the assembled clergymen making known God's will: the new pope must be a penitent named Gregory, isolated for seventeen years on a rock

---

[12] The battle episode is very limited in B_1, rather extensive in all MSS of group A, and even more so in B_2 and B_3.

at sea. They look for him and happen upon the house of the mocking fisherman. He serves them fish for dinner, and in its stomach he finds the key he had thrown into the sea. He understands his mistake and is seized with remorse. The fisherman consents to show them where he had left Gregory, but doubts that he is still alive. The Roman envoys call out to Gregory when they reach the rock, and the saint answers. When they explain the angel's message, Gregory thinks it is another bad joke, but the envoys convince him and carry him to Rome, once they have located the tablets (1813-2078). (B$_1$ stops here.)

(Magnificent ceremonies and numerous miracles accompany Gregory's rise to the pontifical throne. During his pontificate a countess of Aquitaine arrives imploring forgiveness for her sins. She is none other than Gregory's mother and finds peace in the knowledge that their sins have been absolved. She remains in a convent in Rome. When Gregory dies, God makes a place for him among the saints. That is the recompense for hope and faith. This Gregory was one of the creators of the musical chant. [13] May God deliver us from sin and give us eternal life in the name of Gregory (2079-2376).

---

[13] This is only in A; B$_1$ says the exact opposite; B$_2$ and B$_3$ make no mention of it at all.

HILDEFONSE

"En Tulette, la grant cité"

This brief Life of Hildefonse (114 octosyllabic lines rhyming in couplets) was first brought to notice by J. A. Herbert.[1] The Egerton MS 612, published by Neuhaus, is deficient at the beginning. One of the most popular Latin collections studied by Mussafia is a cycle of 17 Miracles called HM after the first and last in the series (Hildefonsus-Murieldis),[2] the first nine of which correspond to the MS published by Herbert.[3] These should probably be considered the beginning of Adgar's Mary-Legends and be placed in front of the Egerton collection.[4] Neuhaus hints at this probable lack at the beginning of Egerton 612, when he shows that both Latin MSS (Cleop. C. X. fol. 100r-143v, and Arundel 346 fol. 60r-73r) contain a Life of Hildefonse of Toledo.[5]

---

[1] J. A. Herbert, "A New Manuscript of Adgar's Mary Legends," *Romania*, 32 (1903), 401-402.

[2] Adolf Mussafia, *Studien zu den mittelalterlichen Marienlegenden* (Vienna: Tempsky, 1891), III, p. 55.

[3] British Museum, Add. 38664, fol. 3-16v (formerly Hope Edwards 598).

[4] Hilding Kjellman, *La Deuxième Collection anglo-normande des Miracles de la Sainte Vierge et son original latin* (Paris: Champion, 1922), xxiii.

[5] Cleop. compared to Toulouse MS 482 brings Mussafia to the conclusion that a series of 17 Miracles called TS (Toledo-Samstag) represents another important Latin source (*Studien*, III, p. 59). Herbert cites as the Latin source B. Pez (ed.), *Venerabilis Agnetis Blannbekin ... Vita et Revelationes Auctore Anonymo ... Accessit Pothonis Prunveningensis nunc Priflingensis prope Ratisbonam O. S. B. Liber de Miraculis S. Dei Genitricis Mariae* (Vienne: 1731), cap. 1. Mussafia proves the author not to be Potho (*Studien*, I, pp. 22-30, II, pp. 53-55).

Hildefonse, archbishop of Toledo, lived from 607 to 667. The version of his life, as told in the Herbert edition, dates from 1175-80, and runs as follows:

There was an archbishop of Toledo named Hildefonse who loved the Virgin above all. To praise her he wrote a book (1-14). The Virgin appears in person to thank him. The archbishop was so filled with joy that he proclaims the eighth day before Christmas as the Feast of the Virgin, which is still celebrated in that region (15-42). The Virgin gives him a holy vestment and a chair which she brings to him from Paradise, saying that no one else can use them or she will take vengeance (43-62). Hildefonse dies, leaving his people a good example to follow (63-73). Siagrius succeeds him. He sits in the chair and tries to don the vestment, reasoning with himself outloud: "I am bishop as he was, so I can do as he did." (74-91) He falls dead immediately, and the people who saw this were struck with fear. They took the vestment to the treasury of the church where it remains to this day. Whoever truly serves the Virgin will receive the grace of God (92-114).

The similarities to St. Bon are striking. Both are high officials in the Church, both receive a holy vestment from the Virgin, and both are imitated by successors who fail. According to Lozinski, first to notice the similar literary motif, the story of Hildefonse is the inspiration for St. Bon. [6] Louis Réau has treated Hildefonse's iconography. [7]

---

[6] G. Lozinski, "De Saint Bon, évêque de Clermont; Miracle versifié par Gautier de Coinci," *Annales Academiae Scientiarum Fennicae*, n.° B XL 1 (Helsinki, 1938), 16.

[7] Louis Réau, *L'Iconographie des saints*, Vol. III, Pt. 2 of *L'Iconographie de l'art chrétien* (Paris: Presses Universitaires de France, 1958), pp. 676-678.

LAURENCE

"Maistre, a cest besoing vus dreciez"

The anonymous *De Saint Laurent,* composed between 1140-1170,[1] comprises 950 octosyllabic lines rhyming in couplets. Söderhjelm's 1888 edition was based on the then sole MS: Paris, Bibliothèque Nationale, fr. 19525.[2] His subsequent edition made available the only other extant MS of *St. Laurent.*[3] The question of origins of the legend has been treated by Russell (pp. 24-27). The Latin source closest to the Old French version can be found in *Analecta Bollandiana,* 51 (1933), 70-71, called the *Passio Polychronii* from the fifth century. Despite the innate interest of the poem, it has received scant treatment by literary critics.[4]

---

[1] See D. W. Russell's critical edition, *La Vie de Saint Laurent. An Anglo-Norman Poem of the Twelfth Century. Anglo-Norman Text Society,* n.º 34 (London, 1976), pp. 22-23.

[2] Werner Söderhjelm, *De Saint Laurent, poème anglo-normand du XIIème siècle, publié pour la première fois d'après le manuscrit unique de Paris* (Paris: Welter, 1888), xvi, believed it to be of the second half of the twelfth century. Paul Meyer disagreed, placing the date of composition at the beginning of the thirteenth century. However, he did not give his reasons for doing so ("Notice du manuscrit Egerton 2710 du Musée Britannique," *Bulletin de la Société des Anciens Textes,* 15 [1889], 72-97.

[3] W. Söderhjelm, "Le Poème de Saint Laurent dans Egerton 2710," *Mémoires de la Société Néophilologique à Helsingfors,* 1 (1893), 21-31. Söderhjelm did not consider this second MS different enough to be termed a second version. D. W. Russell's edition, based on both MSS, brings the necessary emendations. For the editor, it is probable that each scribe copied separately from a common source.

[4] Arthur Robert Harden, "The *Ubi sunt* Theme in Three Anglo-Norman Saints' Lives," *Romance Notes,* 1 (1959), 63-64.

The historical figure of St. Laurence has been analyzed by Abbé Labosse and H. Delehaye.[5] Toward the end of the fourth century the martyr became a subject of Latin poetry. Louis Réau has treated Laurence's iconography.[6]

The story is as follows:

Life is brief and death is just for all. Let us pray to. St. Laurence for his grace (1-74). His deeds are an example for us. There was an evil man in Rome, named Decius Caesar, envious of the power of the good Pope Syxtus, and desirous of destroying the Church. During a confrontation Syxtus dethrones an idol in the temple of Mars, and is decapitated for this by Decius (75-242). Laurence, the diacre, is called before Decius to hand over the church treasure he must guard. He refuses and is imprisoned. There he baptizes Lucillus who is then given sight. A pagan prison guard, Hippolytus, is also converted (243-380). Decius summons Laurence who condemns the idols and preaches the word of God. Decius becomes insensed and has Laurence tortured, hoping to force him to abandon his "mad" faith. During one exchange Decius implores him to give him the treasure and Laurence retorts that treasure for him is his faith (381-613). The torture continues and brings but joy to the martyr, and conversion to Christianity for the pagans in attendance. He is finally decapitated, but continues to speak and comfort those who are saddened by his death. Laurence is subjected to hot coals, yet no technique tried gives him any pain. His soul goes straight to Paradise. His friends bury him and keep vigil for three days. Let us pray that we shall be given joy and sustenance as well. (614-950).

[5] Abbé Labosse, *Histoire de Saint Laurent, diacre et martyr* (Lille, 1862) and H. Delehaye, "Recherches sur le légendier romain," *Analecta Bollandiana*, 51 (1933), 34-72.
[6] Louis Réau, *L'Iconographie des saints*, Vol. III, Pt. 2 of *L'Iconographie de l'art chrétien* (Paris: Presses Universitaires de France, 1958), pp. 787-792.

MARGARET

"A l'onor Deu et a s'aïe"

The legend of Saint Margaret of Antioch is its own fact, since there is a complete absence of historical evidence for her existence of martyrdom. The oldest Syrian martyrology makes no mention of her. Perhaps sprouting from the legends of Pelagia the Penitent, the historical Pelagia of Antioch and the cult of Catherine of Alexandria, Margaret was well-known in the Middle Ages with versions of her life extant in most vernaculars. [1]

The most popular Latin rendition dating from the tenth century comes from the library of the Saint-Pierre Abbey in Moissac. [2] The author, Theotimus, claims to have been an eye-witness to the events he relates. This version probably derives from a Greek version of the seventh or eighth century where Margaret is known as Marina. [3] Both are apocryphal. E. A. Francis believes this Latin version to be the probable source for Wace's Old French version, and the

---

[1] For the questions of historicity and development of the legend, see D. Guido Tammi, *Due versioni della leggenda di S. Margherita d'Antiocha* (Piacenza: Scuola Artigiana dal Libro, 1958).

[2] MS: Paris, Bibliothèque nationale, Lat. 17002. See B. Mombritius, *Catalogus Codicum Hagiographicorum Latinorum Biblio. Nat. Parisiensis,* 1643; rpt. Paris, 1910), II, p. 190, and by C. H. Gerould, "A New Text of the *Passio Sancta Margaritae* with Some Account of its Latin and English Relations," *PMLA,* 39 (1924), 525-556. Also printed in E. A. Francis' edition, *Wace: La Vie de Sainte Marguerite* (Paris: Champion, 1932). For a complete discussion of all Greek and Latin versions, see D. Tammi, *op. cit.,* pp. 29-52.

[3] See H. Usener, *Acta Sanctae Marinae et Sancti Christophori* (Bonn, 1886).

comparison between the Latin and French has been done by both Francis (pp. viii, ix) and Josef Merk. [4]

The iconography has been fully treated by Tammi and Réau. [5]

Wace himself is well-known. The few historical facts we know of him come from his works, primarily the *Roman de Rou*. Gaston Paris outlines Wace's life: [6] born around 1110 in Jersey, he came to Caen while still young, studied in Paris (perhaps Chartres), and was a "clerc lisant" before the death of Henry I (1135). He was probably a nobleman, and received a stipend from Henry II as encouragement to write.

Marguerite is a simple biography, less ambitious a work than Wace's other religious poems (*Vie de St. Nicolas* and *Conception Notre Dame*), and based on its style was probably the first of the three, composed between 1135 and 1150.

The Life is extant in three MSS:

1) A.—Paris, Arsenal, 3516, fol. 125r-126v. [7]

2) T.—Troyes, Bibliothèque municipale, 1905, fol. 155v-175v. [8]

3) M.—Tours, Bibliothèque municipale, 927 (formerly of Marmoutier Abbey), fol. 205r-216v. [9]

Francis publishes both M and A side by side (both have many lacunae), T when M and A are both lacking, and the Latin version at the bottom of the page. In the following summary, the events

---

[4] Josef Merk, *Die literarische Gestaltung der altfranzösischen Heiligenleben bis Ende des 12. Jahrunderts* (Affoltern am Albis: J. Weiss, 1946).

[5] Tammi, *op. cit.*, pp. 77-81; L. Réau, *L'Iconographie des saints*, Vol. III, Pt. 2 of *L'Iconographie de l'art chrétien* (Paris: Presses Universitaires de France, 1958), pp. 877-882.

[6] G. Paris, in *Romania*, 9 (1880), 592ff; see also Francis, iv-vii, and Urban T. Holmes, "Norman Literature and Wace," in *Medieval Secular Literature, Four Essays*, ed. William Matthews, *UCLA Center for Medieval and Renaissance Studies, Contributions I* (University of California Press, 1965).

[7] For a description see *Catalogue général des manuscrits. Bibliothèques publiques en France, Bibliothèque de l'Arsenal*, III (Paris, 1887), p. 395; Waters, xviii.

[8] For a description see *Catalogue général... Bibliothèque de Troyes*, 787.

[9] For a description see Dorange, *Catalogue général... Bibliothèque de Tours*. Francis believes this to be the work of two copyists, along with V. Luzarche and W. Foerster.

occur in both MSS M and A, unless otherwise indicated. The 746 octosyllabic lines rhyming in couplets tell the following story:

To honor God I shall tell you the story of a beautiful, saintly young virgin who clung steadfastly to her faith. Her name was Margaret because, I think, she was a beautiful as a daisy. She was like a precious gem and vowed to keep her chastity. She was born in Antioch of noble parents; her father, Theodosius, was a pagan priest, greatly honored in the city. He was a pagan because in those times there were not many Christians. Despite the faith of her father, Margaret was filled with the Holy Spirit. Her father entrusted her care to a nursemaid when the mother fell ill. Upon learning of Margaret's Christian faith, Theodosius is infuriated and asks her to take up his law. But the love of her father is less than that of the Lord of all things. At fifteen she loved God and her nursemaid. It was a time of persecutions. Those who believed in God were often seized and killed. When Margaret heard of their suffering, she vowed to remain chaste. She stayed in the fields, guarding sheep (A 1-84).

One day Olybrius saw her and fell in love. He was provost of Antioch, very powerful and responsible for the persecution of Christians. He ordered his men to bring Margaret to him; if unmarried he would make her his wife, if married, his concubine. Margaret cried out to Christ for help in remaining chaste. Olybrius was angered at hearing of her response and had her brought to him. — "Who were your parents?" — "Noble people of Antioch." — "What is your name?" — "Margaret" — "What God do you adore?" — "Jesus Christ" — "Christ whom the Jews killed?" — "Yes, He always takes care of me." — "How can he help you since he was crucified?" — "He died to save his people from Hell. You will never be able to make me deviate from the way of the truth." The provost answered in anger, "You will tell me soon whether you want to adore our gods. I shall torture you, put your body to fire. If you renounce your faith I shall make you rich and shall put you in my bed." — "You may torture me, my soul will be saved." He ordered her to be hanged and beaten with rods. Margaret spoke to Christ for strength. Her body was beaten and bloody. Olybrius asked her to recant. Those watching pitied her and asked what good could come of her death. She answered, "My soul will be in Paradise for the suffering of my body. You should believe in God, the doors of

Paradise are opened for his friends. I shall never believe in your gods." (A 85-224)

"You should adore the God who is all-powerful. You, dog of a provost, shameless, whatever you do, nothing elevates you. You serve the devil." Olybrius was full of rage and again ordered torture. Margaret prayed to God to give her hope and strength, and to send her a dove to help guard her virginity (T 225-248).

Margaret was in prayer while the felons beat her. Olybrius and others had to cover their eyes for they could not stand to see her tender flesh bleed. The provost asked why she does not pray to his gods, and why she does not do his will in order not to die. She answers that her soul would go to hell and that she accepts bodily torture for the sake of her soul (A 249-272).

When her entrails were spilling out of her wounds, she was taken to prison and left alone. She crossed herself and prayed to God: "Hear my prayer. I have no brother or sister. My father left me because I love you. But you will never abandon me." (M, T 273-288). "I am being wrongly tormented and I complain to you alone. Help me chase away the enemy who punishes Christians." (A, T 289-294)

The virgin offered this prayer often. The nursemaid brought her bread and wine which she passed through a window. There she could hear Margaret pray. One day Margaret saw a dragon in the corner. He was black, with fire darting out of his nose; his beard was golden, his teeth of iron, his eyes like a serpent's; he terrified others with his sword. He was angered, and started to huff and throw fire in the cell. The virgin was afraid but had trust in God. She knelt down and prayed: "God, you who have power over sky, earth, air and sea, give me strength through my prayer to resist this enemy so that he will not take me away to his den." She armed herself with the holy cross and when the devil opened his mouth to swallow her, he died. She never felt any pain. She turned to her left to find another devil whose hands and feet, however, were tied. Margaret gives thanks to her Lord: "I vanquished the devil, and put fear behind me. The dove came from the sky to give me confort. It is the Holy Spirit that I was waiting for." (A 295-360)

The devil rose: "I can no longer live. I sent you my brother, Rufon, who resembles a dragon, to deflower you. But you killed him with the cross. I ask you not to inflict the same on me." The virgin threw him to the ground, put her right foot on his head and said: "Don't ever try to tarnish my virginity again. I am the spouse of God." She had not finished speaking when the sun brightened her cell. She saw the cross of Christ and the dove who spoke: "You are a good virgin. You have conquered the dragon. There is nothing hindering your entrance into Paradise." (A, M 361-398)

Margaret gave thanks to God and turned to the devil asking his name. He answered: "I shall tell you what you want, if you take your foot off me." She agreed. "My name is Beelzeb (Belgibus, Belsabut). I fight against the men of this world and was never vanquished until I met you. I see that you deserve glory in the heavens. I am the one who battles good men, who makes them forget their savior, who counsels them in sin. What shame that a virgin has conquered me." Margaret asked where his power comes from. The devil first wants to know why her faith is so strong. Margaret answers that what she knows is by the grace of God who may do what He wishes with her. The devil continues: "Our king is Satan, who fell from Heaven where he is known as Lucifer. I dare not tell you more for I see that you are with God. I ask that you not touch me." Margaret sends the devil away, the earth opens up and swallows him. She is called before Olybrius, who asks her to renounce her faith but she refuses (A, M 399-516).

The provost has her burned, but the Holy Spirit extinguishes the fire and Margaret feels no pain. Olybrius tied her hands and feet, and plunged her head into oil. The virgin looked to the heavens and prayed that the Holy Spirit take her away from this peril. No sooner had she spoken than thunder struck and the dove appeared announcing that the company of God awaited her. Hands and feet miraculously untied, Margaret escapes the oil unharmed. More than five thousand converted at the sight of the miracle (A, M 517-576).

Olybrius ordered her decapitation outside the city. The executioner asks her forgiveness. She requests a few moments for prayer. She thanks God for keeping her a virgin, pure and free of torment and asks that He pardon sins. She makes a special plea for healthy children and pregnant mothers.[10] While she is still on her knees,

---

[10] M. D. Legge points out that copies of the *Life of Saint Margaret* were given to women in childbirth as a charm, in *Anglo-Norman Literature and its Background* (Oxford: Clarendon Press, 1963), 258.

thunder was heard and all fell to their knees. The dove appeared telling Margaret that her wishes would be granted: all those who pray to Margaret will have their sins forgiven. Margaret turned to the sergeant asking him to strike the fatal blow. He hesitated: "How can I, when an angel of God speaks to you?" — "If you don't kill me, you will not go to Paradise. Do what has been ordered." He decapitated her with one blow, asking for mercy. Angels from the heavens arrived singing her praises (A, M 577-712).

All the sick who touched her were cured. Theotimus took her body and buried it in Antioch. This Theotimus was the same who had brought her food in prison, had heard her suffer, and has put down in writing what he saw and heard. Let us pray to God for forgiveness (M, T 713-746).

MARY I

"Oiés, seignor, une raison"

Peter Dembowski's recent critical edition and introduction to the French versions of this legend permit us to abstain from a lengthy discussion of the origins, development and manuscript tradition.[1] It suffices here to summarize his findings.[2]

The oldest version is a Greek narrative attributed to Sophronius.[3] F. Delmas suggests the second half of the fifth century as the earliest possible date of the legend's origin.[4] Of the Latin versions, A[5] is considered the most faithful rendition of Sophronius, and by previous scholars to be the source for the subsequent French versions. Dembowski remains unconvinced and concludes on this point:

> L'étude des versions latines de la *Vie,* de leur classement ainsi que de leurs rapports exacts avec les différentes versions françaises reste à faire.[6]

This version (called T by Dembowski) is extant in six MSS and two fragments:

---

[1] P. F. Dembowski, *La Vie de Sainte Marie l'Egyptienne, versions en ancien et en moyen français* (Geneva: Droz, 1976).

[2] *Ibid.,* pp. 13-18.

[3] Found in *Acta Sanctorum,* Apr. I, Appendix, xi-xviii, and in J. P. Migne, *Patrologiae Cursus Completus. Series graeca,* LXXXVII, pars III, col. 3697-3725.

[4] F. Delmas, "Remarques sur la *Vie de Sainte Marie l'Egyptienne,*" *Echos d'Orient,* 4 (1902), 35-42, and 5 (1903), 15-17.

[5] *Acta Sanctorum,* Apr. I, pp. 77-84.

[6] Dembowski, *op. cit.,* p. 16.

1) A—Paris, Bibliothèque nationale, fr. 23112, fol. 334c-344a. [7]

2) B—Oxford, Bodleian Library, Cononici. Misc. 74, fol. 109r-120r.

3) C—Oxford, Corpus Christi 232, fol. 35r-64v.

4) D—Paris, Bibliothèque nationale, fr. 19525, fol. 15b-26b.

5) E—Paris, Arsenal 3516, fol. 113v-117v.

6) L—London, British Museum, Add. 26614, fol. 271c-284c.

7) F¹—Manchester, John Rylands, French 6, fol. 8b-8d.

8) F²—Anglo-Norman fragment of 38 lines corresponding to lines 967-1004 in Dembowski's edition. [8]

Dembowski remains unconvinced by Baker's arguments in favor of its Anglo-Norman origins. [9]

The author is unknown. Based on linguistic evidence the date of composition is agreed to be the last quarter of the 12th century, contemporary to Adgar's version. [10]

Margareta Wietzorek has discussed this legend as well as that of Thais. [11] The iconography has been treated by Louis Réau. [12]

The 1532 octosyllabic lines in rhyming couplets relate the following story:

Listen to the true story of Mary the Egyptian. There is no repentant sinner whom God does not forgive, and there is no man however wise who has not sinned at some time. All iniquity vanishes when one says, "I repent." (1-53)

This woman of whom I speak was born in Egypt and was shameful even in her youth. She was enamored of pleasure and gave herself to all men. It's a wonder her parents did not die of

---

[7] For a description of all MSS, see Dembowski, pp. 25-27.

[8] Published by Adolf Tobler, "Bruchstücke altfranzösischer Dichtung aus den in der Kubbet in Damaskus gefundenen Handschriften, 2. Ein Bruchstück eines Lebens der h. Maria aus Aegypten," *Sitzungsberichte der königlich-preussischen Akademie der Wissenschaften*, Phil.-Hist. Klasse, Berlin, LXIII, 966-969. Cited by Dembowski.

[9] A. T. Baker, "La Vie de Sainte Marie l'Egyptienne," *Revue des Langues Romanes*, 59 (1916-1917), 145-401; Dembowski, pp. 28-30.

[10] Dembowski, pp. 16-17.

[11] M. Wietzorek, *Die Legenden der Thais und der Maria Aegyptica in den romanischen Literaturen vornehmlich des Mitteralters* (Lingerich: Westf, 1938).

[12] Louis Réau, *L'Iconographie des saints,* Vol. III, Pt. 2 of *L'Iconographie de l'art chrétien* (Paris: Presses universitaires de France, 1958), pp. 884-888.

grief. Her mother implored her to leave this life and to accept a rich husband (54-96). When Mary heard also of the wrath of her father, at the age of 12 she left her family to follow her own desires and was never to see them again. She came to Alexandria and there in a bordello she gave herself to men not only for the money but for her pleasure as well. Sometimes the young men would fight over her, but she was never frightened by blood (97-148).

At seventeen there was no countess or queen more beautiful than she. Her ears were round and white, her eyes clear and smiling, her mouth small and her face tender as a rose. Her beauty was perfect. She received many presents of beautiful clothes. The townspeople loved her for her beauty while the old and the wise lamented her foolish ways (149-216).

One day in May, she went to the port where a ship of pilgrims was arriving. She asks to go with them to Jerusalem for she has been too long in Alexandria, offering to pay her passage with her body. When they laugh at her offer she turns to the young pilgrims and appeals to their sense of charity. They accept her on board, but cannot sleep, because Mary begins to kiss and caress them (217-306). To satisfy her desires, she went to all the beds that night. Upon arriving in Jerusalem, Mary felt lost and sad for she knew no one. The young men of the city were taken by her beauty. Shortly after it was the Feast of the Ascension. Mary joined a procession of pilgrims but, unlike the others, she was barred entry into the temple. She retreated to a corner where she begins to think. She finally comes to a realization of her sins, begins to sigh and weep and cries for mercy (307-408).

She looked toward a statue of the Virgin and began to pray. After a long prayer for mercy, Mary rose and entered the temple without difficulty. There a statue speaks to her: "Go to the Church of St. John, cross the river Jordan, then spend the rest of your life in the desert." (409-560)

She made the sign of the cross, started on her way, and bought three rolls from a pilgrim. That was all she had as sustenance. That night she slept near the banks of the Jordan, ate half of a roll and drank holy water. She felt cleansed of all her sins. The next morning she went to the church and received communion. She crossed the river, walked all day and rested under a tree for the night. The following day she continued East, deeper and deeper into the wild, never forgetting to pray to the Virgin. Her clothes were torn, and what had been skin white as a flower turned black. Her hair whitened, and her body became black as coal. She trimmed her long nails with her teeth. She was wounded in many places by thorns, but for this she was grateful. She led a very harsh life (561-662).

For more than forty years she lived nude, eating of her rolls and then grasses from the field, like an animal. The devil would try to tempt her, recalling her past loves. She persisted in her solitary, spiritual existence (663-700).

Let us leave Mary now and speak of an abbey where monks led an ascetic life, wearing hair shirts, going barefoot and eating very poorly. They had no property; God was their treasure. At Lent the abbot assembled everyone for communion and prayer, and then sent all but two out into the desert to renew their eremitic existence. Two remained to take care of the needs of the abbey. When the monks would see each other in the desert, they would flee in order to remain in solitude with God. They would all return to the abbey for Palm Sunday. One of the monks who lived a saintly life was Zozima. Once during a noon prayer in the desert, he noticed a shadow and prayed to God to keep him from temptation. Zozima and Mary look at each other; she is clothed only in her hair which has grown down to her feet. The wind rose and revealed her flesh burned by sun and frost. Mary took to flight, with Zozima running close behind despite his age. He calls out to God, Mary stops upon hearing this, and they begin to speak once Zozima has given her a cloth to wrap herself in. She tells him of her penitence for her sins, and Zozima is moved to tears. They exchange benedictions, each feeling the other is more worthy (701-952).

When Mary inquires about the state of the world, Zozima replies that it is in great need of prayer. As she prays, Zozima was frightened, for there was a full two and one half feet between her and the ground. He starts to run, but Mary calls him back reassuring him that there is nothing to fear. She recounts her life to him, and predicts that he will be sick the following year during Lent, but that he will be able to return to her to give her communion (953-1082).

When she turned and left, the holy man was grieved at the loss and praised her virtue. He returned to the abbey. The following year Mary's prophecy was realized. He sees no sign of her until

the bank of the Jordan. They pray together and he gives her communion. Zozima leaves her some food before returning. Mary
returns to the place where Zozima first saw her and prays for
the peace of death. Her body lies on the desert exposed to the
elements but does not decompose nor emit any odor. The poor will
be happy, for they have the kingdom of God (1083-1327).

When another year had passed, Zozima went to look for Mary.
He was unable to find her, feared that she was dead and prayed
to God that He show him the way so that he might bury her.
Zozima is led to Mary's body by a bright light and finds a letter
near her, addressed to him: "Zozima, take Mary's body and bury
it with the help of God. When you have done so, pray for her."
The earth was hard and he had brought no instrument with him.
A lion came up to him, licked his feet and made it known that
he was there to serve. The lion dug out the grave according to
Zozima's directions. Zozima took her head, the lion her feet, and
they lowered her into the grave. The lion disappeared into the
great desert (1328-1482).

Zozima offers a prayer, and returns to his church where he
recounts the life of Mary the Egyptian. We pray that Mary will
intercede for us and ask God to forgive our sins. Amen (1483-1532).

MARY II

(Adgar)

"Ci truis escrit la sainte vie"

This second version of the Life of Saint Mary the Egyptian is considerably briefer and is Miracle n.° 31 of the Egerton MS 612, fol. 59c-61a, which contains Adgar's Mary-Legends. [1] According to Mussafia, the Latin source is found in chapter 17 of the Salisbury MS, the version by William of Malmesbury. [2] Neuhaus also proposes a theory in a study we were unable to locate, [3] but Dembowski feels that no Latin *Vita* has been proven to be the source for any of the OF versions. [4] Neither the Cleop. nor the Arundel MSS contains a rendition of the legend. [5] Adgar has been dated toward the end of the twelfth century. [6]

Both T and W fall into the category where Mary plays the principal role and Zozima a secondary one. [7] Here in W, although Zozima is subordinate to the saint, Mary's repentance is seen as an indication of the Virgin's powers of forgiveness.

The 140 octosyllabic lines tell simply the bare outline of the story:

Here is the holy life of Mary the Egyptian who wasted her time living in sin. She gave herself to anyone, for pleasure not for money.

---

[1] Carl Neuhaus, pp. 193-197; also Dembowski, pp. 153-158. Called W.
[2] Mussafia, IV, p. 83.
[3] C. Neuhaus, *Das Dulwick'er Adgar-Fragment* (Aschersleben, 1887).
[4] Dembowski, p. 16.
[5] Neuhaus, xxvii.
[6] *Ibid.*, xlv-xlvii; Dembowski agrees (p. 18).
[7] Dembowski, pp. 21-22.

One day she crossed the sea to Jerusalem, where her companions entered a church. Her feminine sins kept her from entering. She saw an image of the Virgin and repented in tears, promising to change. She could then enter the church without difficulty (1-74). The Virgin promised her peace provided she cross the Jordan river. She bought three loaves of bread before entering the desert where she lived off the land like an animal. Zozima spoke with her once and they took communion. When he returned, he found her dead, and buried her with the help of a lion (75-118). This is an example of the compassion of the Virgin who forgives repentant sinners (119-140).

The only discussions of this legend include the one alluded to in our Appendix of Mary I (p. 278 n. 11), and Ebel's study on the genre of the miracle. [8]

---

[8] See our Appendix on St. Bon, p. 210 n. 18. The complete bibliography for Adgar can be found in this same appendix.

NICHOLAS

"A ces qui n'unt lectres aprises"

The story of St. Nicholas survived through oral tradition until the ninth century when two Greek versions were first compiled.[1] In the third quarter of the ninth century, John the Deacon composed the first known Latin version.[2] To this *Vita* were added the accounts of several miracles inspired by Nicholas, bishop of Pinara (d. 564).[3] Later Greek and Latin versions existed as did Latin hymns, celebrating the miracles of the saint. The cult was well known in the West during the early eleventh century and was particularly well-rooted in Normandy.[4] In 1087, some Norman merchants living in Southern Italy seized the relics of the saint and transported them to Bari en Pouille which soon became a center of pilgrimages.[5] Patron saint of sailors, merchants and children,

---

[1] *Vita per Michaelem* and *Methodius ad Theodorum*, the latter written by Method, patriarch of Constantinople from 842 to 846. Both versions can be found in G. Anrich, *Hagios Nikolaos, der heilige Nikolaus in der griechischen Kirche, Texte und Untersuchungen*, 2 vols. (Berlin, 1913-17).

[2] Boninus Mombritius, *Vitae Sanctorum* (Rpt. as *Sanctuarium seu Vitae Sanctorum, Novam Hanc Editionem Curaverunt Duo Monachi Solesmenses* [Paris: 1910], II, 296-309). Charles W. Jones discusses Latin liturgical texts derived from John the Deacon's *Vita* in *The Saint Nicholas Liturgy and its Literary Relationships (9th to 12th Centuries)* (Berkeley: University of California Press, 1963).

[3] Nicolaus Carminius Falconius, *Sancti Confessoris Pontificis et Celeberrimi Thaumaturgi Nicolai Acta Primigenia* (Naples, 1751), pp. 112-126.

[4] See O. Albrecht, *Four Latin Plays of Saint Nicholas* (Diss. Philadelphia, 1935) and K. Meisen, *Nikolauskult und Nikolausbrauch im Abendlande, eine kultgeographisch-volkskundliche Untersuchung. Forschungen zur Volkskunde*, n.º 9-12 (Düsseldorf, 1931), p. 71 ff.

[5] This transferal of the relics was recounted in 1088 by Johannes Archidiaconus Barensis, *De Translatione Sancti Nicolai Episcopi*, in L. Surius,

Nicholas became perhaps the most popular saint of Christendom. It is natural that a Norman be the first author of the vernacular version. He names himself at the beginning:

> Jo sui Normanz s'ai a non Guace.
>
> (35)

All that is known of the life of Wace has been brought to light by Gaston Paris and Urban T. Holmes. [6]

E. Ronsjö has done a comparative study of all of Wace's extant works in attempting to date the composition of the *Vie de St. Nicolas*. He concludes that it was composed around 1150 and that there elapsed only a brief period of time between its composition and the completion of the *Roman de Brut* in 1155. [7]

The probable Latin source is one of numerous Latin MSS containing a fusion of the two *Vitae* found in Mombritius and Falconius. [8] This fused version does not account for six of the miracles, however, whose sources remain for the most part uncertain. [9]

Wace's rendering is preserved in five MSS; all but *A* (picard) are anglo-normand:

1) B.—Paris, Bibliothèque nationale, français 902 (formerly 7268³·³ and Colbert 3745), fol. 117v-125v. [10]

De Probatis Sanctorum Historiis. Coloniae Aggripinae, n.º 7, 1618, pp. 116-121. See Meisen, p. 94 ff. and K. Fissen, *Das Leben des heiligen Nikolaus in der altfranzösischen Literatur und seine Quellen* (Diss. Göttingen, 1921), p. 62.

[6] Gaston Paris, review of Andresen' edition of the *Roman de Rou, Romania,* 9 (1880), 592 ff, and Urban T. Holmes, "Norman Literatur and Wace," in *Medieval Secular Literatur, Four Essays,* ed. William Matthews, *UCLA Center for Medieval and Renaissance Studies, Contributions I* (University of California Press, 1965). For details see our appendix on Margaret.

[7] E. Ronsjö, *La Vie de Saint Nicolas par Wace. Etudes romanes de Lund,* n.º 5 (Lund: Gleerup and Munksgaard, 1942), pp. 18-26.

[8] *Ibid.,* p. 32. Ronsjö disproves the conclusions of Fissen and Ida Del Valle de Paz, *La leggenda di S. Nicolas nella tradizione poetica medioevale in Francia* (Florence, 1921).

[9] Ronsjö has found a Latin MS which Wace could have known for some of these miracles (Paris, Bibliothèque nationale, Lat. 5290); for others the source is uncertain, pp. 34-45. For a comparison with the Latin, see also Josef Merk's chapter on Nicholas.

[10] For a description see Ronsjö, pp. 46-52; M. S. Crawford, *The Life of Saint Nicholas* (Philadelphia, 1924), p. 24 ff.; *Catalogue général... Bibliothèque Nationale* (Paris, 1868), I, p. 152. Paul Meyer discusses all the MSS in *Romania,* 32 (1903), 20 ff. This is Ronsjö's base MS.

2) D.—Oxford, Bodleian 21844, Douce 270, fol. 91v-106v.

3) A.—Paris, Bibliothèque de l'Arsenal 3516 (formerly BLF 283), fol. 69v-73v. [11]

4) O.—Oxford, Bodleian 1687, Digby 86, fol. 150r-161r. [12]

5) C.—Cambridge, Trinity College B 14.39-40, fol. 48r-57v. [13]

To establish with certainty the line of demarcation between legend and history is difficult. It is believed that Nicholas lived during the fourth century, [14] in Asia Minor where he was bishop of Myra in Lycia; even this is uncertain and the rest is legend.

As patron of children he is the origin of Father Christmas, our American Santa Claus having derived from the Dutch form of his name, Sinte Claas. His feast day, December 6, is still celebrated in some countries through the giving of presents. [15]

Only three scholars have studied the Nicholas legend recently. A. De Groot delves into the behavioral sciences for an explanation of Nicholas' appeal, [16] G. F. Carr shows the symmetrical, architectonic structure of the Prologue, [17] and Leger Brosnahan discusses Wace's use of proverbs. [18] Ida Del Valle de Paz studied the different forms this legend took in medieval French literature, [19] and it should be mentioned here that the first dramatized Saint's Life in French

---

[11] Described by Ronsjö, *op. cit.*, and E. G. R. Waters, *The Anglo-Norman Voyage of Saint Brendan* (Oxford: Clarendon Press, 1928), xvii ff. and in *Catalogue général . . . Bibliothèque de l'Arsenal* (Paris, 1887), III, p. 395 ff.

[12] See Ronsjö, *op. cit.*, and Stengel, *Codicem Manuscriptum Digby 86 . . . Descripsit* (Halle, 1871); W. D. Macray, *Codices a Kenelm Digby Anno 1634 Donati, Catalogi Codd. Manuscr. Bibl. Bodleianae* (Oxford, 1883), IX, 91 ff; F. Madan, *A Summary Catalogue of Western Manuscripts in the Bodleian Library*, II, i, pp. 72-73. Cited by Ronsjö.

[13] See Ronsjö, *op. cit.*; M. R. James, *Catalogue of the Western Manuscripts in the Library of the Trinity College, Cambridge*, I, p. 438 ff. Cited by Ronsjö.

[14] Anrich, *op. cit.*, p. 509 ff.

[15] His late feast day explains the fact that the Bollandists have not yet treated him at length in *Acta Sanctorum*.

[16] Adriaan De Groot, *Saint Nicholas, a Psychoanalytic Study of his History and Myth* (Paris: Mouton, 1965).

[17] Gerald F. Carr, "The Prologue to Wace's *Vie de St. Nicolas*: A Structural Analysis," *Philological Quarterly*, 47 (1968), 1-7.

[18] L. Brosnahan, "Wace's Use of Proverbs," *Speculum*, 39 (1964), 444-473.

[19] See note 8.

literature is the *Jeu de saint Nicolas* by Jean Bodel (1200 or 1201). [20]
Louis Réau has fully treated the iconography. [21]

Wace's version contains 1,562 octosyllabic lines rhyming in pairs,
the last one of which is in Latin, followed by Amen, as is often
the case. The story he tells is as follows:

One should speak of saints for the benefit of those who cannot
read. God endows different men with different gifts, but all can
learn from the saints and should have faith in God. The strong
should help the weak; "Petit prendra qui se[me] petit" (line 33) as
the Scripture says (1-34).

I am Norman, my name is Wace. I shall tell you of the life
and miracles of St. Nicholas, "en romanz" for those who do not
understand Latin. He was born of rich and noble parents in Patras.
As an only child, so filled with the grace of God was he that on
Wednesdays and Fridays he accepted his mother's milk only once
a day. After his education, he gave his entire inheritance to the
poor (35-80).

A poor man and his daughters were living in misery. Nicholas
takes pity on them, throwing gold to them through their window
at night and finding husbands for the daughters. On the third night
Nicholas is recognized but refuses their gratitude, exhorting them
to praise God. Thus he saved them from poverty and the daughters
from "putée" (81-120).

Nicholas proceeds to Myra where the archbishop has just died.
At the assembly of bishops, an angel appears saying that the first
man to enter the church should be named bishop. His name will
be Nicholas (121-156).

A woman goes to church, leaving her child in a basin of water
on the fire. The water begins to boil, yet the child remains unharmed. This miracle enhanced the reputation of St. Nicholas
(157-194).

I do not wish to belabor the recounting of his miracles. Suffice
it to say that Nicholas was charitable and pious, and spent his night
in prayer, his days in fast (195-204).

Nicholas cured a child possessed by the devil (205-212).

---

[20] F. J. Warne, *Le Jeu de Saint Nicolas* (Oxford, 1963), xvi.
[21] L. Réau, *L'Iconographie des saints*, Vol. III, Pt. 2 of *L'Iconographie
de l'art chrétien* (Paris: Presses Universitaires de France, 1958), pp. 976-988.

Three students who have been assassinated by an inn-keeper are brought back to life by the saint (213-226).

A violent storm threatens the lives of sailors. They implore Nicholas to come to their aid; he calms the sea and saves them. He worked many miracles like this one (227-274).

Famine ravishes the country and Nicholas asks some passing ships to share their wheat. At first they refuse, saying the cargo is for the emperor Constantine in Alexandria, but when the saint promises them a full load upon their arrival, they agree. Nicholas multiplies the grain, thus ending the famine, yet leaving the initial quantity intact (275-336).

Pagan gods are worshipped in Myra. Troubled by this, Nicholas destroys a statue of Diana. She plots her vengeance, disguises herself as a nun and gives sailors some inflammable oil to bring to the church of St. Nicholas. The saint appears to them in a vision and shows them the treachery of Diana (337-444).

Constantine enprisons three counts who had previously served Nicholas. They pray to the saint who then appears to Constantine in a dream-vision, promising that the emperor will meet death in a battle if he does not free the three counts. This dream kept him awake all night. The counts are unable to furnish an explanation until the emperor asks if they know St. Nicholas. Constantine repents and sends the three with gifts for the saint (445-600).

It would be too long to tell of all his miracles. He restored health to many and delivered several from the devil. He was a good man (601-610).

On the day of his death he cures a sick woman. He dies a natural death and his soul is carried to heaven. From his tomb flows a miraculous oil which cures many sick people. When Nicholas' successor was exiled, the oil ceases and begins again only upon his return (611-650).

The people were greatly saddened at the death of Nicholas and made a statue of him. This was pillaged by invading pagans, one of whom used it to guard his worldly treasure. Some thieves steal the treasure despite Nicholas' surveyance, thus infuriating the pagan who beats the statue. Nicholas intervenes, admonishes the thieves to return the goods or they will be tortured. The pagan repents and many others are converted at the sight of this miracle (651-722).

A Christian borrows money from a Jew using as security a statue of Nicholas. He later denies having borrowed the money which he has hidden in his walking stick. He swears that he has returned the money while the Jew is holding the stick. On his way home, he falls asleep in the road, is run over by an ox-driven cart and dies. The stick is broken, the gold spills out on the road, and the Jew and his household convert to Christianity (723-806).

A man has a silver cup made for the saint. He finds it so beautiful that he keeps it himself and has another made, not as heavy nor well made as the first. He sets sail with his wife and child to present his gift to Nicholas. His son falls into the sea while washing the beautiful cup and disappears. Upon their arrival at Myra, they offer the second cup which falls repeatedly to the ground. Frightened at having their true feelings discovered, they repent and confess their sin. The child, who had been saved by Nicholas, arrives carrying the first cup which they offer in praise to the saint (807-934).

In the city of Escorande, Getro and his wife can have no children. Getro goes on a pilgrimage to pray for Nicholas' intervention and is saddened to learn that the saint is dead. He requests some of Nicholas' clothes, returns home and has a church built to house the relic. Before a year had passed, a son is born to Getro and his wife, on the very day of the saint's feast day. They name him Deudoné for he was a gift of God. However the child is stolen and sold to a pagan emperor who mistreats him when the child starts to cry and remember how his birthday was celebrated with his parents. Nicholas appears, brings him back miraculously to the parents who continue to serve and honor the saint (935-1092).

A rich merchant, on a pilgrimage to bring Nicholas all his wealth, stops for the night at an inn. The innkeeper strangles him during the night and cuts his body into pieces which he preserves in salt. Nicholas comes to the same inn disguised as a wealthy knight and restores the merchant to life. The following morning the merchant greets the innkeeper who is struck dumb by the miracle, repents and is converted (1093-1156).

A common enemy of all people is the devil. In Lombardy, a man and his wife celebrated the saints every day. One morning the wife tells of a frightening vision: a wolf was eating her breast and drinking her blood. They go to church despite her fears, leaving their child at home alone. The devil comes in the guise of a penitent, asks for a piece of bread and then strangles the child. Returning from church, the parents lament the loss of their child; the mother now understands the meaning of her vision. Nicholas hears their lamentations, visits them dressed as a pilgrim and resuscitates the child (1157-1376).

The miraculous oil from the saint's tomb outside of Myra cures the ailments of all the pilgrims who come to his shrine. The king sends one of his men to bring back some relics. The messenger asks for some holy oil in a cup and finds to his joy one of the saint's teeth. He guards it carefully in a closed box. Nicholas appears to him in a dream, requests that he not take the tooth away since the saint wishes to remain intact. The king's envoy cannot find the tooth in the morning (1377-1484).

A crippled man who was so weak and in such pain that he couldn't stand alone was brought to Nicholas by horse. The saint was still alive at that time. He took some oil from a lamp and prayed for the man, who was instantly cured (1485-1518).

Shortly thereafter Nicholas delivered a man from the power of the devil by making the sign of the cross over him (1519-1545).

Wace put this life of Nicholas into the vernacular at the request of Robert, son of Tiout, who loved Nicholas very much. The author had wanted to tell of Nicholas' life and miracles for a long time. Let us pray to God, Our Lord, to be forgiven for our sins (1546-1562).

SILVESTER

"Qui de cuer i voldra entendre"

The twelfth-century version of the *Life of St. Silvester* is preserved in a single MS which is in parts quite mutilated.[1] The MS contains two separate stories, the legend of Silvester (1-572) followed by the Invention of the Holy Cross (573-1480), with no noticeable division in the MS.[2] The section on Silvester is in octosyllabic rhyming couplets. Some entire lines are lacking, others illegible.

The Latin source exists in several MSS and has been published by Mombritius.[3] The Old French version, in turn, is the only recognized source for Jacobus of Voragine's *Legenda Aurea*.[4]

Silvester was Pope from 313 to 335. According to legend, as bishop of Rome, he baptized the emperor Constantine and in return received a donation: primacy of his see over all other bishops. This legend was, however, invented in the ninth century when Charlemagne was being encouraged to do likewise.

As a builder of churches, Silvester is the patron saint of masons and stone-cutters.

---

[1] The MS belongs to the Marquis of Villoutrey, fol. 1-14. For a description see L. Delisle, "Description de la *Vie de Saint Silvestre*," *Bibliothèque de l'Ecole des Chartes*, 54 (1898), 533-37.

[2] The editor, A. Planchenault, *Cartulaire du Chapitre de Saint-Laud d'Angers* (Angers, 1903), marks the separation at line 593.

[3] *Sanctuarium*, II. The beginning can also be found in P. Meyer's article, "La Vie de Saint Silvestre en vers français," *Romania*, 28 (1899), 280-286.

[4] Analyzed by M. Graf, *Roma nella memoria e nelle imaginazini del medio evo*, 81 ff. Cited by P. Meyer, see note 3 above.

His feast day is December 31. [5] The blood bath of emperor Constantine is the most frequent of iconographical representations. [6]

Dating from the late twelfth century, [7] and composed in the region of Anjou, this fragment recounts the following story:

Whoever is willing to put his faith in God, and to listen to my story will find more aid than in wealth or lineage (1-48).

Constantine was persecuting the Christians. The bishop of Rome had to retreat to Mount Soract. Constantine contracted leprosy as punishment for his cruelty. His pagan priests advised him to bathe in the blood of children. Three thousand children were gathered to be slaughtered, their blood to fill the emperor's swimming pool, when suddenly Constantine was moved to compassion at the sight of the grieving mothers. He delivers a speech, stating that he would rather die than be cured at the cost of innocent lives, especially since he was not certain that this treatment would work (49-256).

The following night St. Peter and St. Paul appear to him and give him new instructions: he is to summon Silvester who has been hiding in the mountains. The saint will tell him where he can find a swimming pool. The emperor will be cured after bathing in it three times. Constantine agrees and is converted. At his baptism he is immediately cured. Silvester becomes the chief bishop and Constantine builds a basilica (257-573). [Constantine sends his men on a mission to find the Holy Cross, and the second story begins.]

---

[5] The date accounts for the lack of materials concerning this saint by the Bollandists.

[6] For a complete account of the iconography, see Louis Réau, L'Iconographie des saints, Vol. III, Pt. 3 of L'Iconographie de l'art chrétien (Paris: Presses Universitaires de France, 1958), pp. 1217-1220.

[7] P. Meyer, op. cit., p. 280.

THEOPHILE

"Meint bel sermun ai descrit"

The legend of Theophile is first found in the vernacular in the collection of Mary-Legends by Adgar.[1] Composed around 1165-70, it comprises 1,102 octosyllabic lines rhyming in couplets. In the Egerton MS 612 it is Miracle 17, fol. 21-32. A fragment among the MSS at Dulwich, Alleyne College 13, contains the latter half of the legend (lines 559-1102) and was edited by Neuhaus in 1887.[2] This edition is extremely rare, neither the British Museum nor the Bibliothèque Nationale has one.

The Latin source was published by Neuhaus, Cleop., Miracle 4.[3] The legend was a popular one as attested by the numerous versions listed in Neuhaus, pp. 80-81, but Adgar's remains the only extant rendition from the twelfth century. The only discussion known to us of the sources and development of the legend can be found in a review by Henri Strohmayer.[4] Louis Réau has treated its iconography.[5]

The *Life* itself is preceded by a prologue and tells the following story:

---

[1] Carl Neuhaus, *Adgar's Marienlegenden* (Heilbronn: Henninger, 1886), pp. 79-115.

[2] C. Neuhaus, *Das Dulwich'er Adgar-Fragment* (Aschersleben, 1887).

[3] Carl Neuhaus, *Die lateinischen Vorlagen zu den Adgar'schen Marienlegenden*, 2 vols. (Heilbronn: Henninger, 1886, 1890).

[4] H. Strohmayer, in *Romania*, 23 (1894), 601-607.

[5] Louis Réau, *L'Iconographie des saints*, Vol. III, Pt. 3 of *L'Iconographie de l'art chrétien* (Paris: Presses Universitaires de France, 1958), p. 1257.

I have written many beautiful sermons, and I continue to serve God in translating the life of Theophile. Now listen to the truth (1-18). In the city of Adana in Cilicia lived a very religious and well respected "vidame" named Theophile. He was well educated and served his bishop (19-60). When the latter died, the people ask that the good Theophile be elected to replace him. Theophile refuses repeatedly out of humility to accept such an honor, even after three days of introspection (61-126). Another is named bishop, who, at the request of officers in the church, has Theophile replaced as "vidame", who in turn accepts his fate. The devil grieves over the goodness of Theophile and incites him to prefer worldly honor and glory (127-164). In the same city lived a Jew, an agent of the devil, who receives Theophile one night and agrees to help him. When Theophile complains of the unfairness of the new bishop, the Jew promises him great power were he to obey the devil. The following night Theophile performs the ritual of refusing to make the sign of the cross, and the Jew takes Theophile to the devil, explaining his desire. The devil promises him mastery over the bishop (165-256). Theophile kisses the feet of the Prince of Darkness and denounces the Virgin, God and Christ. He becomes "vidame" again and is so powerful that all are afraid of him. The Jew is condemned to death as Theophile will be delivered to eternal torment (257-332). God remembers the former good works of Theophile who then repents, laments his wrong-doing and wonders where to turn. His sin is so great that he sees no one who could intercede in his behalf. He accuses the devil of surprising him (333-432). In the throes of guilt Theophile finds hope in the goodness of God and cries out for help to the Virgin, promising to fast and to pray until he is forgiven. Doubt besets him again, for he finds himself unworthy of addressing the Virgin. He finally puts all his trust in her and spends forty days of penitence in the chapel (433-512). The Virgin appears to him at night, asking many questions: how can I intercede for such a great sinner without incurring the wrath of my Son? Theophile reminds her that he cannot pray directly to Christ and that she has already interceded in behalf of other sinners, recalling specifically Ninivin, David, St. Peter and Saint Justine (513-656). The Virgin is persuaded to help him and explains that if he prays in good faith God will listen to him. Theophile then recites his credo (657-754). The Virgin leaves to plead his case with Christ while Theophile prays for three days. She returns to say that his penitence is sufficient, and he requests her aid in recovering the charter he had signed with the devil. He prays again for three days during her absence, and she returns with the signed charter (755-854). Theophile confesses his sin publicly, whereupon the bishop rejoices and proclaims a miracle, stressing how tears of repentance can bring remission of sin. We are all weak, but the example of Theophile proves the goodness of God (855-1018). Ordered by the bishop, Theophile burns the charter, and the congregation praises God and the Virgin. Theophile returns to the place of his vision, remains three days in prayer, gives all his belongings to the poor and dies. Virgin Mary, hear our prayers and help us sinners (1019-1102).

BECKET I

"Tuit li fysicïen ne sunt adès bon mire"

This earliest vernacular version of the Life of Thomas Becket, archbishop of Canterbury is unique in several ways:

1) The 6,180 lines are alexandrine, grouped in mono-rhymed 5-line stanzas.

2) The author, Guernes de Pont-Sainte-Maxence, was the first to write about a contemporary.

3) Because of this, Guernes makes a conscious attempt at historicity; yet he is wearing two hats, those of historiographer and composer of legend.

The scant information about the author has been provided by E. Walberg.[1] Guernes names himself twice (ll. 5877, 6156) and thus we know that he was from the small town of Pont-Sainte-Maxence in the north of the Ile-de-France near Picardy. From line 2491 on and the epilogue, we know that he was a wandering cleric with a good command of Latin.

Shortly after Becket's murder on December 29, 1170, Guernes begins his Life in verse. Dissatisfied with his first rendition, he goes to Canterbury to inform himself directly through contact with eye witnesses. This first version is lost and it is only the second,

---

[1] Emmanuel Walberg, *La Vie de Saint Thomas Becket par Guernes de Pont-Sainte-Maxence* (Paris: Champion, 1969), iv, and by the same author, *La Tradition hagiographique de saint Thomas Becket avant la fin du XIIème siècle* (Paris: Droz, 1929), pp. 82-84.

written in England from 1172 to 1174, which has come down to us. [2]

There are six MSS and one fragment of this version:

1) B—Wolfenbüttel, Duck of Brunswick Library, August, fol. 1r-84v.

2) H—London, British Museum, Harley 270, fol. 1r-122v.

3) P—Paris, Bibliothèque nationale, français 13513, fol. 1-98.

4) W—Welbeck Abbey, Library of the Duke of Portland, iCi, fol. 9r-50v.

5) C—Cheltenham, Thirlestaine House, Phillips Collection, 8113, fol. 16r-130r.

6) D—London, British Museum, Cotton, Comitien XI, fol. 25r-43v.

7) Fragment, Oxford, Bodleian, Rawlinson C 641, fol. 10-13. [3]

All the MSS were copied by Anglo-Norman scribes, which accounts for the slight Anglo-Norman coloration of the language. Yet Guernes' language is relatively free of dialectal traits, and Walberg concludes that he wrote in the literary language of the period. [4]

The Latin sources of the poem have been fully studied by both Walberg and J. Merk. [5] Walberg concludes that Guernes' principal sources are Edward Grim's *Vita Sancti Thomae* (1172) and William of Canterbury's *Vita Sancti Thomae* (1172-74); some details he borrowed from Benoit of Canterbury, also known as Benoit of Peterborough (1173 or 1174) and William Fitz-Stephen (1173-74). At least one Latin version, that of Roger de Pontigny (1176 or 1177) used Guernes as a source.

Both Walberg and Merk have studied in detail the parts of the poem which are historically valid and those where the poet's imagination and creativity (or perhaps simply the tradition of hagiog-

---

[2] *Ibid.,* edition, iv, v.

[3] For a description of the contents of each MS see Walberg, edition, xiv, xv.

[4] *Ibid.,* xxi.

[5] Walberg's findings in *Tradition* differ noticeably from those of M. L. Halphen, "Les Biographes de Thomas Becket," *Revue Historique,* 102 (1909), 35-45; Josef Merk, *Die literarische Gestaltung der altfranzösischen Heiligenleben bis Ende des 12. Jahrhunderts* (Affoltern am Albis: J. Weiss, 1946).

raphy with its stock elements) emerge dominant. [6] Becket was born in London of well-to-do Norman parents in 1118. In 1142 he entered the service of Archbishop Theobald of Canterbury. In 1155 he was chosen by King Henry II to be royal chancellor, and in 1162 appointed Archbishop of Canterbury. When the friendship between Henry and Becket turned to conflict, the latter fled to France. Shortly after his return to France six years later, he was killed in the chapel of Canterbury Cathedral on December 29, 1170. In 1173, Pope Alexander III canonized him formally. The iconography has been analyzed by Louis Réau. [7] The development of the cult and the impact that the saint had on society have been treated in depth. [8]

Guernes' version recounts the following story:

I shall tell you the story of saint Thomas, the martyr. I have worked on this for four years and do not lie (1-165). Thomas was born "de nette gent" (170), Gilbert and Mahalt Becket after a dream that his mother had. He went to school at an early age and played with his friends (166-245). Thomas enters the service of Theobald of Canterbury, gains his confidence and is named archdeacon of Canterbury when Roger de Pont-l'Evêque becomes archbishop upon the death of William of York (246-280). Theobald recommends Becket to King Henry II, who names the latter as his chancellor. Becket fulfills his duties with zeal, never forgetting his allegiance to God and the Church. His wealth and power grow, the king has limitless confidence in him and entrusts to him the education of his son (281-430).

With the support of the king, Becket is elected archbishop of Canterbury at the death of Theobald. He undergoes a great change, adopting an ascetic existence and giving his complete devotion to God. He progressively loses favor with the king (431-740).

---

[6] Walberg, *Tradition*, pp. 135-185; Merk, *op. cit.* The Latin versions have been published twice: J. C. Robertson, *Materials for the History of Thomas Becket,* 7 vols. (London: Rolls Series, n.º 67, 1875-85), and by Migne in *Patrologia Latina.*

[7] Louis Réau, *L'Iconographie des saints,* Vol. III, Pt. 3 of *L'Iconographie de l'art chrétien* (Paris: Presses Universitaires de France, 1958), pp. 1272-77.

[8] See R. Foreville, *Thomas Becket. Actes du Colloque international de Sédières* (Paris, 1975), and Christine Renardy, "Notes concernant le culte de Saint Thomas Becket dans le diocèse de Liège aux 12ème et 13ème siècles," *Revue Belge de Philologie et d'Histoire,* 55 (1977), pp. 381-389.

Henry's anger is explained. In one instance Becket yields to the king: Henry wants to reinstate certain customs which the bishops refuse. During a ceremony at Clarendon, Becket promises finally to respect these customs, but against his better judgment. When the king puts in writing the sixteen articles of Clarendon, Becket refuses to sign, and Pope Alexander III supports the archbishop. The king vents his anger by condemning church officials through the secular judicial system (741-1180).

Other prelates abandon Thomas in his struggle against Henry. Feeling alone in a desperate cause, Becket leaves England, but the crew brings him back out of fear of the king. At Northampton the archbishop is sentenced to prison, but he escapes during the night. He hides in England for a short time before fleeing to Soissons, where he meets King Louis of France and cardinal Henry of Pisa (1181-2160).

Henry sends messengers requesting that Becket be refused all hospitality and aid. Louis, however, treats him well and refers him to the Pope. Despite intervention by Henry's envoys, Pope Alexander welcomes Becket at Sens. He remains there one month before retiring to the abbey at Pontigny upon the advice of the Pope (2161-2560).

Across the channel, Henry banishes the family and friends of Becket and seizes their possessions. He forbids other bishops to leave England and to correspond with the Pope. All comply except Roger of Worcester who joins Thomas in exile. Guernes transcribes the edict of Henry into French (2561-2745).

The young king is crowned by the archbishop of York, which constitutes a violation of the priviledges of the archbishop of Canterbury and brings about a papal condemnation. Guernes then summarizes the contents of letters exchanged between Becket and the bishops, and those between Henry and Becket (2746-3565).

During Becket's two years at Pontigny, he has divine visions and works miracles. Forced to leave by Henry, Becket accepts Louis' invitation to stay at the Benedictine abbey of Sainte-Colombe, near Sens, where, despite the opposition of Henry, he remains for four years (3566-3980).

Many attempts at reconciliation are carried out by Louis and envoys of the Pope: at Pontoise, Nogent-le-Retrou, Montmirail, Montmartre, Fréteval, Tours and finally at Amboise where the terms of the accord are agreed upon and put in writing (3981-4525).

Becket returns to England acclaimed by all. He goes to London to salute the king but is refused an audience. He returns to Canterbury where he profers an anathema against the bishops who had crowned the young king (4526-4970).

Henry is furious and indignant against the archbishop. Four knights, Renaud Fils-Ours, William of Tracy, Hugh of Moreville and Richard the Breton, accompanied by others, go to Canterbury and accuse Becket of machinations against the young king. Becket is taken to the cloister for safety by the monks, but the archbishop unlocks the doors and faces his enemies. All of Becket's companions take flight except for Edward Grim. When the attack begins, Grim is wounded in the arm; Becket offers no resistance and dies after being stabbed four times (4971-5634).

Guernes laments such a crime and recounts proof of the martyr's sanctity. Miracles occur on the tomb of the saint. The king repents. The author exhorts the king to continue his good ways and tells of a dream which foresees the king's immanent conversion. Guernes names himself, tells of the circumstances of the writing of this Life, and affirms that its truth is absolute (5635-6180).

BECKET II

"Al Deu loenge e sun servise"

This second version of the *Life of St. Thomas Becket* offers a more schematic as well as a more earth-bound portrait of the martyr than that of Guernes. It is the first poem in Old French hagiography to be composed in six-line stanzas of tail-rhyme. [1]

Little is known about the author: Beneit was a Benedictine monk at the Abbey of St. Alban, [2] writing between 1183 and 1189, probably in 1184. [3] In the introduction to his edition of the *Life*, Schlyter presents linguistic evidence in support of the historical findings of Walberg. [4]

Through a comparative study of Beneit's version and an Icelandic version (*Thomas Saga Erkibyskups*), [5] Walberg discovered that both versions came from the same source: a lost Life by Robert of Cricklade. [6] His *Vita Sancti Thomae* was composed before 1180, probably shortly after 1172 while he was prior of St. Frideswide's (1140-1177), now Christ Church at Oxford.

Beneit's version is preserved in six MSS, all executed by Anglo-Norman scribes:

---

[1] M. D. Legge, *Anglo-Norman Literature and its Background* (Oxford: Clarendon Press, 1963), p. 250.

[2] Emmanuel Walberg, *La Tradition hagiographique de Saint Thomas Becket avant la fin du XIIème siècle* (Paris: Droz, 1929), pp. 12-13.

[3] *Ibid.,* pp. 14-21.

[4] Börje Schlyter, *La Vie de Thomas Becket par Beneit. Etudes romanes de Lund,* n.º 4 (Lund: Gleerup and Munksgaard, 1941), pp. 23-73.

[5] E. Magnusson, *Thomas Saga Erkibyskups. A Life of Archbishop Thomas Becket in Icelandic* (London: Rolls Series, n.º 65, 1875-83).

[6] Walberg, *op. cit.,* pp. 21-33.

1) C—Cambridge, Clare College, Kk. 3:13, fol. 1-4v, 230-233v. [7]

2) T—Cheltenham, Thirlestaine House, Collection Phillipps-Fenwick, 8113 (formerly Heber 322.2), fol. 1-15v.

3) P—Paris, Bibliothèque nationale, fr. 902, fol. 129v-135r.

4) B—London, British Museum, Cotton, Vespasian B XIV, fol. 95v-113r.

5) D—London, British Museum, Cotton, Vespasian D IV, fol. 149-171r. [8]

6) H—London, British Museum, Harley 3775, fol. 1-14r.

A summary of the story as Beneit tells it in 2,124 lines follows.

I want to sing the praises of saint Thomas who died an honorable death. He was born to noble parents in London, after a dream the mother had just before his birth. She dedicates her son to the Church and soon he enters the service of Theobald of Canterbury who later names him archdeacon (1-90).

The king makes Thomas his chancellor and showers him with gifts. Becket gives his riches to the poor and displays other virtues of a man of God. At the death of Theobald, Thomas is elected archbishop of Canterbury after lengthy debate. He doesn't consider himself worth of such a position and at first refuses. He finally relents, because it is the will of God (91-366).

Becket experiences a change in attitude and habits which will eventually lead to a schism between the king and the archbishop. Henry calls a meeting at Clarendon where he demands that secular justice apply to church officials. Becket takes a stand against Henry. At a subsequent meeting in Northampton, Thomas again declares the superiority of the Church over royal power in a long, allegorical speech (367-672).

Becket appeals to the Pope whom he meets in Sens. The Pope is struck by Thomas' humility and urges him to pursue his ecclesiastical career. Becket is then warmly received by the King of

---

[7] For a description of C see M. R. Jones, *A Descriptive Catalogue of the Western Manuscripts in the Library of Clare College*, p. 21 ff. Cited by Schlyter.

[8] For a description see H. Delaborde, *Etude sur la chronique en prose de Guillaume le Breton* (Paris: Thorin, 1881), p. 11 ff.

France. Henry's messengers plead with the Pope in an attempt to exonerate the king (673-918).

Enjoying the protection of the French king, Thomas retires to the Abbey at Pontigny where he is a model of virtue. He has a vision during which a celestial voice predicts his martyrdom. English bishops try to bring about a reconciliation between Henry and Becket, but the archbishop remains firm in his refusal of customs which have not been approved by Rome. Angered, the king takes revenge by banishing Becket's family. Despite the Pope's intervention, a new attempt at reconciliation in Montmartre fails when Becket refuses to give the kiss of peace to the king (919-1170).

Thomas leaves Pontigny for Sens. Henry has his son crowned king by the archbishop of York, in violation of the rights of the archbishop of Canterbury. Thomas complains to the Pope who recommends patience. After many negociations, Thomas and Henry are reconciled at Fréteval and the former returns to England. He immediately reprimands the bishops who had participated in the coronation ceremony (1171-1308).

Becket goes to Canterbury where he delivers a sermon, and then to London where he is refused access to the young king. The archbishop chooses some messengers to intercede on his behalf, among them the abbot Simon, prior of St. Alban's, the author's immediate superior. The messengers fail. Thomas is saddened and returns to Canterbury. The three ex-communicated bishops are now declared enemies of the archbishop, and manage to provoke the king into pronouncing threatening words against Becket (1309-1560).

Four knights come to Canterbury ordering Thomas to submit to the young king. Becket refuses. The knights leave momentarily to arm themselves while the monks try to persuade Becket to protect himself by locking the doors. The archbishop states that he is ready to die. The knights enter the church and stab Becket who asks them to spare the monks. One of the knights plunges his sword into the head of Becket, already dead. They pillage the palace (1561-1782).

The monks carefully prepare the martyr's body for burial. Becket died on the fourth Calends of January, 1171. The Church would have perished if Thomas had not purged it of the vicissitudes which had plagued it since ancient times. After his death, Becket performs miracles: he ressurects the dead, cures lepers, and restores the sight and health to a young man of Bedford. We must all pray for the king and the royal family, as we should try to keep from sin. I am brother Beneit who translated this from the Latin. May we one day all find ourselves in paradise with Becket (1783-2124).

APPROXIMATE DATES OF TWELFTH-CENTURY SAINTS' LIVES

We should like to be able to furnish a definitive list of the dates of composition for the Saints' Lives studied here, but there exist so many variants and unknowns that it is impossible. The dating of a manuscript by qualified paleographers, however reliable, does not provide information concerning the date of composition of the texts it may contain. Literary historians, critics and editors have in turn sought to shed light on this problem with differing results. We are indebted to all those scholars before us who have wrestled with this question and defer to their findings. In cases of discrepancies, the choice (in bold type) between diverging opinions in ours.

		Date	*Reference*
1.	Alexis I	in or before 1119	Storey (ed.), Legge (1) (both rely on Pächt)
2.	Alexis II	twelfth century	Paris, Pannier (ed.)
3.	Bon	first written 1165-70; second version **1175-80**	Legge (1)
		c. 1160-70	Vising
4.	Brendan	**c. 1120**	Payen
		c. 1122	Vising
		perhaps the earliest	Legge (1)
		probably 1112	Ritchie
		1121	Waters (ed.), Walberg (3)
5.	Catherine	**1163-89**	MacBain (ed.)
		c. 1150-60	Vising
		late twelfth century	Legge (1)
6.	Edmond I	**perhaps before 1150**	Legge (1)
		1150-60	Vising
		second half twelfth century	Nabert (ed.)

		Date	Reference
7.	Edmund II	not before 1175, or even 1190	Haxo
		end of twelfth century	Legge (1)
		c. 1170-80	Vising
		1190-1200	Ravenel (ed.)
		1175	Levy
		c. 1170	Kjellman (ed.)
8.	Edward	**1163-69**	Legge (1)
		1170	Södergard (ed.)
9.	Evroul	1165-80	Danne (ed.)
10.	Genevieve	1200	Bohm (ed.)
11.	George I	**just before or after Crusade in 1188**	Legge (1)
		end of twelfth century	Matzke (ed.)
		late twelfth century	Vising
		1199	Levy
12.	George II	written around the same time as George I	Petersen
13.	Giles	**c. 1190**	Legge (1)
		1185	Levy
		second half 12th c.	Vising
		1170 at earliest	Paris, Bos (ed.)
14.	Gregory	c. 1145	Payen (2)
		second half 12th c.	Telger (ed.)
15.	Hildefonse	first written 1165-70	Legge (1)
		second version 1175-80	
		c. 1160-70	Vising
16.	Laurence	**third quarter 12th c.**	Russell (ed.)
		beginning second half 12th c.	Söderhjelm
		early thirteenth c.	Vising
		twelfth century	Legge (1)
17.	Margaret	**1135**	Levy
		twelfth century	Francis (ed.)
		thirteenth century	Legge (1)
18.	Mary I	twelfth c., seems younger than Giles (1170)	Baker (ed.)
		last quarter 12th c.	Dembowski (ed.)
19.	Mary II	first written 1165-70; second version 1175-80	Legge (1)
		c. 1160-70	Vising
		end 12th c., beg. 13th c.	Neuhaus (ed.)
		contemporary to Mary I	Dembowski (ed.)
20.	Nicholas	**c. 1150**	Ronsjö (ed.)
		1153	Levy
21.	Silvester	late twelfth century	Planchnault (ed.)
22.	Theophile	**first version 1165-70;** second version 1175-80	Legge (1)
		c. 1160-70	Vising

		Date	Reference
23.	Becket I	1174	Levy, Legge (1), Walberg (ed.), Payen (2)
24.	Becket II	**1184**	Legge (1), Walberg (3), Schlyter (ed.)
		1185	Vising
		1189	Levy

We should mention that some texts have been eliminated from this study on the basis of recent scholarship which places them in the thirteenth century (all five versions of *Le Purgatoire de St. Patrice, St. Osith, St. Modwenna, Fragment d'une Vie de Becket,* Moïse l'Ethiopien and Thais contained in *Le Poème moral,* and *Josephat et les Sept Dormants*). *Guillaume d'Angleterre* finds no place in this study since it is essentially a romance, despite its promising hagiographical tone at the beginning.

Appendix B

Whether a text is Anglo-Norman or continental remains a difficult problem and has not always been satisfactorily resolved. The entire question of dialects is in itself a moot point for some scholars. Clear lines cannot be drawn, and the language of the author, tainted by that of the scribe, is more often a conglomerate of dialects, typical of the wandering bards of the Middle Ages and their methods of transmission. Some travelled more than others, some were churchmen and others laymen, but most assuredly all, at one time or other, heard dialects or languages different from their own. There was perhaps even a "literary language" of the period (see Walberg, *La Vie de St. Thomas Becket,* v) devoid of any dialectal demarcations.

We have attempted here to draw up two lists: 1) those works generally agreed to be Anglo-Norman, and 2) those considered continental. We again defer to recent scholarship and are indebted to research of those mentioned.

Anglo-Norman

Alexis I	Lege (1) (Manuscript yes, text no), **Storey** (ed.)
Bon	Legge (1), Vising
Brendan	Legge (1), Vising, Ritchie, Waters (ed.), Payen (2)
Catherine	Legge (1), Vising, MacBain (ed.)
Edmund I	Legge (1), Vising, Nabert (ed.)
Edmund II	Legge (1), Vising, Ravenel (ed.), Haxo, Kjellman (ed.)
Edward	Legge (1), Södergard (ed.)
George I	Legge (1), Vising, Matzke (ed.)
Giles	Legge (1), Vising, Paris and Bos (ed.)
Hildefonse	Legge (1), Vising
Laurence	Legge (1), Vising, Söderhjelm (ed.)

Mary II	Legge (1), Vising, Neuhaus (ed.), Dembowski (ed.)
Theophile	Legge (1), Vising
Becket I	influenced by Anglo-Norman (Legge)
	Walberg (ed.)
Becket II	Legge (1), Vising, Walberg (3), Schlyter (ed.)

Continental

Alexis II	Paris and Pannier (ed.)
Evroul	Danne (ed.)
Genevieve	Bohm (ed.)
George II	Luzarche (ed.), Petersen
Gregory	"Norman" (Meyer), Telger (ed.)
Margaret	Francis (ed.)
Mary I	more Norman than Anglo-Norman **(Vising)**
	Anglo-Norman (Baker), neither is proven (Dembowski)
Nicholas	Ronsjö (ed.) calls it Anglo-Norman, but attributes it to Wace (generally accepted). Wace wrote in Caen.
Silvester	Planchenault (ed.)

BIBLIOGRAPHY

Aarne-Thompson. *Types of the Folk-Tale. Folklore Fellows Communications,* no. 74. Helsingfors, 1928.

Abbo of Fleury. *Vita et Passio Sancti Eadmundi.* Migne, *PL,* CXXXIX, 507-520.

Acta Sanctorum. Brussels: 1643...

Aigrain, René. *L'Hagiographie.* Paris: Bloud & Gay, 1953.

Albrecht, O. *Four Latin Plays of Saint Nicholas.* Diss. Philadelphia, 1935.

Amiaud, A. *La Légende syriaque de Saint Alexis.* Paris: Bouillon, 1889.

Anrich, G. *Hagios Nikolaos, der heilige Nikolaus in der griechischen Kirche, Texte und Untersuchungen.* 2 vols. Berlin, 1913-1917.

Anson, Peter F. *The Call of the Desert. The Solitary Life in the Christian Church.* London: 1964.

Archer, J. "Sur un calembour méconnu de Simund de Freine." *Zeitschrift für romanische Philologie,* 34 (1910), 211-212.

D'Arcq, Douet. "Inventaire du trésor de la cathédrale de Clermont-Ferrand." *Revue archéologique,* 10 (1853), 160-174.

Arndt, Wilhelm. *Berichte über die Verhandlungen der K. Sächs. Gesellschaft der Wissenschaften zu Leipzig.* Phil.-Hist. Klasse, 1875.

Arnold, Thomas. *Memorials of St. Edmund's Abbey.* 3 vols. London: Rolls Series, 1890-1896.

———. *Le Roman de Brut de Wace.* 2 vols. Paris: Société des Anciens Textes Français, 1938-1940.

Aston, S. C. "The Saint in Medieval Literature." *Modern Language Review,* 65 (1970), xxv-xlii.

Auerbach, Eric. *Literatursprache und Publikum in der lateinischen Spätantike und in Mittelalter.* Bern: Francke Verlag, 1958.

Bachelard, Gaston. *La Poétique de la rêverie.* Paris: Presses Universitaires de France, 1960.

———. *La Terre et les rêveries du repos.* Paris: José Corti, 1948.

Baker, A. T. "Fragment of an Anglo-Norman Life of Edward the Confessor." *Modern Language Review,* 3 (1907-1908), 374-375.

———. "Saints' Lives Written in Anglo-French: Their Historical, Social and Literary Importance." *Transactions of the Royal Society of Literature of the United Kingdom,* New Series 4 (1924), 119-156.

312 LE VAIN SIECLE GUERPIR

Baker, A. T. "La Vie de Sainte Marie l'Egyptienne". *Revue des Langues Romanes,* 59 (1916-1917), 145-401.

Barensis, Johannes Archidiaconus. *De Translatione Sancti Nicolai Episcopi* in Surius, L. *De Probatis Sanctorum Historiis Coloniae Agrippinae,* no. 7, 1618, pp. 116-121.

Beaujouan, Guy. "Le Symbolisme des nombres à l'époque romane." *Cahiers de Civilisation Médiévale,* 4 (1961), 159-160.

Bédier, Joseph. *Légendes épiques.* Paris, 1908-1913. Vol. 3.

Bernard of Clairvaux. *The Twelve Degrees of Humility.* Trans. Mills, Barton R. R. London, 1929.

Bernheimer, Richard. *Wild Men in the Middle Ages.* Cambridge: Harvard University Press, 1952.

Bieling, H. *Ein Beitrag zur Uberlieferung der Gregorlegende. Altfranzösischen Bibliothek,* n. 9. Berlin, 1874.

Bienvenu, J. M. "Pauvreté, misères et charité en Anjou aux XIème et XIIème siècles." *Moyen Age,* 72 (1966), 389-424, 73 (1967), 5-34.

Bohm, Lennart. *La Vie de sainte Geneviève de Paris.* Upsala, 1955.

The Book of Saints. A Dictionary of Persons Canonized or Beatified by the Catholic Church. Ed. St. Augustine's Abbey. Ramsgate: Crowell, 1921.

Bos, Alphonse, and Paris, Gaston. *La Vie de saint Gilles par Guillaume de Berneville, poème du XIIème siècle publié d'après le manuscrit unique de Florence.* Paris: Société des Anciens Textes Français, no. 14, 1881.

Bouly De Lesdain, A. M. "Les Manuscrits didactiques antérieurs au XIVème siècle: Essai d'inventaire." *Bulletin de l'Institut de Recherche et d'Histoire des Textes,* no. 14. Paris, 1966.

Brandin, Louis. "Un Fragment de la *Vie de saint Gilles* en vers français." *Romania,* 33 (1904), 94-98.

Brémond, Henri. *Prière et poésie.* Paris: Grasset, 1926.

Bronzini, Giovanni. *La Leggenda di S. Caterina d'Alessandria. Passioni greche e latine. Atti della accad. naz. dei Lincei, Memorie, Cl. di Scienze morale, stor. et filol.,* Ser. 8, Vol. 9, Fasc. 2. Rome, 1960.

Brosnahan, Leger. "Wace's Use of Proverbs." *Speculum,* 39 (1964), 444-473.

Brown, James Baldwin. *Stoics and Saints. Lectures on the Later Heathen Moralists, and on Some Aspects of the Life of the Medieval Church.* New York: Macmillan, 1893.

Budge, E. A. Wallis. *The Martyrdom and Miracles of Saint George of Cappadocia. The Coptic Text Edited with an English Translation.* London, 1885.

Bulatkin, Eleanor W. "The Arithmetic Structure of the Old French *Vie de Saint Alexis." Publications of the Modern Language Association,* 74 (1959), 495-502.

Camproux, C. *"The Life of St. Catherine* ed. par William MacBain." *Revue des Langues romanes,* 108 (1966), 220.

Carr, Gerald F. "The Prologue to Wace's *Vie de St. Nicholas*: A Structural Analysis." *Philological Quarterly,* 47 (1968), 1-7.

Catalogue Général des Manuscrits des Bibliothèques Publiques en France. Paris, 1887.

Catalogue of Additions to the Manuscripts in the British Museum in the Years 1836-1840. London, 1843.

Caulkins, J. Hillier. "Les Notations numériques et temporelles dans la *Navigation de Saint Brendan* de Benedeit." *Moyen Age,* 80 (1974), 245-260.

Chenu, M. D. *L'Eveil de la conscience dans la civilisation médiévale*. Montreal: Institut d'Etudes Médiévales, 1969.

————. *La Théologie au XIIème siècle*. Paris: Vrin, 1957.

Constable, Giles. "Twelfth-Century Spirituality and the Late Middle Ages." *Medieval and Renaissance Studies*, 5 (1971), 27-60.

Crawford, M. S. *The Life of Saint Nicholas*. Philadelphia, 1924.

Curtius, Ernst Robert. *Europäische Literatur und lateinisches Mittelalter*. Bern: Francke Verlag, ed. 1961.

————. "Zur Interpretation des Alexiusliedes." *Zeitschrift für romanische Philologie*, 56 (1936), 113-137.

Danne, Ferdinand. "Das altfranzösische Ebrulfusleben, eine Dichtung aus dem 12. Jahrhundert nach dem Manuskript 19867 der national Bibliothek zu Paris." *Romanische Forschungen*, 32 (1913), 748-893.

Davy, M. M. *Essai sur la symbolique romane*. Paris: Flammarion, 1955.

Delaborde, H. *Etude sur la chronique en prose de Guillaume le Breton* (Paris: Thorin, 1881).

Delaruelle, Etienne. "La Culture religieuse des laïcs en France aux XIème et XIIème siècles." *Miscellanea del Centro di Studi Medioevali*, 5 (1968), 548-581.

————. "Les Ermites et la spiritualité populaire." *Miscellanea del Centro di Studi Medioevali*, 4 (1967), 212-241.

————. "L'Idée de croisade dans la littérature clunisienne du XIème siècle et l'abbaye de Moissac." *Annales du Midi*, 75 (1963), 419-439.

Delehaye, H. *Les Légendes hagiographiques*. 3rd. ed. Brussels: Société des Bollandistes, 1927.

————. "Recherches sur le légendier romain." *Analecta Bollandiana*, 51 (1933), 34-72.

Delhaye, Philippe. "Les Perspectives morales de Richard de Saint Victor." *Mélanges Offerts à René Crozet à l'Occasion de son 70ème Anniversaire*. Poitiers: Société d'Etudes Médiévales, 1966. 851-862.

Delisle, L. "Description de la *Vie de Saint Silvestre*." *Bibliothèque de l'Ecole des Chartes*, 54 (1898), 533-537.

————. "Notices." *Romania*, 2 (1873), 91-95.

Delmas, F. "Remarques sur la *Vie de Sainte Marie l'Egyptienne*." *Echos d'Orient*, 4 (1902), 35-42, and 5 (1903), 15-17.

Dembowski, Peter F. *La Vie de Sainte Marie l'Egyptienne, versions en ancien et en moyen français*. Geneva: Droz, 1976.

————. "Literary Problem of Hagiography in Old French." *Medievalia et Humanistica*, 7 (1975), 117-130.

Dillman. "Uber die apokryphischen Märtyrergeschichten des Cyriacus mit Julitta und des Georgius." *Sitzb. d. k. preuss. Acad. d. Wiss. zu Berlin*. Phil.-Hist. Klasse, 1887. Cited by Matzke.

Dirickx van der Straeten, Hermine. *La Vie de Saint Jehan Bouche d'Or et la vie de Dieudonnée, sa mère*. Liège: Vaillant-Carmanne, 1931.

Dorange. *Catalogue des manuscrits de Tours*.

Duchesne, W. L. "Les Légendes chrétiennes de l'Aventin." *Mélanges d'Archéologie et d'Histoire*, 10 (1890), 234-235.

Ebel, Uda. *Das altromanische Mirakel. Ursprung und Geschichte einer literarischen Gattung*. Studia Romanica, no. 8. Heidelberg: Carl Winter Universitätsverlag, 1965.

Einenckel, E. *The Life of Saint Katherine*. London, 1884.

Erasmus, Desiderius. "Stultitiae Laus." *Opera Omnia*, vol. 4. London, 1962.

314   LE VAIN SIECLE GUERPIR

Erdmann, Carl. *Entstehung des Kreuzzugsgedantens.* Stuttgart: Kohlhammer, 1965.

Esposito, Marius. "Inventaire des anciens manuscrits français des bibliothèques de Dublin." *Revue des Bibliothèques,* 24 (1914), 185-198.

Falconius, Nicholaus Carminius. *Sancti Confessoris Pontificis et Celeberrimi Thaumaturgi Nicolai Acta Primigenia.* Naples, 1751.

Fantier-Jones, E. C. "Les Vies de sainte Catherine d'Alexandrie." *Romania,* 56 (1930), 80-104.

Fawtier, R. "Les Reliques rouennaises de sainte Catherine d'Alexandrie." *Analecta Bollandiana,* 41 (1923), 357-368.

Ferguson, Wallace K. "The Church in a Changing World: A Contribution of the Interpretation of the Renaissance." *The Role of Religion in Modern European History.* New York, 1964, pp. 10-28.

Festugière, André-Jean. *Les Moines d'Orient.* Paris, 1961.

Fissen, K. *Das Leben des heiligen Nikolaus in der altfranzösischen Literatur und seine Quellen.* Diss. Göttingen, 1921.

Fitzell, J. *The Hermit in German Literatur: From Lessing to Eichendorff. Studies in the Germanic Languages and Literature,* no. 30. Chapel Hill: University of North Carolina Press, 1961.

Fliche A., Foreville, R., Rousset, J. *Histoire de l'Eglise.* ed. E. Amann, A. Dumas. Vols. 7, 8. Paris: Bloud & Gay, 1940.

Ford, J. D. M. "The Saints' Life in Vernacular Literature of the Middle Ages." *Catholic Historical Review,* 17 (1931-1932), 268-277.

Foreville, Raymonde. *Thomas Becket. Actes du Colloque International de Sédières* (Paris, 1975).

Francis, Elizabeth A. *Wace: La Vie de Sainte Marguerite. Classiques Français du Moyen Age.* Paris: Champion, 1932.

Frappier, Jean. *Chrétien de Troyes.* Paris: Hatier, 1957.

Fritz, R. *Uber Verfasser und Quellen der altfranzösischen Estoire de Seint Aeward le Rei.* Heidelberg: Marcus Zöller, 1910.

Gaiffier, Baudouin de. "*Intactam sponsari relinquens.* A propos de !a *Vie de Saint Alexis.*" *Analecta Bollandiana,* 65 (1947), 157-195.

————. "La Légende de Charlemagne, le péché de l'empereur et son pardon." In *Recueil de Travaux offerts à M. Clovis Brunel.* Paris: Société de l'Ecole des Chartes, 1955. Vol. I, pp. 490-503.

Gallia Christiana, VII. Cited by Bohm.

Gams. *Series Episcoporum Ecclesiae Catholicae.* Ratisbonne, 1873.

Geraldi Cambrensis Opera. Rolls Series, I. Cited by Matzke.

Gerould, C. H. "A New Text of the *Passio Sancta Margaritae* with Some Account of its Latin and English Relations." *Publications of the Modern Language Association,* 39 (1924), 525-556.

Geschière, Léon. "Un passage obscur de la *Vie de Sainte Catherine.*" *Festschrift Wartburg zum 80. Geburtstag, 18 mai, 1968.* Tübingen: Niemeyer, 1968. Vol. I, pp. 343-358.

Ghellinck, Joseph de. *L'Essor de la littérature latine au XIIème siècle.* Brussels: Desclée de Brouwer, 1955.

Gibbs, M. *Early Charters of St. Paul's Cathedral.* Camden Society, 3rd Series, 1939.

Gierden, Karlheinz. *Das altfranzösische Alexiuslied der Handschrift L. Ein Interpretation unter dem Gesichtspunkt von Trauer und Freude. Untersuchungen zur romanischen Philologie,* I. Meisenheim am Glan: Anton Hain, 1967.

BIBLIOGRAPHY 315

Glasser, Richard. *Time in French Life and Thought.* trans. C. G. Pearson. Totowas, New Jersey: Manchester University Press, 1972.

Gnädinger, Louise. *Eremitica. Studien zur altfranzösischen Heiligenvita des 12. und 13. Jahrhunderts. Beihefte zur Zeitschrift für romanische Philologie,* n.º 130. Tübingen: Niemeyer, 1972.

Goldschmidt, A. *Der Albani-Psalter in Hildesheim.* Berlin, 1895.

Goubert, Danièle. "Recherche sur les pauvres et la pauvreté." *Centre de Recherche et d'Histoire du Moyen Age,* 4 (1965-1966), 1-8.

Graf, M. *Roma nella memoria e nelle imaginazini del medio evo.* Cited by Paul Meyer, "*La Vie de Saint Silvestre* en vers français. *Romania* 28 (1899), 281.

Gröber, G. *Grundiss der romanischen Philologie.* I (1888), II (1893-1902). Strasburg.

Groot, Adriaan De. *Saint Nicholas, a Psychoanalytic Study of his History and Myth.* Paris: Mouton, 1965.

Györy, Jean. "Hagiographie hétérodoxe." *Acta ethnographica Academiae Scientiarum Hungaricae,* 2 (1962), 375-390.

Halphen, M. L. "Les Biographes de Thomas Becket." *Revue Historique,* 102 (1909), 34-45.

Harris, J. Rendell. "A New Christian Apology." *Bulletin of the John Rylands Library* 7, 8, 9 (1923-1925).

Harden, Arthur Robert. "The *Ubi sunt* Theme in Three Anglo-Norman Saints' Lives." *Romance Notes,* 1 (1959), 63-64.

Haxo, Henry. "Denis Piramus: *La Vie Seint Edmunt.*" *Modern Philology,* 12 (1914), 345-366, 13 (1915), 559-583.

Henri, Albert. "Séquence de Sainte Eulalie." *Chrestomatie de la Littérature en Ancien Français.* 2nd ed., Bern: Francke, 1960, pp. 2-3.

Herbert, J. A. "A New Manuscript of Adgar's Mary Legends." *Romania,* 32 (1903), 401-402.

Holmes, U. T. "Norman Literature and Wace." In *Medieval Secular Literature, Four Essays,* ed. W. Matthews, *University of California at Los Angeles Center for Medieval and Renaissance Studies,* Contributions I, University of California Press, 1965.

Hopper, V. Foster. *Medieval Number Symbolism: Its Sources, Meaning, and Influence on Thought and Expression.* New York: Columbia University Press, 1938.

Houck, Margaret. *Sources of the Roman de Brut of Wace.* University of California Publication in English, no. 5, 1940-1944.

Howard, Donald Roy. "The Contempt of the World: A Study in the Ideology of Latin Christendom with Emphasis on Fourteenth-Century English Literature." Diss. University of Florida, 1954.

Hugh of Saint Victor, in *Patrologia Latina,* 177, p. 585.

Jackson, W. T. H. "Problems of Communication in the Romances of Chrétien de Troyes." *Medieval Literature and Folklore Studies: Essays in Honor of Francis Lee Utley.* New Jersey: Rutgers University Press, 1970, pp. 39-50.

James, M. R. *Catalogue of the Western Manuscripts in the Library of the Trinity College.* Cambridge. Cited by Ronsjö.

Jarnik, J. U. *Dvé verse starofrancouské legendy o sv. Kateriné Alexandrinské.* Prague, 1894.

Javelet, Robert. *Psychologie des auteurs spirituels du XIIème siècle.* Strasburg: Muh. Le Roux, 1959.

316 LE VAIN SIECLE GUERPIR

Jirmounsky, M. Malkiel. "Essai d'analyse des procédés littéraires de Wace." *Revue des Langues Romanes,* 63 (1925-1926) 261-296.

Jolles, André. *Einfache Formen: Legende/Sage/Mythe/Rätsel/Spruch/Kasus/ Memorabile/Märchen/Witz.* 2nd. ed. Tübingen: Niemeyer, 1958.

Jones, C. W. *The Saint Nicholas Liturgy and its Literary Relationships (9th to 12th Centuries).* Berkeley: University of California Press, 1963.

Jones, E. C. *Saint Gilles. Essai d'histoire littéraire.* Paris: Champion, 1914.

Jones, M. R. *A Descriptive Catalogue of the Western Manuscripts in the Library of Clare College.* Cited by Schlyter.

Keller, Hans-Erich. "Quelques réflexions sur la poésie hagiographique en ancien français: A propos de deux nouveaux manuscrits de la *Conception Nostre Dame* de Wace." *Vox Romanica,* 34 (1975), 94-123.

Kjellman, Hilding. *La Deuxième Collection anglo-normande des Miracles de la Sainte Vierge et son original latin.* Paris: Champion, 1922.

————. *La Vie Seint Edmund le Rei, poème anglo-normand du XIIème siècle par Denis Piramus.* Göteborg: Wettergren and Kerbor, 1935.

Knowles, David. *Christian Monasticism.* New York: McGraw-Hill, 1969.

Kohler, C. *Etude critique sur le texte de la vie latine de Sainte Geneviève de Paris, avec deux textes de cette vie. Bibliothèque de l'Ecole des Hautes Etudes,* no. 48. Paris: Vieweg, 1881.

Krappe, Alexander Haggerty. "La Légende de Saint Grégoire." *Moyen Age,* 46 (1936), 161-177.

Kraus, Gerd. *Die Hanschrift von Cambrai der altfranzösischen Vie de Saint Grégoire.* Diss. Halle, 1932.

Kuchenbäcker, K. *Uber die Sprache des altfranzösischen Gregor B.* Diss. Halle, 1886.

Labosse, Abbé. *Histoire de Saint Laurent, diacre et martyr.* Lille, 1862.

Ladner, G. B. "Greatness in Medieval History." *Catholic Historical Review,* 50 (1964), 1-26.

Langfors, E. *Romania,* 46 (1915-1917), 102-103.

————. *Notices et Extraits des Manuscrits de la Bibliothèque Nationale,* vol. 33.

Larmat, Jean. "Le Réel et l'imaginaire dans la *Navigation de Saint Brendan.*" *Senefiance,* 2 (1976), 169-182.

Lea, H. C. *A History of Auricular Confession and Indulgences in the Latin Church.* 3 vols. London, 1896.

Leclercq, Jean. *L'Amour des lettres et le désir de Dieu: Initiation aux auteurs monastiques du moyen âge.* Paris: Le Cerf, 1957.

————. *Etudes sur le vocabulaire monastique du moyen âge. Studia Anselmiana,* no. 48. Rome: Pontificum Institutum S. Anselmi, 1961.

Lefèvre, Yves. *L'Elucidarium et les lucidaires.* Paris: Boccard, 1954.

Legge, Mary Dominica. *Anglo-Norman Literature and its Background.* Oxford: Clarendon Press, 1963.

————. *Anglo-Norman in the Cloisters: The Influence of the Orders upon Anglo-Norman Literature.* Edinburgh: Edinburgh University Press, 1950.

————. "Archaism and the Conquest." *Modern Language Review,* 51 (1956), 227-229.

Le Goff, Jacques. *La Civilisation de l'occident médiéval.* Paris: Arthaud, 1964.

Lejeune, Rita. "Le Péché de Charlemagne et la *Chanson de Roland.*" *Studia Philologica, Homenaje Ofrecido a Dámaso Alonso.* Madrid: 1961. Vol. 2, pp. 339-371.

Lekai, Louis J. "Motives and Ideals of the Eleventh-Century Monastic Renewal." *Cistercian Studies,* 4 (1969), 3-20.

Levy, Raphael. "Chronologie approximative de la littérature française du Moyen Age." *Beihefte zur Zeitschrift für romanische Philologie.* Tübingen: Niemeyer, 1957, pp. 13-17.

Linskill, Jos. *Saint Léger: Etude de la langue du manuscrit de Clermont-Ferrand, suivie d'une édition critique du texte avec commentaire et glossaire.* Diss. Strasbourg, 1937.

Little, Lester K. "Pride goes before Avarice: Social Change and the Vices in Latin Christendom." *American Historical Review,* 76 (1971), 16-49.

Loomis, C. G. *White Magic: An Introduction to the Folklore of Christian Legend.* Cambridge: Medieval Academy of America, 1948.

Loomis, Grant. "The Growth of the Saint Edmund Legend." *Harvard Studies and Notes in Philology and Literature,* 4 (1932), 83-113.

Lozinski, Grigorii L. *De Saint Bon, Névêque de Clermont: Miracle versifié par Gautier de Coinci. Annales Academiae Scientiarum Fennicae,* n.º B XL 1 (Helsinki, 1938).

Luzarche, Victor. *La Vie du Pape Grégoire le Grand.* Tours, 1857.

――――. *La Vie de la Vierge Marie, par Wace, suivie de la Vie de Saint Georges.* Tours: Bouserez, 1858.

MacBain, William. *The Life of Saint Catherine by Clemence of Barking. Anglo-Norman Text Society,* no. 18, Oxford, 1964.

――――. "The Literary Apprenticeship of Clemence of Barking." *Journal of the Australasian Universities Language and Literature Association,* 9 (1958), 3-22.

Macray, W. D. *Codices a Kenelm Digby Anno 1634. Donati Catalogi Codd. Manuscr. Bibl. Bodleiannae.* Oxford, 1883.

Madan, F. *A Summary Catalogue of Western Manuscripts in the Bodleian Library.* Cited by Ronsjö.

Maddox, Donald. "Pilgrimage Narrative and Meaning in Manuscripts L and A of the *Vie de Saint Alexis.*" *Romance Philology,* 27 (1973), 143-157.

Magnusson, E. *Thomas Saga Erkibyskups. A Life of Archbishop Thomas Becket in Icelandic.* London: Rolls Series, n.º 65, 1875-1883.

Manger, K. *Die französischen Bearbeitungen der Legende der h. Katharina von Alexandrien.* Tübingen: Niemeyer, 1901.

Manselli, Raoul. *La Religion populaire au moyen âge. Problèmes de méthode et d'histoire.* Institut d'Etudes Médiévales Albert le Grand: Montreal, 1975.

Mansi, J. D. *Sacrorum Conciliorum.* Paris: Muguet, 1903.

Mason, M. E. *Active Life and Contemplative Life. A Study of the Concepts from Plato to the Present.* Milwaukee: Marquette University Press, 1961.

Matzke, John E. "The Anglo-Norman Poet Simund de Freine." *Transactions and Proceedings of the American Philological Association,* 33 (1902).

――――. "Contributions to the History of the Legend of Saint George, with Special Reference to the Sources of the French, German and Anglo-Saxon Metrical Versions." *Publications of the Modern Language Association,* 17 (1902), 464-535, and 18 (1903), 99-171.

――――. *Les Oeuvres de Simund de Freine, publiées d'après tous les textes manuscrits connus.* Paris: Société des Anciens Textes Français, 1909.

McKeehan, Irene P. "Saint Edmund of East Anglia: The Development of a Romantic Legend." *University of Colorado Studies,* 15 (1925), 13-74.

318   LE VAIN SIECLE GUERPIR

Meisen, K. *Nikolauskult und Nikolausbrauch im Abendlande, eine kultgeographischvolkskundliche Untersuchung.* Forschungen zur Volkskunde, Nos. 9-12, Düsseldorf, 1931.

Merk, Josef. *Die literarische Gestaltung der altfranzösischen Heiligenleben bis Ende des 12. Jahrhunderts.* Affoltern am Albis: J. Weiss, 1946.

Meyer, Paul. "Légendes hagiographiques en français." *Histoire Littéraire de la France,* 33 (1906), 328-378.

——. *Romania,* 22 (1893), 170.

——. *Romania,* 36 (1915).

——. "La Vie de Saint Silvestre en vers français." *Romania,* 28 (1899), 280-286.

Miehle, W. *Das Verhältnis der Handschriften des altfranzösischen Gregorius.* Diss. Halle, 1886.

Migne, J. P. *Patrologiae cursus completus, Series graeca.* Paris, 1857-1866. 166 vols. and 3 vols. tables, 1912, 1928, 1939.

——. *Patrologiae cursus completus, Patres ecclesiae latinae.* Paris, 1844-1855. 217 vols., 4 vols. of tables, 1855-1864.

Mombritus, Boninus. *Vitae Sanctorum.* Rpt. as *Sanctuarium seu Vitae Sanctorum, Novam Hanc Editionem Curaverunt Duo Monachi Solesmenses.* Paris, 1910.

——. *Catalogus Codicum Hagiographicorum Latinorum Biblio. Nat. Parisiensis.* 1643; rpt. Paris, 1910.

Monfrin, J. "MacBain's The Life of Saint Catherine." *Zeitschrift für romanische Philologie,* 83 (1967), 132-135.

Morris, Colin. *The Discovery of the Individual, 1050-1200.* New York: Harper and Row, 1972.

Mussafia, Adolf. *Studien zu den mittelalterischen Marienlegenden.* Vienna: Tempsky, 1891.

Nabert, Albert. *La Passium de Seint Edmund. Ein anglonormannisches Gedicht aus dem 12. Jahrhundert.* Greifswald, 1915.

Neuhaus, Carl. *Adgars Marienlegenden.* Heilbronn: Henninger, 1886.

——. *Das Dulwich'er Adgar-Fragment.* Aschersleben, 1887.

——. *Die lateinischen Vorlagen zu den Adgar'schen Marienlegenden.* 2 vols. Heilbronn: Henninger, 1886, 1890.

Oskamp, H. P. A. *The Voyage of Máel Dúin. A Study in Early Irish Voyage Literature.* Groningen: Wolters-Noordhoff, 1970.

Owen, Douglas David. *The Vision of Hell: Infernal Journeys in Medieval French Literature.* Edinburgh: Scottish Academic Press, 1970.

Paris, Gaston. *L'Histoire poétique de Charlemagne.* Paris: Franck, 1863.

——, and Pannier, L. *La Vie de Saint Alexis.* Paris: Franck, 1872.

——, and Bos, Alphonse. *La Vie de Saint Gilles par Guillaume de Berneville, poème du XIIème siècle publié d'après le manuscrit unique de Florence.* Paris: Société des Anciens Textes Français, 1881.

——. "Review of Andresen's edition of the *Roman de Rou.*" *Romania,* 9 (1880), 592ff.

Payen, Jean-Charles. *Le Motif du repentir dans la littérature française médiévale.* Geneva: Droz, 1968.

——. *Le Moyen Age. Vol. 1: Des Origines à 1300.* Paris: Arthaud, 1970.

Petersen, Holger. "Une Vie inédite de Saint Georges en vers français du Moyen Age." *Neuphilologische Mitteilungen,* 28 (1926), 1-7.

Petit. *Charles de Valois.* Cited by Bohm.

Plaine, Fr. *Vie inédite de Saint Malo, écrite au IXème siècle par Bili.* Rennes: Arth. de la Broderie, 1804.

Planchenault, Adrien. "La Vie de Saint Silvestre et l'invention de la Sainte Croix: poème français du XIIème siècle." *Cartulaire du Chapitre de Saint-Laud d'Angers, Actes du XIème et du XIIème siècles.* Angers, 1903.

Porter, M. E. and Baltzell, J. H. "The Old French Lives of Saint Edmund, King of East Anglia." *Romanic Review,* 45 (1954), 81-88.

Prior, O. H. *Cambridge Anglo-Norman Texts.* London: Cambridge University Press, 1924, vi-xxviii.

Réau, Louis. *L'Iconographie des saints,* Vol. III, Pts. 1-3 of *L'Iconographie de l'art chrétien.* Paris: Presses Universitaires de France, 1958.

Rembry, Ernest. *Saint Gilles, sa vie, ses reliques, son culte dans la Belgique et le nord de la France.* 2 vols. Bruges: Gaillard, 1881.

Renardy, Christine. "Notes concernant le culte de Saint Thomas Becket dans le diocèse de Liège aux XIIème et XIIIème siècles." *Revue Belge de Philologie et d'Histoire,* 55 (1977), 381-389.

Riché, Paul. "Recherches sur l'instruction des laïcs du IXème au XIIème siècle." *Cahiers de Civilisation Médiévale,* 5 (1962), 175-182.

Ritchie, R. L. G. "The Date of the *Voyage de Saint Brendan.*" *Medium Aevum,* 19 (1950), 64-66.

Robertson, Howard S. "*La Vie de Saint Alexis*: Meaning and Manuscript A." *Studies in Philology,* 67 (1970), 419-438.

Robertson, J. C. *Materials for the History of Thomas Becket.* 7 vols., London: Rolls Series n. 67, 1875-1885.

Robinson, J. A. "The Passion of Saint Catherine and the Romance of Barlaam and Josaphat." *Journal of Theological Studies,* 25 (1924).

Ronsjö, Einar. *La Vie de Saint Nicolas par Wace: Poème religieux du XIIème siècle publié d'après tous les manuscrits. Etudes romanes de Lund,* No. 5. Lund: Gleerup and Munksgaard, 1942.

Roques, Mario. "Notes pour l'édition de la *Vie de Saint Grégoire* en ancien français." *Romania,* 77 (1956), 1-25.

———. "Sur deux particularités métriques de la *Vie de Saint Grégoire* en ancien français." *Romania,* 48 (1929), 41-59.

Rousset, Paul. "La Croyance en la justice immanente à l'époque féodale." *Moyen Age,* 54 (1948), 225-248.

———. "Le Sens du merveilleux à l'époque féodale." *Moyen Age,* 62 (1956), 25-37.

———. "Recherches sur l'émotivité à l'époque féodale." *Cahiers de Civilisation Médiévale,* 2 (1959), 53-67.

Russell, D. W. *La Vie de Saint Laurent. An Anglo-Norman Poem of the Twelfth Century.* London: Anglo-Norman Text Society, No. 34, 1976.

Ryding, W. *Structure in Medieval Narrative. De Proprietatibus Litterarum. Series Major,* No. 12. Paris, 1971.

Saints d'hier et sainteté d'aujourd'hui. Centre Catholique des Intellectuels Français. Paris: Desclée de Brouwer, 1966.

Schirmer, G. *Zur Brendanus-Legende.* Leipzig: Habilitationsschrift, 1888.

Schlyter, Börje. *La Vie de Thomas Becket par Beneit: Poème anglo-normand du XIIème siècle publié d'après tous les manuscrits. Etudes romanes de Lund,* No. 4. Lund: Gleerup and Munksgaard, 1941.

Sckommodau, Hans. "Das Alexiuslied. Die Datierungsfrage und das Problem der Askese." *Medium Aevum Romanicum Festschrift für Hans Rheinfelder.* Munich, 1963, 208-304, 325-338.
————. "Zum altfranzösischen Alexiuslied." *Zeitschrift für romanische Philologie,* 70 (1954), 161-203.
Selmer, Carl. "The Beginnings of the Brendan Legend on the Continent." *Catholic Historical Review,* 29 (1943), 169-176.
————. "The Vernacular Translations of the *Navigatio:* A Bibliographical Study." *Medieval Studies,* 18 (1956), 145-157.
Simon, Edith. *The Saints.* London: Weidenfeld and Nicholson, 1968.
Sinclair, K. V. "Anglo-Norman Studies: The Last Twenty Years." *Australian Journal of French Studies,* 2 (1965), 113-155, 225-278.
Snyder, Susan. "The Left Hand of God: Despair in Medieval and Renaissance Tradition." *Studies in the Renaissance,* 12 (1965), 18-59.
Söderhjelm, Werner. "Le Poème de Saint Laurent dans Egerton 2710." *Mémoires de la Société Néophilologique à Helsingfors,* 1 (1893), 21-31.
————. *De Saint Laurent, poème anglo-normand du XIIème siècle, publié pour la première fois d'après le manuscrit unique de Paris.* Paris: Welter, 1888.
Södergärd, Osten. *La Vie Seinte Audrée, poème anglo-normand du XIIème siècle.* Upsala, 1955.
————. *La Vie d'Edouard le Confesseur, poème anglo-normand du XIIème siècle.* Upsala, 1948.
Southern, R. W. "The English Origins of the *Miracles of the Virgin*." *Medieval and Renaissance Studies,* 4 (1958), 176-216.
————. "The Place of England in the Twelfth-Century Renaissance." *History,* 45 (1960), 201-216.
————. *Western Society and the Church in the Middle Ages.* London: Harmondsworth, 1970.
Spitzer, Leo. "Erhellung des Polyeucte durch das Alexiuslied." *Archivum Romanicum,* 16 (1932), 473-500.
Sprissler, Manfred. *Das rhythmische Gedicht "Pater Deus ingenite" (IIJH) und das altfranzösische Alexiuslied.* Munich: Aschendorff, 1966.
Stebbins, C. E. "Les Origines de la légende de Saint Alexis." *Revue Belge de Philologie et d'Histoire,* 51 (1973), 497-507.
Steinweg, C. "Die handschriftlichen Gestaltungen der lateinischen *Navigatio Brendani.*" *Romanische Forschungen,* 7 (1891).
Stengel. *Codicem Manuscriptum Digby 86...Descripsit.* Halle, 1871.
Storey, Christopher. *La Vie de Saint Alexis.* Paris: Minard, 1968.
Strohmayer, Henri. *Romania,* 23 (1894), 601-607.
Strong, A. *A Catalogue of Letters and Other Historical Documents Exhibited in the Library of Welbeck Abbey.* London, 1903.
Tammi, D. Guido. *Due versioni della leggenda di S. Margherita d'Antiochia.* Piacenza: Scuola Artigiana dal Libro, 1958.
Telger, Gerta. *Die altfranzösische Gregoriuslegende nach der londoner Handschrift zum ersten Male herausgeben. Arbeiten zur romanische Philologie,* No. 5. Paris: Droz, 1933.
Tobler, Adolf. "Bruchstücke altfranzösischer Dichtung aus den in der Kubbet in Damaskus gefundenen Handschriften, 2. Ein Bruchstück eines Lebens der h. Maria aus Aegypten." *Sitzungsberichte der königlichpreussischen Akademie der Wissenschaften.* Phil-Hist. Klasse. 63. Berlin, pp. 966-969. Cited by Dembowski.

Tyssens, Madeleine. "Le Prologue de la *Vie de Saint Alexis* dans le manuscrit de Hildesheim." *Studi in onore di Italo Siciliano.* Florence, 1966, pp. 1165-1177.

Uitti, Karl D. "The Clerky Narrator Figure in Old French Hagiography and Romance." *Medioevo Romanzo,* 2 (1975), 394-408.

——. "The Old-French *Vie de Saint Alexis:* Paradigm, Legend, Meaning." *Romance Philology,* 20 (1966), 263-295.

Usener, H. *Acta Sanctae Marinae et Sancti Christophori.* Bonn, 1886.

Ussher, Archbishop. *Works,* 6, 1654. *Index. Chron.,* An. DXIV. Cited by Wahlund.

Vacant, Mangenot, Amaan, E. *Dictionnaire de Théologie Catholique.* Paris: Letouzey, 1939. Vol. 14.

Valle de la Paz, Ida del. *La leggenda di S. Nicola nella tradizione poetica medioevale in Francia.* Florence, 1921.

Vicaire, M.-H. *L'Imitation des apôtres: Moines, chanoines, mendiants (IVème-XIIIème siècles).* Paris: Le Cerf, 1963.

Vie des Pères du Désert. Lettres Chrétiennes, No. 4. Paris: Grasset, 1961.

Vielliard, Françoise. *Bibliotheca Bodmeriana. Manuscrits français du moyen âge.* Geneva: Fondation Martin Bodmer, 1975.

Vincent, P. R. "The Dramatic Aspect of the Old French *Vie de Saint Alexis.*" *Studies in Philology,* 60 (1963), 525-541.

Vising, Johan. *Anglo-Norman Language and Literature.* London: Oxford University Press, 1923.

Wahlund, C. *Die altfranzösische Prosaübersetzung von Brendans Meerfahrt, nach der Pariser Hdschr. Nat.-Bibl. fr. 1553.* Upsala, 1900; Slatkine Reprints, 1974.

Walberg, Emmanuel. *Quelques aspects de la littérature anglo-normande.* Paris: Droz, 1936.

——. "Sur le nom de l'auteur du *Voyage de Saint Brendan.*" *Studia Neophilologica,* 12 (1939), 46-55.

——. *La Tradition hagiographique de Saint Thomas Becket avant la fin du XIIème siècle.* Paris: Droz, 1929.

——. *La Vie de Saint Thomas Becket par Guernes de Pont-Sainte-Maxence.* Paris: Champion, 1969.

Warne, F. J. *Le Jeu de Saint Nicolas.* Oxford, 1963.

Waters, E. G. R. *The Anglo-Norman Voyage of Saint Brendan by Benedeit.* Oxford: Clarendon Press, 1928.

Weaver, Charles P. *The Hermit in English Literature from the Beginnings to 1660.* Nashville, Tenn.: George Peabody College for Teachers, 1924.

Weber, C. "Uber die Sprache und Quelle des altfrz. hl. Georg." *Zeitschrift für romanische Philologie,* 5 (1881), 498-520.

Weitzorek, Margareta. *Die Legenden der Thais und der Maria Aegyptica en den romanischen Literaturen vornehmlich des Mittelalters.* Lingerich: Westf, 1938.

Wormald, Francis, Dodwell, C. R., and Pächt, Otto. *The St. Albans Psalter.* London: The Warburg Institute, 1960.

Zaal, Z. W. B. *A lei francesca: Etude sur les chansons de saints gallo-romanes du XIème siècle.* Leiden: Brill, 1962.

Zumthor, Paul. *Essai de poétique médiévale.* Paris: Seuil, 1972.

NORTH CAROLINA STUDIES IN THE ROMANCE LANGUAGES AND LITERATURES

I.S.B.N. Prefix 0-8078-

Recent Titles

When ordering please cite the *ISBN Prefix* plus the last four digits for each title.

Send orders to: University of North Carolina Press
Chapel Hill
North Carolina 27514
U. S. A.

NORTH CAROLINA STUDIES IN THE ROMANCE LANGUAGES AND LITERATURES

I.S.B.N. Prefix 0-8078-

Recent Titles

THE THEATER OF ARTHUR ADAMOV, by John J. McCann. 1975. (Essays, No. 13). *-013-0.*

AN ANATOMY OF POESIS: THE PROSE POEMS OF STÉPHANE MALLARMÉ, by Ursula Franklin. 1976. (Essays, No. 16). *-016-5.*

LAS MEMORIAS DE GONZALO FERNÁNDEZ DE OVIEDO, Vols. I and II, by Juan Bautista Avalle-Arce. 1974. (Texts, Textual Studies, and Translations, Nos. 1 and 2). *-401-2; 402-0.*

GIACOMO LEOPARDI: THE WAR OF THE MICE AND THE CRABS, translated, introduced and annotated by Ernesto G. Caserta. 1976. (Texts, Textual Studies. and Translations, No. 4). *-404-7.*

LUIS VÉLEZ DE GUEVARA: A CRITICAL BIBLIOGRAPHY, by Mary G. Hauer. 1975. (Texts, Textual Studies, and Translations, No. 5). *-405-5.*

UN TRÍPTICO DEL PERÚ VIRREINAL: "EL VIRREY AMAT, EL MARQUÉS DE SOTO FLORIDO Y LA PERRICHOLI". EL "DRAMA DE DOS PALANGANAS" Y SU CIRCUNSTANCIA, estudio preliminar, reedición y notas por Guillermo Lohmann Villena. 1976. (Texts, Textual Studies, and Translation, No. 15). *-415-2.*

LOS NARRADORES HISPANOAMERICANOS DE HOY, edited by Juan Bautista Avalle-Arce. 1973. (Symposia, No. 1). *-951-0.*

ESTUDIOS DE LITERATURA HISPANOAMERICANA EN HONOR A JOSÉ J. ARROM, edited by Andrew P. Debicki and Enrique Pupo-Walker. 1975. (Symposia, No. 2). *-952-9.*

MEDIEVAL MANUSCRIPTS AND TEXTUAL CRITICISM, edited by Christopher Kleinhenz. 1976. (Symposia, No. 4). *-954-5.*

SAMUEL BECKETT. THE ART OF RHETORIC. edited by Edouard Morot-Sir. Howard Harper, and Dougald McMillan III. 1976. (Symposia, No. 5). *-955-3.*

DELIE. CONCORDANCE, by Jerry Nash. 1976. 2 Volumes. (No. 174).

FIGURES OF REPETITION IN THE OLD PROVENÇAL LYRIC: A STUDY IN THE STYLE OF THE TROUBADOURS, by Nathaniel B. Smith. 1976. (No. 176). *-9176-2.*

A CRITICAL EDITION OF LE REGIME TRESUTILE ET TRESPROUFITABLE POUR CONSERVER ET GARDER LA SANTE DU CORPS HUMAIN, by Patricia Willett Cummins. 1977. (No. 177).

THE DRAMA OF SELF IN GUILLAUME APOLLINAIRE'S "ALCOOLS", by Richard Howard Stamelman. 1976. (No. 178). *-9178-9.*

A CRITICAL EDITION OF "LA PASSION NOSTRE SEIGNEUR" FROM MANUSCRIPT 1131 FROM THE BIBLIOTHEQUE SAINTE-GENEVIEVE, PARIS, by Edward J. Gallagher. 1976. (No. 179). *-9179-7.*

A QUANTITATIVE AND COMPARATIVE STUDY OF THE VOCALISM OF THE LATIN INSCRIPTIONS OF NORTH AFRICA, BRITAIN, DALMATIA, AND THE BALKANS, by Stephen William Omeltchenko. 1977. (No. 180). *-9180-0.*

OCTAVIEN DE SAINT-GELAIS "LE SEJOUR D'HONNEUR", edited by Joseph A. James. 1977. (No. 181). *-9181-9.*

A STUDY OF NOMINAL INFLECTION IN LATIN INSCRIPTIONS, by Paul A. Gaeng. 1977. (No. 182). *-9182-7.*

THE LIFE AND WORKS OF LUIS CARLOS LÓPEZ, by Martha S. Bazik. 1977. (No. 183). *-9183-5.*

"THE CORT D'AMOR". A THIRTEENTH-CENTURY ALLEGORICAL ART OF LOVE, by Lowanne E. Jones. 1977. (No. 185). *-9185-1.*

When ordering please cite the *ISBN Prefix* plus the last four digits for each title.

Send orders to: University of North Carolina Press
Chapel Hill
North Carolina 27514
U. S. A.

NORTH CAROLINA STUDIES IN THE ROMANCE LANGUAGES AND LITERATURES

I.S.B.N. Prefix 0-8078-

Recent Titles

PHYTONYMIC DERIVATIONAL SYSTEMS IN THE ROMANCE LANGUAGES: STUDIES IN THEIR ORIGIN AND DEVELOPMENT, by Walter E. Geiger. 1978. (No. 187). *-9187-8.*

LANGUAGE IN GIOVANNI VERGA'S EARLY NOVELS, by Nicholas Patruno. 1977. (No. 188). *-9188-6.*

BLAS DE OTERO EN SU POESÍA, by Moraima de Semprún Donahue. 1977. (No. 189). *-9189-4.*

LA ANATOMÍA DE "EL DIABLO COJUELO": DESLINDES DEL GÉNERO ANATOMÍSTICO, por C. George Peale. 1977. (No. 191). *-9191-6.*

RICHARD SANS PEUR, EDITED FROM "LE ROMANT DE RICHART" AND FROM GILLES CORROZET'S "RICHART SANS PAOUR", by Denis Joseph Conlon. 1977. (No. 192). *-9192-4.*

MARCEL PROUST'S GRASSET PROOFS. *Commentary and Variants,* by Douglas Alden. 1978. (No. 193). *-9193-2.*

MONTAIGNE AND FEMINISM, by Cecile Insdorf. 1977. (No. ;94). *-9194-0.*

SANTIAGO F. PUGLIA, AN EARLY PHILADELPHIA PROPAGANDIST FOR SPANISH AMERICAN INDEPENDENCE, by Merle S. Simmons. 1977. (No. 195). *-9195-9.*

BAROQUE FICTION-MAKING. A STUDY OF GOMBERVILLE'S "POLEXANDRE", by Edward Baron Turk. 1978. (No. 196). *-9196-7.*

THE TRAGIC FALL: DON ÁLVARO DE LUNA AND OTHER FAVORITES IN SPANISH GOLDEN AGE DRAMA, by Raymond R. MacCurdy. 1978. (No. 197). *-9197-5.*

A BAHIAN HERITAGE. An Ethnolinguistic Study of African Influences on Bahian Portuguese, by William W. Megenney. 1978. (No. 198). *-9198-3.*

"LA QUERELLE DE LA ROSE: Letters and Documents", by Joseph L. Baird and John R. Kane. 1978. (No. 199). *-9199-1.*

TWO AGAINST TIME. *A Study of the very present worlds of Paul Claudel and Charles Péguy,* by Joy Nachod Humes. 1978. (No. 200). *-9200-9.*

TECHNIQUES OF IRONY IN ANATOLE FRANCE. Essay on *Les sept femmes de la Barbe-Bleue,* by Diane Wolfe Levy. 1978. (No. 201). *-9201-7.*

THE PERIPHRASTIC FUTURES FORMED BY THE ROMANCE REFLEXES OF "VADO (AD)" "PLUS INFINITIVE, by James Joseph Champion. 1978 (No. 202). *-9202-5.*

THE EVOLUTION OF THE LATIN /b/-/ʉ/ MERGER: A Quantitative and Comparative Analysis of the *B-V* Alternation in Latin Inscriptions, by Joseph Louis Barbarino. 1978 (No. 203). *-9203-3.*

METAPHORIC NARRATION: THE STRUCTURE AND FUNCTION OF METAPHORS IN "A LA RECHERCHE DU TEMPS PERDU", by Inge Karalus Crosman. 1978 (No. 204). *-9204-1.*

LE VAIN SIECLE GUERPIR. A Literary Approach to Sainthood through Old French Hagiography of the Twelfth Century, by Phyllis Johnson and Brigitte Cazelles. 1979. (No. 205). *-9205-X.*

THE POETRY OF CHANGE: A STUDY OF THE SURREALIST WORKS OF BENJAMIN PÉRET, by Julia Field Costich. 1979. (No. 206). *-9206-8.*

NARRATIVE PERSPECTIVE IN THE POST-CIVIL WAR NOVELS OF FRANCISCO AYALA "MUERTES DE PERRO" AND "EL FONDO DEL VASO", by Maryellen Bieder. 1979. (No. 207). *-9207-6.*

RABELAIS: HOMO LOGOS, by Alice Fiola Berry. 1979. (No. 208). *-9208-4.*

"DUEÑAS" AND "DONCELLAS": A STUDY OF THE "DOÑA RODRÍGUEZ" EPISODE IN "DON QUIJOTE", by Conchita Herdman Marianella. 1979. (No. 209). *-9209-2.*

PIERRE BOAISTUAU'S "HISTOIRES TRAGIQUES": A STUDY OF NARRATIVE FORM AND TRAGIC VISION, by Richard A. Carr. 1979. (No. 210). *-9210-6.*

When ordering please cite the *ISBN Prefix* plus the last four digits for each title.

Send orders to: University of North Carolina Press
Chapel Hill
North Carolina 27514
U. S. A.